CANTERING THE COUNTRY

The Geography Unit Study for Young Learners

Loreé Pettit & Dari Mullins

Published by Geography Matters, Inc., Nancy KY, USA

Programs utilized during production: Serif Page Plus 8, Puzzle Power, Art Explosion, ClipTures volume 4

ISBN 978-1-931397-56-8
Previous ISBN 1-931397-33-3

Library of Congress Control Number: 2005923082

Printed in the United States of America

Geography Matters, Inc.
800-426-4650
www.geomatters.com

Dedication

Cantering the Country is lovingly dedicated to our children, Jason and Aaron Pettit and Artie, Autumn, and Aspen Mullins. The five of you are the biggest blessings in our lives. We are so thankful that God has given us the privilege of being your moms.

Acknowledgements

I would like to thank God for enabling me to do more than I ever dreamed possible. Several years ago when I was at the lowest point of my life, You promised to bring beauty from ashes. True to your nature, You have done so abundantly, exceedingly more than I ever thought. To my husband and best friend, Ralph, thank you for being there and encouraging me. God definitely knew what He was doing when He put us together. To my heart sister, Dari, you are one of the "abundantly, exceedingly more than I ever thought" gifts from God. Thank you for all of your hard work on this book. But mostly, thank you for your friendship. — Loreé

I would like to thank the Lord for His providential hand in my life. Thank you for continuing to lead us, even when we can't see or understand the road ahead. To my husband, Allen, for continuing to support, love and encourage me in the most challenging times. To my best friend and sister- in-the-Lord, Loreé, as each year passes the value of your friendship grows. I appreciate your dedication to homeschooling no matter what the circumstances. I also want to thank Josh and Cindy Wiggers for their advice, friendship and prayers during the last several years. — Dari

Cantering the Country

Table of Contents

Instructions

Objective

Cantering the Country's main objective is to introduce students to the fifty states and District of Columbia. While studying the geography of the states, students will meet various historical figures, leaders, and other important people from each state. They will learn about trees, flowers, birds, rocks/minerals, and various other scientific topics from each state. They will also study traits taken from state mottoes and preambles to help instill noble character qualities. This study is designed for students in the first to sixth grade levels. It can be easily adapted for older children by using a few companion texts.

Brief Overview

This United States unit study is designed to be completed in one to three years. All subjects except math and spelling are covered. The unit for each state includes:

- **General Reference** – General information about the state.
- **Geography** – Geographic terms and physical or topical geographic forms located in the state.
- **History/Biographies** – Historical figures, leaders, authors, artists, and other important people who were born in or have another affiliation with the state.
- **Science** – The major science topics covered are trees, birds, flowers, and rocks/minerals of each state. Also included are other animals native to the state, insects, amphibians, and various science topics related to the state, including: spacecraft, rockets, skyscrapers, bridges, photography, tornadoes, hurricanes, blizzards, thunderstorms, fireworks, hot air balloons, combustion engines, and various ecosystems such as deserts and ponds.
- **Literature** – Lists a variety of quality children's literature that is set in the state, is written by an author from the state, or relates to a topic studied under that state. Also included in this section are books that emphasize a character trait studied.
- **Language Arts** – Suggestions and activities to reinforce language and grammar concepts. The preamble to each state constitution, included in this section, can be used for copywork or vocabulary.
- **Character** – Includes the motto of each state and, when available, the source of the motto. Character traits from these mottoes are studied along with the state flag pledges (if the state has one).
- **Activities** – The main focus of this section is mapping activities and hands-on projects using readily available materials. Also included are fun, easy ideas that relate to topics within the state.
- **Internet Resources** – To enhance your study, Internet links are list throughout. If a link becomes inactive, do your own search on the topic to find something similar.

Getting Started

Before beginning *Cantering the Country*, please be sure your students have basic map skills. If they do not, take time to teach these necessary skills. A good resource to help students learn these foundational skills is *Discovering Maps* published by Hammond.

An atlas and children's dictionary need to be readily available throughout this study. We also recommend access to a set of encyclopedias, either in book form or on the computer. Most of the books used in this program were found in the authors' local library. Please check your library for these or other compatible resources before purchasing books listed.

While none are mandatory, there are a few resources that you may want to buy since they are utilized throughout the course. Besides the added convenience, most of these can be used for many years. These foundational books are:

- *Atlas of the United States* by Geography Matters (or any good U.S. atlas)
- *Geography from A to Z* by Jack Knowlton
- *Earth Science for Every Kid* by Janice Van Cleave
- *Eat Your Way Through the U.S.A.* by Loreé Pettit
- *Profiles from History* - Volume 1 by Ashley M. Wiggers
- *Zoo Guide* by Answers in Genesis
- *Aquarium Guide* by Answers in Genesis

Before beginning *Cantering the Country*, please familiarize yourself with the layout of the book. States are listed alphabetically. Within each state are nine categories, which are further broken down into topics. Topics have recommended books, websites, and activities. Read through the topics and resources and decide which items are right for your family. Some states or topics do not have as many selections, as appropriate resources were not readily available.

Books listed under each topic are only suggestions. Your library or personal collection may have other wonderful resources on the subject. In most sections there are more books suggested than necessary. Choose one to three books per topic depending on your children's ages. The symbol (RA) indicates the selection is most likely suitable to be read aloud to younger students or read by older students.

Books listed in *Cantering the Country* have been reviewed by the authors. We tried to be extremely cautious about content, themes, and language in the selections. Every family has different criteria for appropriate literature. Please preview any books listed and decide if they meet your family criteria.

The authors hold to a young earth creation worldview and tried to find resources that were either in line with that view or neutral on the topic of evolution. However, some books and websites may make reference to the earth being millions of years old or other evolutionary statements. In most cases, these are noted beside the resource cited. You may prefer to preview these resources to determine whether they are acceptable for your family.

Activity CD-ROM

The Activity CD-ROM bound in the back of this book includes printable activities and maps for use with your state studies. Select activities appropriate to your students' abilities. Choose from crosswords, word searches, word scrambles, dot-to-dot, and more. For your convenience a thumbnail image of most activities is provided in the text to give you a glimpse of what is available on the disk. It is helpful if you choose the activities, print those pages, and have them ready at the beginning of each state study. The reproducible pages in the appendix and other BONUS pages are also included on the Activity CD-ROM for easy printing from your computer.

The Activity CD-ROM includes PDF files which can be read by Acrobat Reader and are files for viewing and printing only. If your computer does not have Acrobat Reader installed, you can do so from the CD-ROM or you can download the most recent version free online from adobe.com.

Building Student Notebooks

Cantering the Country utilizes the notebook approach. Each child builds a notebook throughout the length of their journey, encouraging him or her to be a producer rather than a consumer. Some of the benefits of notebooking are:

- Provides a permanent record of learning
- Easy access to studies
- Promotes creativity
- Ability to share with others

Notebooks are unique to each family and individual. Set up your notebooks in a way that works for you and your children. We do give suggestions, but they are suggestions only—there is no "right" way to notebook.

The only supplies needed are a notebook (we suggest 3 ring binder) and dividers for each student. The binder size will depend on the age of the child. Older children will have more work to put in their notebooks and will therefore need a larger one. We recommend a 1½" or 2" binder for younger children and a 3" binder for older. You can make your own dividers from cardstock or purchase them at the store. Personally, we like the tabbed plastic dividers that have pockets.

Notebooks can be set up alphabetically, chronologically, or regionally. To set up a notebook chronologically (the order in which the states joined the Union), please see the Order of Statehood chart in the appendix. To set up a notebook regionally, see chart below.

New England States	ME	MA	NH	VT	CT	RI						
Mid-Atlantic States	NY	NJ	PA	WV	MD	DE	Washington DC					
Southern States	NC	VA	KY	TN	SC	GA	AL	MS	FL	AR	LA	
Midwestern States	OH	MI	IN	IL	WA	MN	IA	MO	ND	SD	NE	KS
Southwestern States	OK	TX	NM	AZ								
Rocky Mountain States	MT	ID	WY	CO	UT	NV						
Pacific Coast States	WA	OR	CA	AK								

As you study a state or subject put the child's work into the appropriate section of the student notebook. Take a picture of any larger project or activity, tape it to a piece of paper, and have the child write or dictate about it. This can be placed into the notebook. Include reproducible pages from the Activity CD-ROM such as maps, puzzles, and notebooking pages for trees, flowers, rocks/minerals, and animals. Many of the websites listed have coloring or activity pages that can be added to your child's notebook.

For more information and ideas on notebooking, go online to www.learningandhavingfun.com and www.geomatters.com (select articles).

Teaching Tips by Topic

Geography

This section covers geographic terms and information about geographic features, national parks, and other monuments found within the state. Use a dictionary, an illustrated geographical terms chart, or *Geography from A to Z* by Jack Knowlton to define geography terms listed. These terms make great vocabulary words for the week.

Once the child learns several geographic terms, he can make a salt dough map of an "imaginary place" utilizing all of the terms mastered. The salt dough recipe and a fun alternative cookie dough map recipe are located in the appendix.

History & Biographies

You will find resources for people or historical events affiliated with the state in this section. The historical figure, leader, author, artist, poet, or musician was born in or lived in the state.

Cantering the Country is meant to introduce some of the key people and events from our country, not to give an exhaustive or chronological overview of our history. If you are adapting this course to a middle or high school student, you may want to supplement with additional history. If doing so, we recommend that you study U.S. history rather than ancient, medieval, or renaissance history, to expand upon knowledge gained from *Cantering the Country*. If your children are preschool to fifth grade, they do not need any additional history. We believe that this age should be introduced to real people who did great things rather than try to learn a bunch of dates. As they get older and study specific time periods, they will remember the friends that they studied and learned about in their early years.

If a topic does not have any references listed, search online or refer to an encyclopedia.

Science

Science covers a tree, bird, flower, and rock/mineral from each state. Many states have the same official state tree, bird, flower, or rock/mineral; therefore, instead of repeating an item we replaced it with another one native to that state. A chart with a complete list of the official tree, bird, and flower for each state is located in the appendix. A broad spectrum of other science-related topics is also included throughout the course. Some of these fun topics are: space travel, bridges, deserts, animals, skyscrapers, photography, and various weather phenomena. A complete list of science topics included for each state can be found in the appendix. These topics are not studied in depth, but are introduced to the young students in order to whet their appetite for science in later years. If your child becomes interested in a specific area, we encourage you to seek out resources and study that topic in more depth for as long as the child exhibits a genuine desire to learn. If you have a middle or high school student, you will need to study these topics in more depth.

Internet sites that include reproducible pages, crafts, projects, and experiments are listed.

If a topic does not have any references listed, search online or refer to an encyclopedia or field guide.

For your convenience, notebooking pages for science topics are included in the appendix and on the Activity CD-ROM. There are pages that the child can draw or paste a picture of whatever is studied and then write about it. There are also pages that the child can simply draw or paste pictures of the tree or flower studied, with little to no writing required.

Literature

This section includes a wide variety of children's literature, from timeless classics to modern stories, set in the state, written by an author from the state, or relating to a topic studied in the state. Also included are books which emphasize character quality. If a book is about a specific character quality, it is denoted with a (†).

While most of the selections chosen are on an elementary reading level, we have also included several chapter books for older children or reading aloud; these books have an (RA) next to the author's name. Several books also include fun activities related to events which happened in the story. Let your children come up with their own fun ideas which relate to the books they read.

Language Arts

The preambles to the state constitutions are included for historical purposes. Our founding fathers subscribed to biblical principles which today seem to be ignored by a large portion of our society. To fully understand how our nation was established, it is important for students to recognize our forefathers believed so deeply in these sound principles that they are even reflected in the preambles throughout the states.

State preambles can be used for copywork and vocabulary. Most of these are too long to be copied at one sitting. Let the child copy one or two sentences at a time. Some of the vocabulary words are too advanced for younger children. Use your own discretion to decide what your child is able to handle.

The language arts section is not a complete grammar and spelling program. If you have middle or high school students you will need to supplement those subjects. The activities and ideas included in this section introduce and reinforce grammar and language concepts and provide opportunities for composition and creative writing. A master list of language arts activities can be found on pages 8-9. For a comprehensive language arts curriculum we recommend *Learning Language Arts Through Literature.*

Character

The focus of this section is character traits derived from the state motto. The source of the motto, if available, is included, as well as an explanation of why certain traits were chosen. Once again, this is meant to introduce the child to good, moral character qualities, not to provide an in-depth study. After studying a specific trait, have your child fill out the Character Trait Report in the appendix. Select from two Character Trait Reports (for either a younger child or an older child), and add it to their notebook.

Some states also have "state flag pledges" and we have provided a copy of those in this section. These pledges can be used for copywork or for more research and study on character traits. If no pledge is listed, an "official" flag pledge was unavailable for that particular state.

General Activities

This is the fun stuff! This curriculum includes lots of activities and hands-on projects using readily available items. Ideas, websites, projects, and craft ideas are listed with each state. Also remember numerous printable activities and maps are included in the CD-ROM bound in this book. Take a picture of larger completed projects to add to the student notebooks. The following activities can be used for all states:

Mapping Activities

Label the capital, major cities, rivers, mountain ranges, and other land forms on a map of the state. State maps are provided on the CD-ROM included with this book.

Canter the Country

Lay out an enlarged floor map of the United States or the region you are studying and use a stick horse to "canter" from state to state. Check your local teacher supply store for a floor map or floor map puzzle.

Salt Map

Draw, trace, or tape an outline of the state on a piece of cardboard. Cover with salt dough. Form mountain ranges and valleys where appropriate. For coastal states, the elevation will be lower along the coast. Allow map to dry overnight. Paint with tempera paint. A cookie dough alternative is listed in the appendix.

Make a Timeline

A timeline is a fun project to do throughout the course. As you study key figures and events from each state, put pictures on a timeline on your wall, in a notebook, or both. The child can make the figure or you can use premade figures such as ones found on *Historical Timeline Figures* CD-ROM by Liberty Wiggers, available through Geography Matters. To help your child remember which state a person is from, have him write the state abbreviation in the corner of the timeline figure. For more information on creating a timeline notebook, look for timeline articles on www.geomatters.com.

Pledge to the State Flag

Some states have a pledge to their state flag. These can be copied on the bottom or the back of the state flag page that the child colors. If it is your home state, you may want to memorize the pledge. If a state has an official state pledge, it can be found after the Character section for that state. We only included pledges officially recognized by the state.

State Song

Most of the states have an official state song. You can use the lyrics as copywork to add to your child's notebook. Got to http://www.50states.com/songs/ for a list of songs and their lyrics. To listen to the state song, click on the state then click on "Listen to MIDI."

Make a Poster

Our children love to make posters, and character traits make great themes. Posters don't have to be large; 8½" x 11" paper works just as well and fits into the student notebook.

State Quarters

In 1999 the U.S. Mint began a ten-year program releasing new quarters each year honoring the fifty states. To learn more about each state's design and why it was chosen, go to http://www.usmint.gov/mint_programs/50sq_program/?flash=yes. For coloring pages of the state quarters and more, go to http://www.usmint.gov/kids/campCoin/coloring.cfm. For more information on other coins, including the National Park quarters, go to http://www.usmint.gov/kids/teachers/.

Cook a Meal - ***Eat Your Way Through the USA***

As you study each state, cook a popular meal from the state, or with ingredients readily available in the state. Bring the child into the kitchen with you and work on valuable life skills. This is also a wonderful time to discuss the various and unique cultures that make our country great. Yummy recipes can be found in *Eat Your Way Through the USA*, by Loree´ Pettit. See Resources for ordering information.

Travel & Tourism Information

Each state's Tourism Board is listed in the appendix. If you contact them, they will send brochures and other information that can be used as reference material. The brochures can also be cut up and used in the student's notebook. Allow 4-6 weeks to receive the information requested.

Website Resources

The websites included below can be utilized throughout the study. Please check them regularly for new additions.

Enchanted Learning

www.enchantedlearning.com – Has a multitude of useful information, including puzzles, printable books, and other items that can be used in the children's notebooks. This website has a paid member section; however, many of the items can be accessed without a membership.

State History Guide Resources

www.SHGResources.com – A great place to get additional information on the states. It has detailed information on state history and emblems and links to state newspapers and other current events data. This website will be very useful in obtaining additional information for an older child utilizing this course.

U.S. Mint

www.usmint.gov – A wonderful site to research information on our national currency. It has links for educators with lesson plans, reproducible sheets, and many other helpful items. There is a link with information and coloring sheets for the state quarters.

Crayola

www.crayola.com/activitybook - A fun site full of printable puzzles and color sheets. You do have to register to use this site, but it is free, and they will not give out your e-mail address.

ABC Teach

www.abcteach.com/directory/theme_units/ - This site is loaded with lesson plans and printable pages for science, history, and geography topics.

Language Arts Guide

- **Copywork**: Use state preamble, quotes from people you are studying, information about the topic you are studying.
- **Simple parts of speech**: nouns, verbs, adjectives, adverbs, articles, etc.

  √ These can be taken from books that you read. They can also be underlined in copywork. For example, if you are covering verbs, have the child underline all of the verbs in that day's copywork.

  √ Figure out the part of speech for the character trait being studied. Can it have more than one function? (Example: Love can be a noun or a verb.) If it can, how does that change the meaning? List the different forms of the word. (Example: creative, creativity, creativeness) Older children can define each form and use it in a sentence.
- **Abstract and concrete nouns**: Character traits are great for studying abstract nouns and comparing them with concrete nouns.
- **Subject and Predicate**: Divide sentences from reading or copywork into subject and predicate. (Example: Delaware / was the first state to join the union.)
- **Types of Sentences**: Learn about the four types of sentences (declarative, interrogative, imperative, and exclamatory)

  √ Have children identify the four types of sentences and the end mark used for each as they come across them in their reading.

  √ Have children identify the four types of sentences and the end mark used for each in their own writing.
- **Quotations**: Learn about and practice using quotation marks in reading and creative writing.

  √ Change a sentence from a statement to a command, question, or a direct quote and vice versa. Does this change the punctuation? How does it change the wording?
- **Synonyms and antonyms**: Be sure to include synonyms and antonyms when studying character traits.
- **Vocabulary**: Use the Dictionary Page in the appendix or a card file system.

  √ To utilize the card file system, write the root word, suffix, or prefix on the top of a 3x5 card, along with its meaning. Every time you encounter a vocabulary word that shares that root, suffix, or prefix, write the word and its meaning on that card and file it in a card file box. For example:

  Astron - star
  Astronomy - the study of stars and the atmosphere beyond the earth

  √ Don't be overwhelmed by finding the root words, suffixes, and prefixes; they are easily located in a good dictionary. F.L.A.G.S. listed below also has an extensive listing of roots, suffixes, and prefixes.
- **Reading and Writing**:

  √ Cut a picture from a magazine of a state, animal, geographical formation, or anything else that you are studying. Glue it to a piece of colored paper. Have the child write a descriptive sentence or paragraph about the picture.

√ Read or write a poem about a flower, insect, bird, or tree that you are studying.

√ Write a story about a character trait you are studying.

√ Write a play about a character trait or Bible story.

√ Write a report on a person, event, or science topic. We really like using the key word approach to writing reports. In this approach, the child makes a list of key words from his reading about a topic, then uses that list to retell, in his own words, what he has read. For example:

On March 6, 1836, the great pioneer and patriot died along with the other brave defenders of the Alamo. He was only forty-nine years old. But in his short lifetime, Davy Crockett carved a legend of skill and courage that will live forever.

Key words: March 6, 1836, died, Alamo, 49 years old, Davy Crockett

Retold as: *Davy Crockett was forty-nine years old when he died on March 6, 1836, defending the Alamo.*

While not as exciting as the original text, all of the important facts are there. As the child gains skill and confidence in his writing ability, his work will improve. Be patient! Learning to write is a skill that takes time and practice.

Resource Suggestions

We recommend purchasing an English handbook to help you with grammar.

For more language arts ideas, see;

- *Learning Language Arts Through Literature* - Debbie Strayer and Susan Simpson
- *A Strong Start in Language* or *The Three R's* - Ruth Beechick
- *Language Arts...The Easy Way* by Cindy Rushton
- *Thematic Copywork Lessons: Lessons From Leaders* compiled and arranged by Sandi Queen
- *Writer's Inc. 2001* - Great Source
- *F.L.A.G.S. (Fundamental Language Arts Game Supplemental)* – Mastery Publications

Teacher Preparation

Every family has its own teaching and learning style. Some families take a more relaxed approach, while others like a lot of structure. Provided below are suggestions that fall somewhere in the middle. Adapt these suggestions to your family and remember there is no "right way" to teach this information.

We recommend using the same atlas throughout the course. Use this to look up information on capital, area, rank, etc. Different sources have different information on the same data; this is why we suggest using the same source consistently. This information will be needed to complete the State Report form located in the appendix.

- Decide approximately how many days you want to spend on a state and break up the activities accordingly. Remember, the younger the child, the more varied the activities should be.
- Before teaching a specific state, decide which activities you will use and plan what the children will include in their notebooks.
- Check the recommended websites listed on page 7 and any websites listed under specific topics. You may want to go ahead and print or copy any printable and reproducible pages from the websites, appendix, and the Activity CD-ROM at this time.
- Make sure that you have all necessary items and ingredients on hand to complete the activities and recipes chosen.
- Gather resources from the library. Remember: if a chosen topic does not have references listed, information can be found online, in an encyclopedia or field guide, or perhaps your local library.
- Read one to three of the literature books on the first day of each state. This will grab the children's interest and make them curious about that state.
- Locate the state on the map daily. Do other mapping activities daily with older children.
- Keeping in mind your child's learning style and temperament; vary your activities throughout the day, alternating written activities with reading and hands-on projects.
- Leave plenty of time to do the fun activities. Some families like to do activities on Friday, while others like to do them throughout the week.
- Remember to be flexible! If your child shows interest in a topic or if an unexpected opportunity presents itself, adjust *your* schedule and go with the flow.

Adapting to Older Students

Cantering the Country can be adapted to older students quite easily. By using a few extra texts, the older student can gain a very in-depth, thorough knowledge of our country. We recommend:

- *Trail Guide to U.S. Geography* by Cindy Wiggers – This guide can be used as the teacher's primary text. Use the suggestions and format provided to give the older student a solid foundation in U.S. geography. Utilize the research ideas listed under each state to include other subjects such as language arts, history, and the arts. Teaching a broad range of ages is very do-able when utilizing *Trail Guide to U.S. Geography* with *Cantering the Country. Trail Guide to U.S. Geography* is arranged by region, while *Cantering the Country* covers states in alphabetical order. Simply choose which order you want to study the states and keep all students on the same states together.
- *Garden Patch of Reproducible Homeschooling Planning and Educational Worksheets* by Debora McGregor – This has a variety of report forms, interview sheets, and research sheets that older students can use in their notebooks.
- *Facts about the States* by Joseph Kane, Steven Anzovin, and Janet Podell – This is a very detailed book including numerous resources that can be used for the older child. There is a list of fiction and nonfiction titles written on an advanced reading level included for each state. These *are not* necessarily written from a Christian perspective and should be previewed by a parent before the child reads them, if this is important to you. This is a very in-depth book and is available in most library reference sections.
- *America the Beautiful Series* - Published by Children's Press, a division of Grolier Publishing, this widely read series has one book for each state and contains very in-depth information. It should be available in your local library.
- *All Through the Ages,* by Christine Miller - Provides organized lists of great literature categorized by place, historical period, and grade level. Use to select books for older students to read.

Preview the items mentioned above and decide on the requirements for your older student.

Giddyup

Finally, remember to have fun! Use *Cantering the Country* as a tool and resource to enhance your home-school journey. Don't be a "slave to the manual," feeling that you must cover every topic and accomplish every activity. Let *Cantering the Country* work for you, not the other way around.

Have a great year and we hope you'll join the discussion group at
http://groups.yahoo.com/group/CanteringTheCountry/

Alabama

Heart of Dixie

On December 14, 1819, Alabama became the 22nd state admitted to the Union. The name "Alabama" originates from a Native American tribe which lived in the region. The tribal name, *Alibamu*, means "clearer of thickets." Alabama is located in the heart of the Deep South, and its capital is Montgomery.

Adopted in 1895, Alabama's flag displays the red cross of St. Andrew that was the principal feature of the Confederate battle flag.

Alabama's climate is hot and wet. The northern part of the state has pine forests, hills, and lakes. In the south, the hills give way to rolling grasslands and fertile farmland. Further south are the swamps and bayous of the Mobile Delta. Along the southern tip, sandy beaches border Mobile Bay and the Gulf of Mexico.

Interesting Facts:

- The first electric street cars in the United States were used in Montgomery in 1866.
- The deepest gorge in the United States east of the Rocky Mountains is at Little River Canyon near Fort Payne, Alabama.
- For decades "King Cotton" dominated Alabama's farm economy. In 1910, boll weevils destroyed the cotton crops, which turned out to be a good thing. The state's farmers learned to grow other crops and not be so dependent on cotton.
- During the Civil War, a company of Alabama soldiers paraded in uniforms trimmed with bits of yellow cloth. This reminded people of the state bird, which has patches of yellow under its wings. From that day on, Alabama troops were known as Yellowhammers.

General Reference

- ❑ *Alabama* - Anne Welsbacher
- ❑ *Alabama* Facts and Symbols - Emily McAuliffe
- ❑ *Alabama* - Dottie Brown (contains evolution)
- ❑ http://www.sos.state.al.us/Kids/index.htm

Geography

- ❑ gulf
  - *Geography from A to Z,* page 22
- ❑ Gulf of Mexico

History & Biographies

- ❑ Booker T. Washington
  - *Booker T. Washington: Leader and Educator* – Patricia and Frederick McKissack
  - *Booker T. Washington* – Thomas Amper
- ❑ George Washington Carver
  - *Pocketful of Goobers* - Barbara Mitchell
  - *A Weed Is a Flower: The Life of George Washington Carver* – Aliki
  - *A Picture Book of George Washington Carver* – David A. Adler
  - http://members.enchantedlearning.com/inventors/page/c/carvercloze.shtml
- ❑ Robert Goddard
  - *Robert Goddard: Pioneer Rocket Boy* - Clyde B. Moore
  - *Book of Explorers* - Usborne
  - http://members.enchantedlearning.com/inventors/page/g/goddardcloze.shtml
- ❑ Jesse Owens
  - *A Picture Book of Jesse Owens* – David A. Adler
  - *Jesse Owens: Olympic Star* – Patricia and Frederick McKissack
  - http://members.enchantedlearning.com/history/us/aframer/owens/print.shtml
  - http://members.enchantedlearning.com/history/us/aframer/owens/cloze.shtml
- ❑ USS Alabama
  - www.ussalabama.com
- ❑ Civil Rights Movement
  - *The Bridge at Selma* – Marilyn Miller
  - *The Montgomery Bus Boycott* – R. Conrad Stein
- ❑ Rosa Parks
  - *Rosa Parks: Fight for Freedom* - Keith Brandt
  - *Young Rosa Parks: Civil Rights Heroine* - Anne Benjamin
  - *A Picture Book of Rosa Parks* - David A. Adler
  - http://members.enchantedlearning.com/history/us/aframer/parks/index.shtml
  - http://members.enchantedlearning.com/history/us/aframer/parks/cloze.shtml

Science

- ❑ yellow hammer (flicker) (state bird)
- ❑ Southern Longleaf Pine (state tree)
- ❑ camellia (state flower)
- ❑ marble (state rock)
- ❑ boll weevil
- ❑ rockets & spacecraft
  - *Spacecraft* - Darlene R. Stille
  - *Flying the Space Shuttles* - Don Dwiggins
  - *Let's Visit a Space Camp* - Edith Alston
  - *Book of Rockets* - Anne Baird
  - *Look Inside Cross-Sections: Space* - Nick Lipscombe & Moira Butterfield
  - *Rocket: How a Toy Launched the Space Age* - Richard Maurer
  - *Space Vehicles* - Anne Rockwell
  - *Book of Explorers* - Usborne
  - http://www.enchantedlearning.com/devices/spaceshuttle/label/

Literature

- ❑ *Judy's Journey* - Lois Lenski (RA)
- ❑ *Ma Dear's Aprons* - Patricia McKissack
- ❑ *Mousehole Cat* - Antonia Barber (†)
- ❑ *Cecil's Story* - George Ella Lyon (†)
- ❑ *Brave Irene* - William Steig (†)

Language Arts

Preamble to the State Constitution:

We, the people of the State of Alabama, in order to establish justice, insure domestic tranquility, and secure the blessings of liberty to ourselves and our posterity, invoking the favor and guidance of Almighty God, do ordain and establish the following Constitution and form of government for the State of Alabama.

1. Refer to Language Arts Guide starting on page 8.
2. Make a list of "loud" adjectives to describe the sound of rockets.
3. Write a story about how it feels to be treated differently.

Character

The Alabama state motto - *We dare defend our rights* - was adopted in 1939 from a poem by Sir William Jones entitled "What Constitutes a State?" The director of the State Archives, Mary Bankhead Owen, was searching for "a phrase that would interpret the spirit of our peoples in a terse and energetic sentence." When she came across the poem by Jones and read the stanza "Men who their duties know. But know their rights, and knowing, dare maintain," she knew that she had found the motto for Alabama. Professor W. B. Saffold of the University of Alabama translated the motto into Latin: *Audemus jura nostra defendere.*

For a people to defend and maintain their rights, they must know what those rights involve and have a love of their country - **patriotism**. They must also be willing to defend those rights, even in the face of opposition - **courage**.

- **Patriotism** - Love of one's country: the passion which aims to serve one's country, either in defending it from invasion or protecting its rights and maintaining its laws and institutions in vigor and purity. Patriotism is the characteristic of a good citizen, the noblest passion that animates a man in the character of a citizen.
- **Courage** - Bravery; intrepidity; that quality of mind which enables men to encounter danger and difficulties with firmness or without fear or depression of spirits; valor; boldness; resolution.

State Flag Pledge

Flag of Alabama I salute thee. To thee I pledge my allegiance, my service, and my life.

Other sources:

- *The Book of Virtues* - William Bennett, pages 441-524. These pages have several short stories, poems, and quotes that relate to courage. Please preread them and use your own discretion as to which ones to read aloud to your children.
- *The Spirit of America* - William Bennett, "Patriotism and Courage," pages 25-97. These are short excerpts from letters, quotes, and poems which deal with patriotism and courage as they relate to the founding of our country. Please use your discretion as to which ones you read aloud to your children.

Activities

1. Color or label a map of Alabama.
2. Label the Gulf of Mexico on a map of the United States.
3. Go to http://www.kidzone.ws/geography/usa/ for printable flag and state symbol coloring pages.
4. Prepare a meal in *Eat Your Way Through the U.S.A.* from the state of Alabama.

5. Make a model rocket.
   - Wrap construction paper around a paper towel tube; tape or glue in place.
   - On one end of the tube, cut four 2-inch slits. The slits should divide the tube into four equal parts.
   - Cut two triangles out of construction paper. Each triangle should be 5 inches long at the base and 4 inches high.
   - Cut a slit halfway through each triangle - one from the top and one from the bottom.
   - Slip the triangle with the slit in the bottom into the rocket's body in two of the slits.
   - Slip the triangle with the slit in the top into the rocket's body in the other two slits. In addition to going onto the rocket, this triangle should also slip into the other triangle. You may have to jiggle the paper a bit to line up the slits. You should now have four "fins" forming a stable base for the rocket.
   - Make a circle by tracing a CD onto a piece of construction paper. Cut it out. Cut a slit from the outer edge of the circle to the center.
   - Form a cone from the circle; use tape or glue to secure. Tape or glue cone onto rocket.
   - Decorate rocket.
6. For instructions on experiments with rockets, go to http://pbskids.org/zoom/activities/sci/.

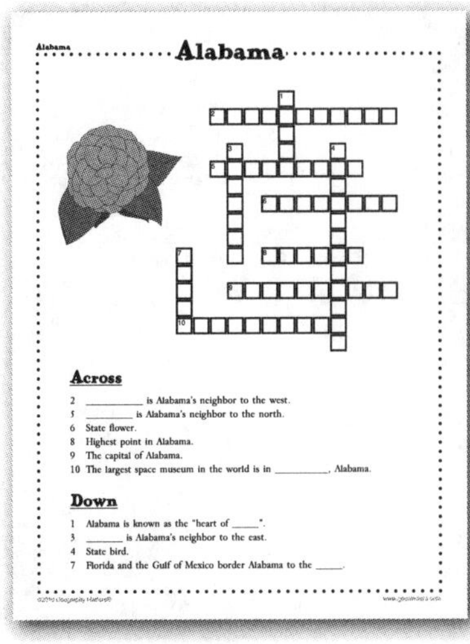

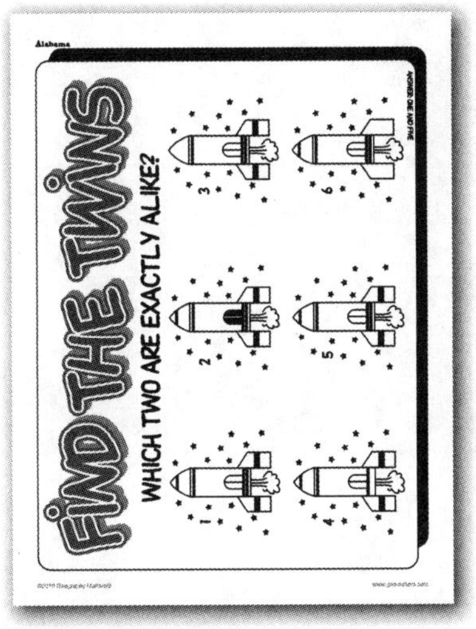

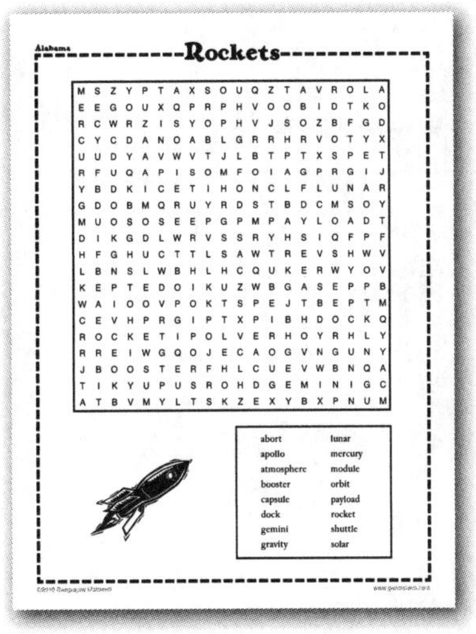

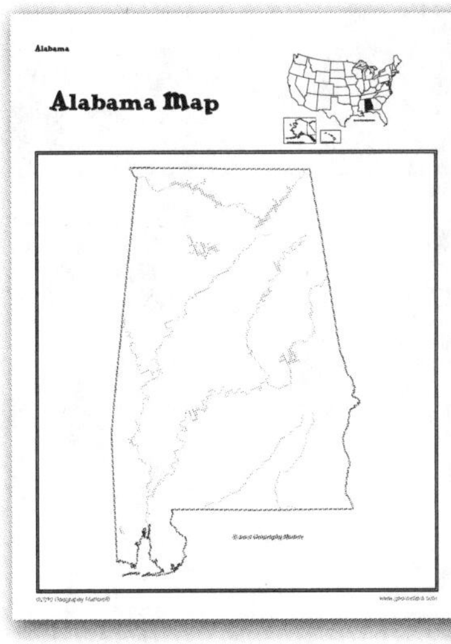

Alaska

The Last Frontier

When Alaska became the 49th state on January 3, 1959, it was the first state to join the Union in 47 years. The name "Alaska" originates from the Native American word ***alakshak***, which means "great land." Alaska, our largest state, is almost a fifth as large as the rest of the states combined and more than twice the size of Texas. At the mainland's westernmost point, Alaska is only 51 miles from Russia. In the Bering Strait, Alaska's Little Diomede Island is only two and a half miles miles from Russia's Big Diomede Island. The capital of Alaska is Juneau.

The flag of Alaska, eight gold stars on a field of blue, was designed in 1926 by a 13-year-old orphan boy from Seward. The blue background represents the sky, the sea, and wild flowers that grow on Alaskan soil. Gold signifies the state's rich gold deposits. The North Star symbolizes Alaska's place as the northernmost location in the United States. The dipper, which is part of the Great Bear constellation, symbolizes strength.

Most of Alaska is a vast, untamed wilderness of frozen tundra and ice fields, and its climate is extremely varied from region to region and from season to season. It is also the only state with land inside the Arctic Circle. At Point Barrow, in the northernmost region, the sun does not set from May 10 to August 2. Famous for its towering mountains and beautiful scenery, Alaska is home to seventeen of the highest mountains in the United States, including the highest peak, Mount McKinley.

Interesting Facts:

- Alaska has the largest coastline in the United States.
- Secretary of State William H. Seward bought Alaska from Russia in 1867 for $7.2 million. That's only 2 cents per acre!
- Alaska is called the Last Frontier because much of the state is not fully settled.
- Alaska is the only state in which polar bears reside in the wild.
- Alaska is home to almost all of the active volcanoes in the United States.
- North America's largest glacier, Malaspina Glacier, is located in Alaska. It is larger than the state of Rhode Island.

Geography

- ❑ glacier
    - *Geography From A to Z,* page 20
    - *Glaciers* – Wendell V. Tangborn
    - *Glaciers* – Michael George (You may want to skip the first page and from page 31 on due to evolution, but the stunning photographs and captivating information made this title too good to pass up.)
    - *Icebergs, Ice Caps, and Glaciers* – Allan Fowler
    - *Earth Science for Every Kid,* Experiment #36
- ❑ iceberg
    - *Geography From A to Z,* page 24
    - *Danger – Icebergs* – Roma Gans
- ❑ crevasse
    - *Geography From A to Z,* page 14
- ❑ tundra
    - *Geography From A to Z,* page 43
    - *Arctic Tundra: Land with No Trees* – Allan Fowler
    - *Tundra* – Philip Steele
    - *Tundra Discoveries* – Ginger Wadsworth

General Reference

- ❑ *Alaska* - Bob Italia
- ❑ *Alaska Facts and Symbols* - Muriel L. Dubois
- ❑ *If You Lived in the Alaska Territory* - Nancy Smiler Levinson
- ❑ *Arctic Hunter* - Diane Hoyt-Goldsmith
- ❑ *A Child's Alaska* - Claire Rudolph Murphy
- ❑ *Alaska* – Joyce Johnston
- ❑ *http://www.statesymbolsusa.org/Alaska/statesymbols.html*

History & Biographies

❑ Eskimo

- *The Eskimo: The Inuit and Yupik People* - Alice Osinski

❑ Klondike Gold Rush

- *Klondike Gold Rush,* The Adventures of Munford series - Jamie Aramini
- *Gold! The Klondike Adventure* – Delia Ray

❑ Jack London

- *Jack London: A Life of Adventure* - Rae Bains

❑ Balto

- *The Bravest Dog Ever: The True Story of Balto* - Natalie Standiford
- *Balto and the Great Race* - Elizabeth Cody Kimmel

❑ Richard E. Byrd

- *Richard E. Byrd: Adventurer to the Poles* - Adele deLeeuw

Science

❑ willow ptarmigan (state bird)

- *Gone Again Ptarmigan* - Jonathan London
- *Marvels of Creation, Breathtaking Birds* - Buddy and Kay Davis
- http://www.coloring.ws/birds.htm

❑ sitka spruce (state tree)

❑ forget-me-not (state flower)

❑ andradite

❑ lemming

❑ sled dogs

- *Sled Dogs: Arctic Athletes* - Elizabeth Ring

❑ Arctic wolves

- *Scruffy* – Jim Brandenburg

❑ polar bears

- *Polar Mammals* – Larry Dane Brimner
- *Polar Bears* - Marcia S. Freeman
- *Polar Bear* - Jason and Jody Stone
- *A Polar Bear Journey* - Debbie S. Miller
- *Zoo Guide,* page 75
- http://www.dltk-teach.com/t.asp?b=m&t=http://www.dltk-teach.com/books/brownbear/clips/bpolarbear.gif

- ❑ seals
  - *The Seal: Furry Swimmer* - Joelle Soler
  - *Seal Journey* - Richard & Jonah Sobol
  - *Harp Seal Pups* - Downs Matthews
  - *Aquarium Guide,* page 201
  - www.coloring.ws/animals.html
- ❑ salmon
- ❑ oil spills
  - *Oil Spill!* - Melvin Berger
  - *Oil Spills* – Laurence Pringle
- ❑ Aurora Borealis
  - *Northern Lights* – D. M. Souza - Conduct experiment on page 17 with bar magnet and iron filings.
  - *Earth Science for Every Kid,* Experiment #28

Literature

- ❑ *Welcome to the Ice House* – Jane Yolen (This is a wonderful selection to open the unit.)
- ❑ *Ice Bear and Little Fox* – Jonathan London
- ❑ *Call of the Wild* - Jack London (RA abridged children's version or book-on-tape)
- ❑ *White Fang* - Jack London (RA abridged children's version or book-on-tape)
- ❑ *Nutik, the Wolf Pup* – Jean Craighead George
- ❑ *Nutik & Amaroq Play Ball* – Jean Craighead George
- ❑ *Arctic Son* – Jean Craighead George
- ❑ *Aunt Lulu* - Daniel Pinkwater
- ❑ *Dog Team* - Gary Paulsen
- ❑ *Year of Miss Agnes* - Kirkpatrick Hill (RA)
- ❑ *Song of the North* – Frank Asch (poetry)

Language Arts

Preamble to the State Constitution:

We the people of Alaska, grateful to God and to those who founded our nation and pioneered this great land, in order to secure and transmit to succeeding generations our heritage of political, civil, and religious liberty within the Union of States, do ordain and establish this constitution for the State of Alaska.

1. Refer to Language Arts Guide starting on page 8.
2. Write a list of adjectives describing cold. Cut out snowflakes and write an adjective on each snowflake.
3. Write a story about competing in a dog sled race.
4. Write a story of adventure in the wilderness of Alaska.

Character

The Alaska state motto - *North to the Future* - was adopted in 1967 during the state's centennial celebration of its purchase from Russia. Richard Peter, a newsman from Alaska, wrote the motto to portray Alaska as a country of promise. Peter said the motto was to be a "reminder that beyond the horizon of urban clutter there is a Great Land beneath our flag that can provide a new tomorrow for this century's huddled masses yearning to be free." The motto is meant to connect the geographic position of Alaska with the bright future potential of the state. In order to achieve these goals, the people of Alaska must have **ambition**.

- **Ambition** – A desire for excellence or superiority.

In a good sense, ambition is used to achieve seemingly impossible tasks. Ambition can also be equated with evil or selfish desires.

State Flag Pledge
Alaska has a state flag song rather than a pledge.

Eight stars of gold on a field of blue,
Alaska's Flag, may it mean to you;
The blue of the sea, the evening sky,
The mountain lakes and the flow'rs nearby;
The gold of the early sourdoughs dreams,
The precious gold of the hills and streams;
The brilliant stars in the northern sky,
The "Bear," the "Dipper," and shining high,
The great North star with its steady light,
O'er land and sea a beacon bright,
Alaska's Flag to Alaskans dear,
The simple flag of the last frontier.

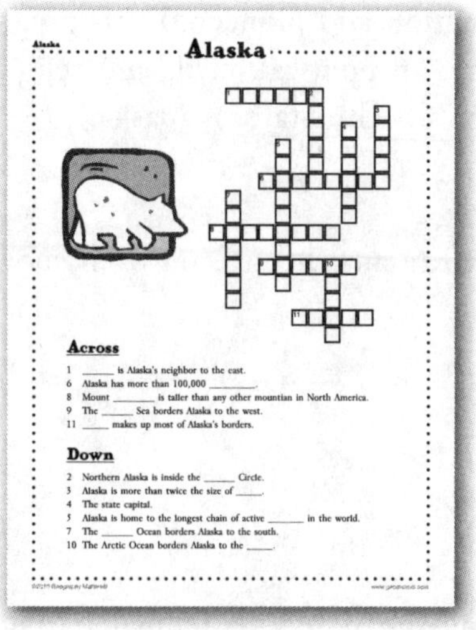

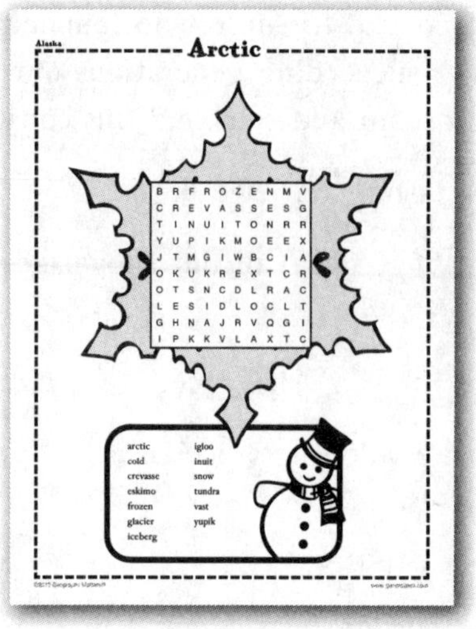

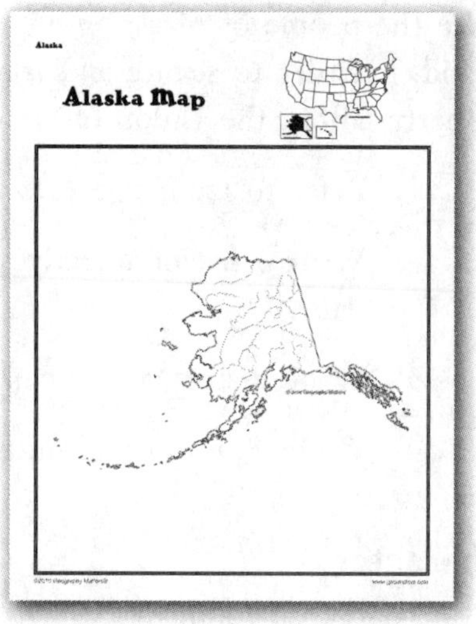

Activities

1. Color or label a map of Alaska.
2. Shade in the tundra on a map of North America. Mark the Arctic Circle with a dashed line; label.
3. Label Mount McKinley and the Bering Strait on a map of the United States.
4. Go to http://www.kidzone.ws/geography/usa/ for printable flag and state symbol coloring pages.
5. Prepare a meal in *Eat Your Way Through the U.S.A.* from the state of Alaska.
6. Watch *Balto* on video. Compare and contrast the cartoon version with the real story.
7. Build an igloo with sugar cubes.
8. Make a snowflake.
   - Twist three white pipe cleaners together in the center to form a six-sided figure. Tie string around the outer edge to make it look like a snowflake.
   - Pour 3-4 cups of boiling water into a wide-mouth Mason jar. Add 3 tablespoons of 20 Mule Team Borax for each cup of water.
   - Cut a few inches of string; it needs to be long enough to suspend the snowflake in the jar. Tie one end of the string around the snowflake and the other end around a pencil.
   - Hang the snowflake in the jar for at least 10 hours.
9. Using a compass, find which direction is north from your house.
10. Label the northern and southern magnetic poles on world map.

Arizona

Grand Canyon State

Home to one of America's most famous natural features, Arizona became the 48th state admitted to the Union on February 14, 1912. The name "Arizona" originates from the Native American words ***arizuma*** and ***arizonac***, which mean "place of little springs." Once thought to be a wasteland of worthless desert, Arizona is now a prosperous and rapidly growing state. The capital of Arizona is Phoenix.

Adopted in 1917, the state flag was designed by Colonel Charles W. Harris, Adjutant General of Arizona. The lower half of the flag is a blue field and the upper half is divided into thirteen rays of yellow and red; in the center is a copper star. The blue field represents liberty, and the rays of the setting sun represent the state's western location. The copper star pays tribute to the metal that first brought a large number of settlers to the state.

While mostly hot and dry, Arizona is more than just desert; in fact more than half the state is covered with mountains and plateaus. The chief mountain ranges are the rugged San Francisco Mountains and the gently sloping White Mountains. The Colorado River and its tributaries have cut beautiful canyons into the flat land. These include Canyon de Chelly, Oak Creek Canyon, and, of course, the Grand Canyon.

Interesting Facts:

- Northeast of Mesa, Arizona, is a special bridge that was built just for sheep.
- Arizona elected two women, Rachel Berry and Francis Munds, to the state legislature in 1914 – before women even had the right to vote.
- The first official rodeo was held on July 4, 1888, in Prescott, Arizona.
- The higher, cooler regions of the state have the largest ponderosa pine forest in the country.
- The Grand Canyon, Petrified Forest, and Painted Desert attract millions of tourists to Arizona each year.

General Reference

- ❑ *Arizona* - Paul Joseph
- ❑ *Arizona Facts and Symbols* - Emily McAuliffe
- ❑ *http://www.azgovernor.gov/kids.asp*
- ❑ *http://www.azsos.gov/public_services/kids/*
- ❑ *http://www.statesymbolsusa.org/Arizona/Arizona_state_symbols.html*

Geography

- ❑ canyon
  - *Geography From A to Z,* page 10
- ❑ Grand Canyon
  - *Grand Canyon National Park* - David Petersen
  - *In Search of the Grand Canyon* – Mary Ann Fraser (contains evolution)

History & Biographies

- ❑ Navajo
  - *The Navajo Nation* - Sandra M. Pasqua
  - *Navajo* - Richard M. Gaines
  - *The Navajos* – Nancy Bonvillain
  - *Songs from the Loom* – Monty Roessel
  - http://www.americanwest.com/pages/navajo2.htm
- ❑ Wyatt Earp
  - *Wyatt Earp* – Carl Green

Science

- ❑ cactus wren (state bird)
  - http://www.coloring.ws/birds.htm
- ❑ palo verde (state tree)
- ❑ saguaro cactus (the blossom is the state flower)
  - *Desert Giant* - Barbara Bash
  - *A Saguaro Cactus* - Jen Green
  - *The 100-Year-Old Cactus* - Anita Holmes
  - *Cactus in the Desert* - Phyllis Busch
  - *Cactus* - Carol Lerner
- ❑ turquoise (state gemstone)

❑ desert ecosystem

- *Geography From A to Z,* page 17
- *One Day in the Desert* – Jean Craighead George
- *Deserts* - Elsa Posell
- *Deserts* – Keith Brandt
- *Welcome to the Sea of Sand* – Jane Yolen
- *Desert* – April Pulley Sayre
- *Earth Science for Every Kid,* Experiment #49

Literature

❑ *The House I'll Build for the Wrens* - Shirley Neitzel

❑ *Brighty of the Grand Canyon* – Marguerite Henry

❑ *My Navajo Sister* – Eleanor Schick

❑ *Navajo Wedding Day* – Eleanor Schick

❑ *Dig, Wait, Listen: A Desert Toad's Tale* - April Pulley Sayre

❑ *Lost* – Paul Brett Johnson and Celeste Lewis

❑ *Boxcar Children: Mystery of the Lost Mine* – Gertrude Chandler Warner (RA)

❑ *Baseball Saved Us* – Ken Mochizuki

❑ *Waterless Mountain* - Laura Adams Armer (RA)

Language Arts

Preamble to the State Constitution:
We, the people of the State of Arizona, grateful to Almighty God for our liberties, do ordain this Constitution.

1. Refer to Language Arts Guide starting on page 8.
2. Write a list of adjectives to describe the desert. Write them with glue and sprinkle with colored sand.
3. The Grand Canyon is the largest canyon in the United States. Make a list of synonyms for "large."
4. Write a story about exploring the Grand Canyon.

Character

Arizona's state motto - *God Enriches* - has remained unchanged since 1864. Introduced by Richard McCormick, the motto has deep religious connotations. It is believed to originate from Genesis 14:23 of the Latin Vulgate version of the Bible. Acknowledging God as the source of blessings demonstrates **thankfulness** and **humility**.

- **Thankfulness** – Expression of gratitude; acknowledgment of a favor.
- **Humility** – Freedom from pride and arrogance; humbleness of mind; a modest estimate of one's own worth.

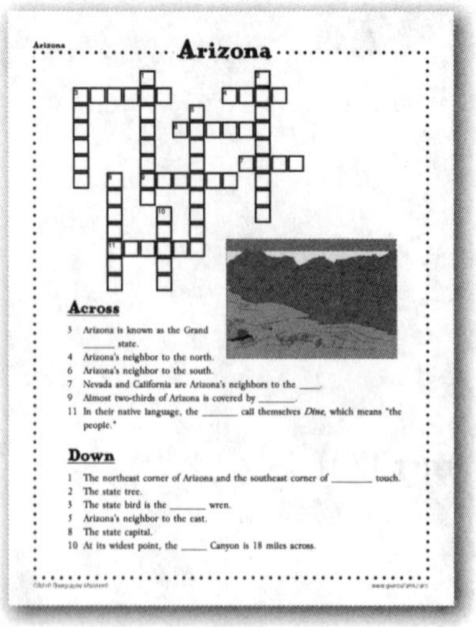

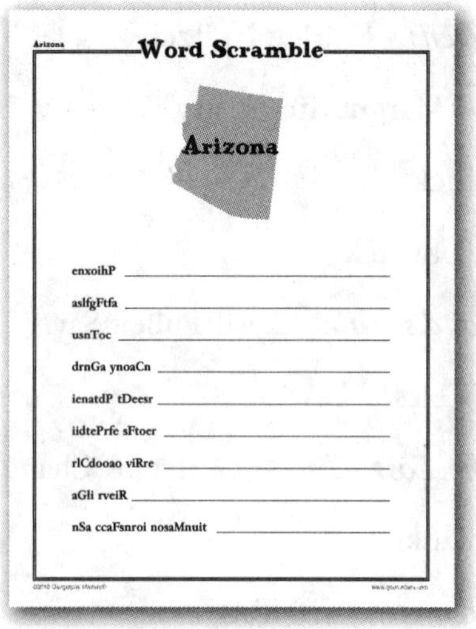

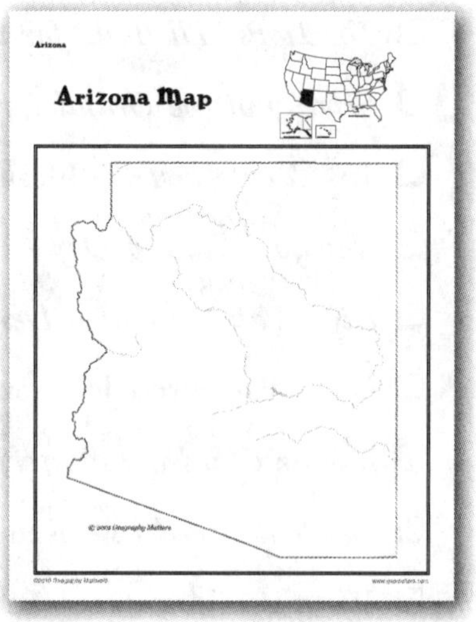

Activities

1. Color or label a map of Arizona.
2. Label a map of the United States with the Grand Canyon and deserts.
3. Go to http://www.kidzone.ws/geography/usa/ for printable flag and state symbol coloring pages.
4. Prepare a meal in *Eat Your Way Through the U.S.A.* from the state of Arizona.
5. Play Tsindl. Instructions are found in the back of *The Navajo Nation.*
6. Learn how desert plants get moisture from sand that appears dry.
   - Dig a hole two feet deep in sandy ground.
   - Place a cup in the bottom of the hole.
   - Cover the hole with a sheet of plastic; fasten down the edges.
   - Put a rock in the center of the plastic sheet, over the cup.
   - The sun will warm the sand in the hole, causing drops of water to form on the underside of the sheet and fall into the cup. Why? The moisture in the sand evaporated and re-formed on the plastic sheet.

7. Experiment with growing plants in different types of soil.
   - Put potting soil in one container, sand in a second container, and dirt from your yard in a third container.
   - Plant a seed in each container.
   - Observe and compare the differences in the plants. Measure and chart their growth.
8. Grow a cactus.
9. Make Navajo Fry Bread.

3 cups flour	1 cup warm water
1 tablespoon baking powder	oil
1/2 teaspoon salt	

Combine dry ingredients in a large mixing bowl. Add warm water and knead until dough is soft but not sticky. If necessary, add more flour or water. Cover bowl and let stand for 30 minutes.

Take an egg-sized piece of dough and pat it out to 1/4-inch thickness.

Fry in hot oil until golden brown on each side.

Serve plain or with ingredients for tacos.

Arkansas

Land of Opportunity

A beautiful land of mountains and valleys, thick forests, and fertile plains, Arkansas became the 25th state admitted to the Union, on June 13, 1836. Arkansas's name originates from the Native American word *Quapaw*, which means "downstream people." The state capital is Little Rock.

The state flag, adopted in 1913, was designed by Miss Willie Hocker, whose design was chosen by the Daughters of the American Revolution in a statewide flag contest. The large diamond represents the only diamond mine in the United States, which is located in Murfreesboro, Arkansas. Twenty-five stars depict Arkansas as the 25th state admitted to the Union, and three stars below the state name represent the three nations that have ruled Arkansas – Spain, France, and the United States. The large star above the name symbolizes the number of years that Arkansas was a member of the Confederacy.

The Ozark and Ouachita mountain ranges in the northern and western portions of Arkansas form the high-lands. The lowlands are in the eastern and southern part of the state. Both regions experience a warm, moist climate with extremely hot summers and cool winters. Its many factories, farms, and mines along with rich natural resources give Arkansas the nickname Land of Opportunity.

Interesting Facts:

- Hope, Arkansas, grows some of the world's largest watermelons; some of them weigh over 250 pounds!
- The Crater of Diamonds, near Murfreesboro, Arkansas, is the only public diamond mine in the United States.
- Arkansas produces more rice than any other state.
- Arkansas is the only state ever to pass a resolution on how to pronounce its name.

General Reference

- ❑ *Arkansas* - Anne Welsbacher
- ❑ *Arkansas Facts and Symbols* - Elaine A. Kule
- ❑ *Arkansas* - Domenica Di Piazza (contains evolution)
- ❑ http://www.soskids.ar.gov/index.html

Geography

- ❑ Ozark Mountains

History & Biographies

- ❑ Douglas MacArthur
  - *Douglas MacArthur: Young Protector* - Laura M. Long
- ❑ Sam Walton
  - *Sam Walton: America's Most Successful Shopkeeper* - Keith Greenberg
- ❑ Bill Clinton
  - www.whitehouse.gov/history/presidents/
  - www.presidentialavenue.com/wc.cfm
  - http://www.homeofheroes.com/e-books/presidents/42_clinton.html

Science

- ❑ mockingbird (state bird)
  - www.enchantedlearning.com/painting/birds.shtml
  - http://www.coloring.ws/birds.htm
- ❑ pine tree (state tree)
  - *Pine Trees* - Marcia S. Freeman
- ❑ apple blossom (state flower)
- ❑ diamonds (state gem)
  - *Diamonds* - Herbert S. Zim
- ❑ trout

Literature

- ❑ *Cotton in My Sack* - Lois Lenski (RA)
- ❑ *Silent Lotus* - Jeanne Lee (†)

Language Arts

Preamble to the State Constitution:

We, the people of the State of Arkansas, grateful to Almighty God for the privilege of choosing our own form of government, for our civil and religious liberty, and desiring to perpetuate its blessings and secure the same to our selves and posterity, do ordain and establish this Constitution.

1. Refer to Language Arts Guide starting on page 8.
2. Write a newspaper article on the 1906 discovery of diamonds in Arkansas.
3. Make a list of adjectives to describe diamonds.

Character

In 1907 the Latin motto for Arkansas was revised from *Regnant Populi* to *Regnat Populus,* which means "The People Rule." The original motto was selected in 1864; however, the origin of the motto is not known.

Since the Arkansas motto focuses on people, the character qualities to be studied are **industriousness** and **self-control/self-government**. These are two qualities which must be present in any people if they are to rule themselves or others effectively.

- **Industriousness** – Diligence in business or study; constantly, regularly, or habitually being occupied in business or a particular pursuit; opposite to slothfulness and idleness. This trait, common in the early citizens of the U.S., is rare in our population today. We should encourage our children to be diligent in every area of their lives now so that they can achieve great things in the future.
- **Self-Control/Self-Government**- Behavior guided from within; internal control; ability to control one's emotions, desires, or actions. Self-government in the modern dictionary means the ability of a group to govern itself, as in a democracy. However, the definition here means the ability of a person to govern himself so that outside restraints are unnecessary. Self-government goes a step further than self-control. A person may be able to demonstrate self-control in one situation, but not in another. Someone who exhibits self-government is consistently making the right choices based on his internal conscience and value system. To teach our children to be self-governed requires years of dedication and consistency in our own lives.

State Flag Pledge

I salute the Arkansas Flag with its diamond and stars. We pledge our loyalty to thee.

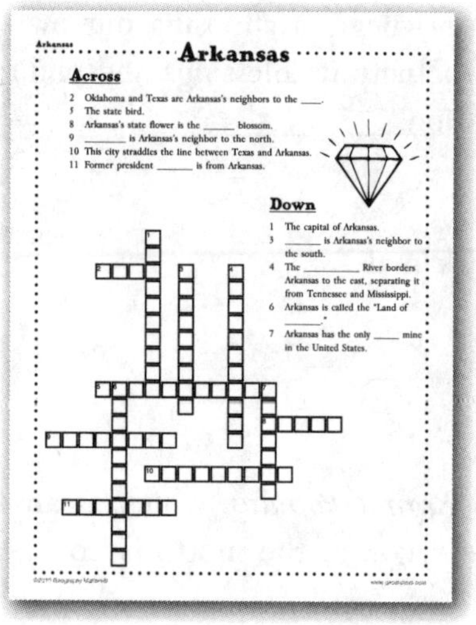

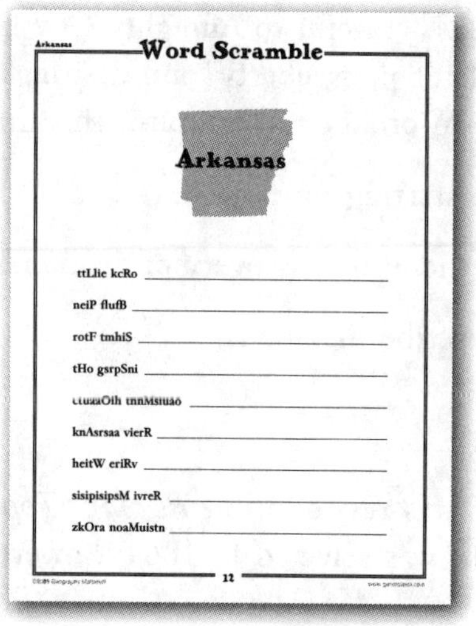

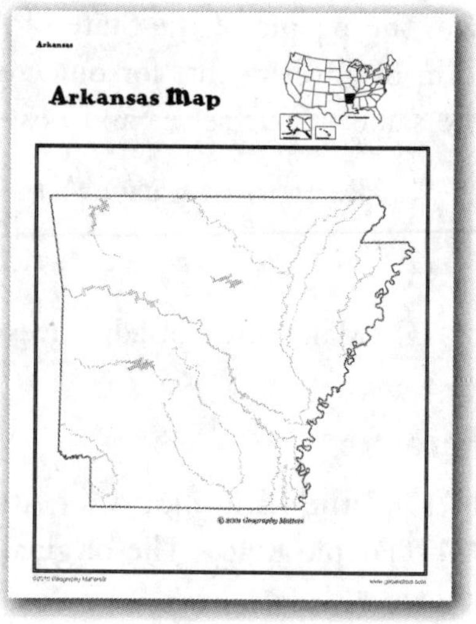

Activities

1. Color or label a map of Arkansas.
2. Label the Ozark Mountains on a map of the United States.
3. Go to http://www.kidzone.ws/geography/usa/ for printable flag and state symbol coloring pages.
4. Prepare a meal in *Eat Your Way Through the U.S.A.* from the state of Arkansas.
5. Visit a local trout farm or fish hatchery.
6. Interview a fisherman or worker at the trout farm or fish hatchery.
7. Trout craft:
    - Flatten and smooth out a coffee filter.
    - Color loosely with markers.
    - Wet coffee filter with a spray bottle. Colors from the markers should run and bleed into one another. Allow to dry for several hours or with the aid of a blow dryer.
    - After the coffee filter is dry, cut out the shape of a fish.
    - Draw on a face.
    - Cut out and glue on small strips and triangles of aluminum foil for fins and gills.
    - Glue fish onto a piece of blue paper.
    - Cover with plastic wrap and secure with glue on back side of blue paper.

California

Golden State

Rich in history and resources, California was the admitted to the Union on September 9, 1850, making it the 31st state. Sixteenth-century explorers named California after a fictional treasure island from a popular story of that day. California, located on the far west coast of the United States, is a state of diverse resources, climates, and people. The capital is Sacramento.

The state flag, adopted in 1911, is modeled after the flag that was raised at Sonoma on June 14, 1846. On that date a small group of settlers declared California a republic, independent of Mexico. The lone star represented California as an independent republic, and the grizzly bear was meant to show great strength and the willingness of the settlers to fight for freedom against Mexico. The flag was removed when it was learned that Mexico and the United States were already at war. Not long after, the California legislature adopted the "bear flag" as the official state flag.

California has four distinct geographic regions: Coast Ranges, the Inland Mountains, the Central Valley, and the Great Basin. The climate in all four regions can be divided into the dry season and the wet season. However, the temperatures, rainfall, and wind speeds vary greatly throughout the regions. Towering mountains which give way to fertile valleys dominate some regions, while others are covered with vast, dry deserts. These varying conditions give California the largest variety of plants and animals found in a single state.

Interesting Facts:

- California's state animal, the grizzly bear, no longer lives in California.
- The highest temperature ever recorded in the United States was in Death Valley on July 10, 1913. The temperature soared to an amazing 134°!
- The Hollywood Bowl is the world's largest outdoor amphitheater.
- California has the largest economy of any state.
- If California's economic size were measured against other countries, it would rank as the 7th largest economy in the world.
- The highest and lowest points in the continental United States are within 100 miles of one another. Mount Whitney measures 14,495 feet, and Bad Water in Death Valley is 282 feet below sea level.

General Reference

- ❑ *California* - Anne Welsbacher
- ❑ *California Facts and Symbols* - Emily McAuliffe
- ❑ *California* – Kathy Pelta (contains evolution)
- ❑ http://www.statesymbolsusa.org/California/StateSymbols.html

Geography

- ❑ Death Valley
- ❑ Sierra Nevada Mountains
- ❑ San Andreas Fault
- ❑ Golden Gate Bridge
  - *The Golden Gate Bridge* – Thomas S. Owens

History & Biographies

- ❑ California Gold Rush
  - *The Story of Gold at Sutter's Mill* - R. Conrad Stein
  - http://score.rims.k12.ca.us/activity/goldrush/
- ❑ Levi Strauss
  - *Mr. Blue Jeans: A Story about Levi Strauss* - Maryann N. Weidt
- ❑ San Francisco and Los Angeles earthquakes
  - *The Story of the San Francisco Earthquake* – R. Conrad Stein
  - *San Francisco Earthquake, 1989* – Victoria Sherrow
  - *Shock Waves Through Los Angeles* – Carole G. Vogel
- ❑ Theodor Seuss Geisel
  - *Dr. Seuss* - Mae Woods
  - *Oh the Places He Went: A Story about Dr. Seuss* - Maryann Weidt
  - *The Boy on Fairfield Street* - Kathleen Krull
  - http://members.enchantedlearning.com/bios/seuss/cloze/
- ❑ Richard M. Nixon
  - www.whitehouse.gov/history/presidents/
  - www.presidentialavenue.com/rn.cfm
  - http://www.homeofheroes.com/e-books/presidents/37_nixon.html
- ❑ Sally Ride
  - *Sally Ride* – Barbara Kramer
  - http://members.enchantedlearning.com/explorers/page/r/ridecloze.shtml

Science

- ❑ quail (state bird)
  - www.enchantedlearning.com/painting/birds.shtml
  - http://www.coloring.ws/birds.htm
  - www.daniellesplace.com/html/birdcrafts.html
- ❑ redwood (state tree)
  - *Redwoods Are the Tallest Trees in the World* – David A. Adler
  - *Redwoods* – Peter Murray
- ❑ California poppy (state flower)
  - http://www.dltk-holidays.com/remembrance/mvflower.html
- ❑ goats
  - *Life on a Goat Farm* - Judy Wolfman
  - www.coloring.ws/animals.html
- ❑ computers
  - *What Is a Computer?* – Jim Drake
  - *Computers for Beginners* – Margaret Stevens & Rebecca Treays
  - *Computers All Around Us* – Jim Drake
  - *The Age of Computers* – World Book
  - *The Internet* – Charles A. Jortberg
  - *Internet* – Lora Koehler
  - *E-Mail* – Larry Dane Brimner
  - *Book of Inventors* - Usborne, page 22
- ❑ gold (state mineral)
  - http://members.enchantedlearning.com/geology/rocks/pages/gold.shtml
- ❑ earthquakes
  - *Earthquakes* – Jane Walker
  - *Earthquake!* - Jules Archer
  - *Earth Science for Every Kid,* Experiments #30-35
  - *Earthquake Games* – Matthys Levy
  - http://pbskids.org/zoom/activities/sci/seismometer.html

Literature

- ❑ *Chang's Paper Pony* - Eleanor Coerr
- ❑ *Wagon Train* - Sydelle Kramer
- ❑ *Red Flower Goes West* - Ann Turner
- ❑ *Snowshoe Thompson* - Nancy Levinson
- ❑ *San Francisco Boy* - Lois Lenski (RA)
- ❑ *Kildee House* - Rutherford Montgomery (RA)
- ❑ *By the Great Horn Spoon* - Sid Fleischman (RA)
- ❑ *Earthquake at Dawn* - Kristiana Gregory (RA)
- ❑ *Earthquake! A Story of Old San Francisco* – Kathleen V. Kudlinski (RA)
- ❑ *Francis: The Earthquake Dog* – Judith Ross Enderle
- ❑ *I Am Lavina Cumming* - Susan Lowell
- ❑ *Tikvah Means Hope* - Patricia Polacco

Language Arts

Preamble to the State Constitution:
We, the People of the State of California, grateful to Almighty God for our freedom, in order to secure and perpetuate its blessings, do establish this Constitution.

1. Refer to Language Arts Guide starting on page 8.
2. Have the child write a news article as if he were a reporter covering the San Francisco earthquake.
3. Write a story of what the world would be like without computers. To research the story, interview parents and grandparents about what life was like without modern technology.
4. Write a friendly letter to a friend or relative and send it via e-mail.
5. If reading Dr. Seuss, make up silly rhymes. Older children can make a story with their rhymes. If they would like, have them illustrate it and make it into a book.

Character

The California state motto – *Eureka* - means "I have found it." This Greek motto was first used on the seal of California when it was designed in 1849. The term was used in reference to the state's admission into the Union or the success of the miners looking for gold. The motto was probably referring to the discovery of gold in 1848. The word *Eureka* has special significance – it is said that the Greek mathematician Archimedes said it when he discovered a method to determine the purity of gold. *Eureka* was made the official state motto in 1963 after several failed attempts to establish "In God We Trust" as California's motto. Since treasure and wealth seem to be a recurring theme in California history, the character traits of **resourcefulness**, **initiative**, and **responsibility** are the focus for this state. **Resourcefulness** was chosen because the Californians who traveled in search of gold had to be resourceful when they discovered there was not enough gold to make everyone rich. **Initiative** was chosen because once a new discovery was made (whether it was gold, the movie industry, or the silicon chip), it took human initiative to pursue that discovery and use it to benefit fellow Californians. **Responsibility** is the most important of the character traits covered here. It takes responsibility to utilize the gifts and resources one is given.

- **Resourcefulness (steadfastness)** – The ability to deal promptly and effectively with problems and difficulties – a source of strength or ability within oneself.
- **Initiative** – The characteristic of originating new ideas or methods; ability to think or act without being urged; enterprise.
- **Responsibility** – The state of being accountable or answerable; liable to account as for a trust reposed.

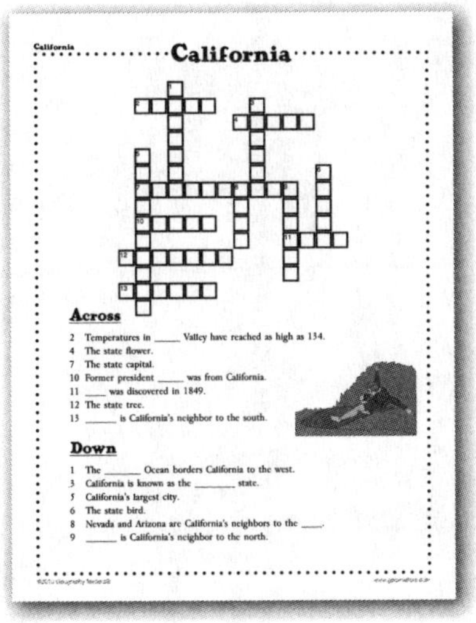

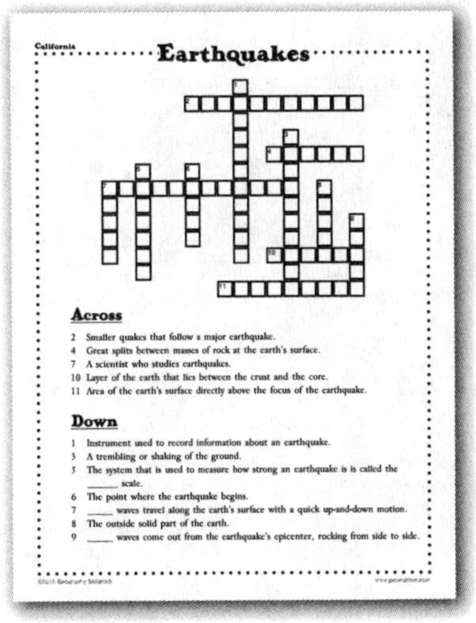

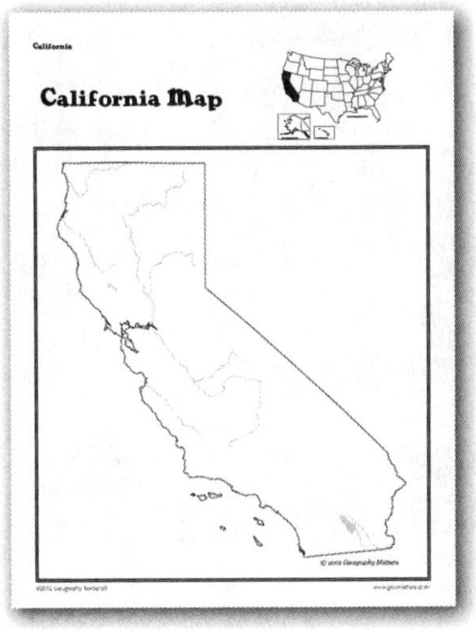

Activities

1. Color or label a map of California.
2. Label the Sierra Nevada Mountains, Death Valley, and the San Andreas Fault on a map of the United States.
3. Go to http://www.kidzone.ws/geography/usa/ for printable flag and state symbol coloring pages.
4. Prepare a meal in *Eat Your Way Through the U.S.A.* from the state of California.
5. Discuss how computers have changed our lives. See #3 under Language Arts.
6. If you read *Tikvah Means Hope,* map how far it is from New Jersey to California.

Colorado

Centennial State

Known as the Centennial State because it joined the Union 100 years after the signing of the Declaration of Independence, Colorado became the 38th state on August 1, 1876. Colorado is a Spanish word meaning "colored red." The name was originally given to the Colorado River because of its path through the red sandstone canyons, and the state took its name from the river. Denver, which houses a U.S. mint, is the capital of Colorado.

The state flag was designed by Andrew Carlisle Johnson and adopted by the General Assembly in 1911. The red "C" stands for Colorado. The gold ball depicts the state's gold deposits.

Colorado is a land of unusual natural beauty. The majestic Rocky Mountains cover over half of the state. The Colorado Rockies are called the Roof of North America because 50-60 peaks reach heights of 14,000 feet or more and are the tallest in the Rocky Mountain chain. The Great Plains stretch to the east, and to the west lie plateaus, hills, and valleys. Colorado's climate is mostly dry with warm days and cool nights. The Rocky Mountain region is considerably cooler, with large quantities of snow.

Interesting Facts:

- The largest silver nugget ever discovered in North America was found in 1894 in Aspen, Colorado. It weighed 1,840 pounds.
- Adolf Hitler owned almost 9,000 acres of land in Colorado at the beginning of World War II.
- The world's highest suspension bridge is located at Royal Gorge, near Canon City.
- The United States government owns a third of Colorado's land and controls grazing, logging, and mining on those lands.

General Reference

- ❑ *Colorado* - Anne Welsbacher
- ❑ *Colorado Facts and Symbols* - Emily McAuliffe
- ❑ http://www.statesymbolsusa.org/Colorado/statesymbols.html
- ❑ http://www.colorado.gov/archive/20080527/colorado-government-services-for/kids-students.html

Geography

- ❑ mountain
  - *Geography From A to Z,* pages 30-31
- ❑ Rocky Mountains
  - *Rocky Mountain National Park* - David Petersen
- ❑ Mesa Verde
  - *Mesa Verde National Park* - David Petersen

History & Biographies

- ❑ Comanche
  - *Comanche* - Richard M. Gaines
- ❑ Quanah Parker
- ❑ Zebulon Pike
  - *Profiles from History* - Volume 1, pages 155-162
  - *Zeb Pike: Boy Traveler* - Augusta Stevenson
  - *Zebulon Pike: Explorer of the Southwest* - William R. Sanford & Carl R. Green
- ❑ Jim Beckwourth
  - *Jim Beckwourth: Adventures of a Mountain Man* - Louis Sabin
- ❑ Katherine Lee Bates

Science

- ❑ lark bunting (state bird)
  - http://www.coloring.ws/birds.htm
- ❑ blue spruce (state tree)
- ❑ columbine (state flower)
- ❑ aquamarine (state gem)
- ❑ pronghorn antelope
  - *Marvels of Creation, Magnificent Mammals* - Buddy and Kay Davis
- ❑ marmot
  - *Woodchucks* - Emilie U. Lepthien, pages 29-34

Literature

- ❑ *Purple Mountain Majesties* - Barbara Younger
- ❑ *Prairie School* – Avi
- ❑ *High as a Hawk* – T. A. Barron

Language Arts

Preamble to the State Constitution:

We, the people of Colorado, with profound reverence for the Supreme Ruler of the Universe, in order to form a more independent and perfect government; establish justice; insure tranquility; provide for the common defense; promote the general welfare and secure the blessings of liberty to ourselves and our posterity, do ordain and establish this constitution for the "State of Colorado."

1. Refer to Language Arts Guide starting on page 8.
2. Have the child keep a journal as if he were a pioneer crossing the Rocky Mountains.
3. Copy the words to "America the Beautiful."

Character

The Colorado state motto - *Nothing without the Deity* - is credited to the first territorial governor, William Gilpin, and was part of the territorial seal. The translation of the original Latin motto has varied throughout Colorado's history. Originally translated as "Nothing without Providence" or "Nothing without God," the official translation was decided upon by the designers and framers of the state seal in 1877.

- **Respect** – That deportment or course of action which proceeds from esteem; regard; due attention; as to treat a person with respect.

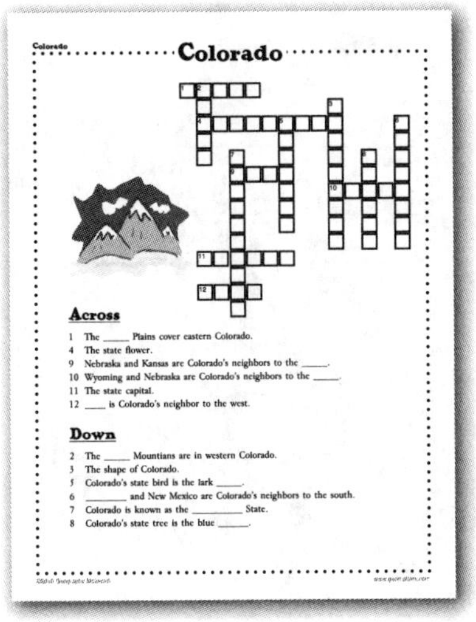

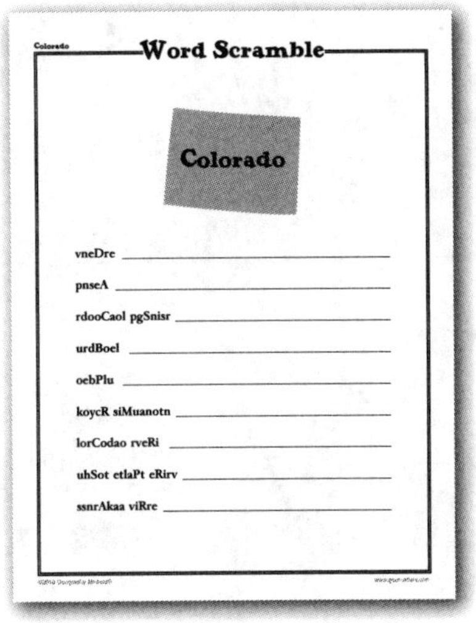

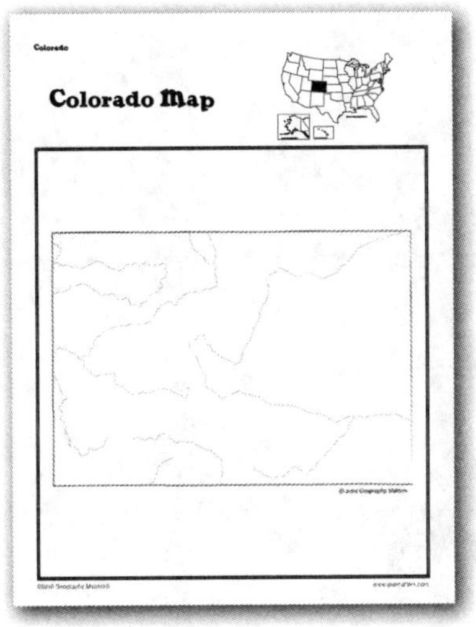

Activities

1. Color or label a map of Colorado.
2. Label the Rocky Mountains and Colorado River on a map of the United States.
3. Go to http://www.kidzone.ws/geography/usa/ for printable flag and state symbol coloring pages.
4. Prepare a meal in *Eat Your Way Through the U.S.A.* from the state of Colorado.
5. Listen to "America the Beautiful." Katherine Lee Bates wrote the song after she visited Pikes Peak.

Connecticut

Constitution State

Connecticut, the southernmost of the New England States, became the 5th state to enter the Union on January 9, 1788. The name is from the Algonquian Indian word *Quonehtacut,* which means "beside the long tidal river." The state capital is Hartford.

Adopted in 1897, the flag is a simple design of a blue background with the state seal and motto in the middle. The three grapevines symbolize the transplanting of the culture and traditions of Europe to the colony of Connecticut.

Covered with rolling hills, valleys, rivers, and lakes, Connecticut is divided by the Connecticut River, which flows into Long Island Sound, the state's outlet to the Atlantic Ocean. Forests, rivers, lakes, waterfalls, and a sandy shore all contribute to Connecticut's natural beauty. Connecticut has a moderate climate with four distinct seasons.

Interesting Facts:

- The nation's first newspaper, *The Connecticut Courant,* was established in 1764. It is still in publication today as *The Hartford Courant.*
- The world's first telephone exchange opened in New Haven in 1878 with 21 subscribers.
- America's first English dictionary was published by Noah Webster in 1806.

General Reference

- ❑ *Connecticut* - Anne Welsbacher
- ❑ *Connecticut Facts and Symbols* - Emily McAuliffe

Geography

- ❑ Connecticut River

History & Biographies

- ❑ Noah Webster
  - *Noah Webster: Boy of Words* - Helen Boyd Higgins
  - *What Do You Mean? A Story About Noah Webster* - Jeri Ferris

- ❑ Harriet Beecher Stowe
    - *A Picture Book of Harriet Beecher Stowe* – David A. Adler
- ❑ Barbara McClintock
- ❑ Gertrude Chandler Warner
    - *Gertrude Chandler Warner* - Joan Wallner
- ❑ Tomie dePaola
    - *26 Fairmount Avenue* - Tomie dePaola
- ❑ Nathan Hale

Science

- ❑ robin (state bird)
    - *The Robins in Your Backyard* - Nancy Carol Willis
    - www.kidzone.ws/animals/birds/american-robin.htm
    - www.enchantedlearning.com/painting/birds.shtml
- ❑ white oak (state tree)
    - *Oak Trees* - Marcia S. Freeman
- ❑ mountain laurel (state flower)
- ❑ garnet (state gem)
- ❑ praying mantis (state insect)
- ❑ skunk
    - *Marvels of Creation, Magnificent Mammals* - Buddy and Kay Davis
    - *Skunks* - Emilie U. Lepthien
    - *Zoo Guide*, page 91
    - www.coloring.ws/animals.html
    - www.dltk-kids.com/animals/mskunk.html
- ❑ genetics/DNA (Barbara McClintock was a leading scientist in genetics.)
    - *DNA Is Here to Stay* – Dr. Fran Balkwill
    - Build model DNA using K'Nex.

Literature

- ❑ *The Boxcar Children* - Gertrude Chandler Warner (RA)
- ❑ *The Art Lesson* - Tomie dePaola
- ❑ *Too Many Hopkins* - Tomie de Paola
- ❑ *My Spring Robin* - Anne Rockwell
- ❑ "Little Robin Redbreast" – Mother Goose rhyme
- ❑ *Adventures of Jimmy Skunk* – Thornton W. Burgess (RA)
- ❑ *Windcatcher* - Avi (RA)

Language Arts

Preamble to the State Constitution:
The people of the State of Connecticut acknowledging with gratitude, the good providence of God, in having permitted them to enjoy a free government; do, in order more effectually to define, secure, and perpetuate the liberties, rights and privileges which they have derived from their ancestors; hereby, after a careful consideration and revision, ordain and establish the following constitution and form of civil government.

1. Refer to Language Arts Guide starting on page 8.
2. *26 Fairmount Avenue* by Tomie dePaola is an autobiography. Discuss the difference between a biography and an autobiography.
3. Learn or review dictionary skills. Be sure to include:
    - guide words
    - entry word
    - definition
    - phonetic spelling

Character

The motto for Connecticut - *Qui Transtulit Sustinet* - is translated as "He who transplanted continues to sustain." The motto has been a part of Connecticut since the creation of the Saybrook Colony Seal and was officially adopted in 1784. The origin of the seal is unknown; however, some historians cite Psalm 80 or Psalm 79:3 as possible sources. Trusting another person to sustain you takes **patience** and **perseverance**.

- **Patience** - The suffering of afflictions, pain, toil, calamity, provocation, or other evil with a calm, unruffled temper; endurance without murmuring or fretfulness. Patience may spring from constitutional fortitude, from a kind of heroic pride, or from Christian submission to the divine will.
- **Perseverance** - Persistence in any thing undertaken; continued pursuit or prosecution of any business or enterprise begun. Like patience, perseverance is often forgotten in our nation. If things start to go wrong or we get tired, we are often told to quit or give up. Our nation would not exist if our forefathers had not persevered through adversity. We need to emphasize the importance of perseverance in our lives.

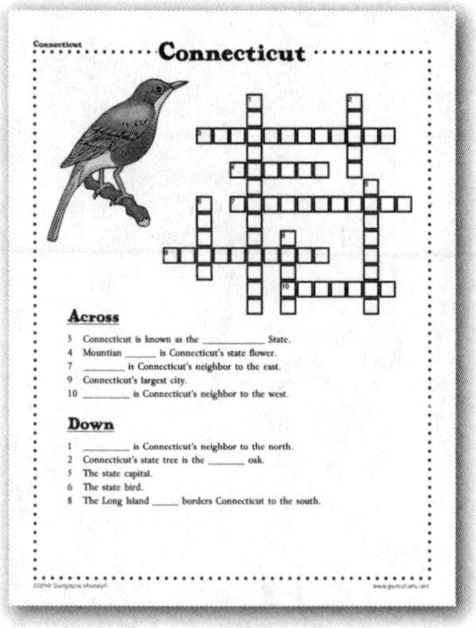

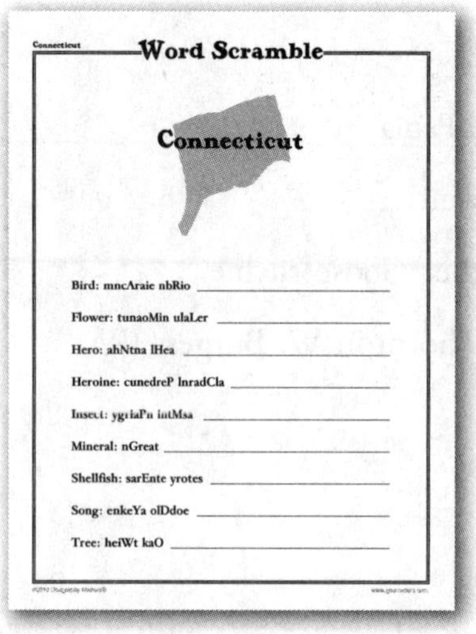

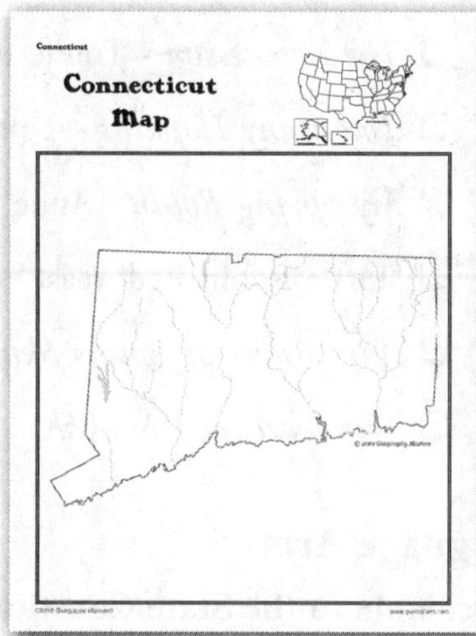

Activities

1. Color or label a map of Connecticut.
2. Label the Connecticut River on a map of the United States.
3. Go to http://www.kidzone.ws/geography/usa/ for printable flag and state symbol coloring pages.
4. Prepare a meal in *Eat Your Way Through the U.S.A.* from the state of Connecticut.
5. Listen to the state song, "Yankee Doodle."
6. Make a *Boxcar Children* diorama.

Delaware

The First State

One of the original thirteen colonies, Delaware became the 1st state admitted into the Union on December 7, 1787. Delaware was named after a governor of Virginia, Lord De La War. The name was first given to the Delaware River and then used by the state. The capital of Delaware is Dover.

The state flag was adopted on July 24, 1913. The shades of buff and colonial blue represent the uniform of General George Washington. The soldier and farmer represent the duties of the people of Delaware both as productive citizens and defenders of their rights. The wheat, corn, and ox represent the importance of agriculture to the state, and the ship represents the commerce industry. Most of the land is flat and only 60 feet above sea level. The state lies almost entirely within the Atlantic Coastal Plain. The northern tip of the state is in the piedmont and has rolling hills and valleys. Portions of Delaware, Maryland, and Virginia form the Delmarva Peninsula.

Interesting Facts:

- The first log cabin in America was built in present-day Delaware in 1638.
- Delaware is known as the chemical capital of the world.
- Pea Patch Island was formed by real peas! When a ship carrying peas became stuck on a sandbar, the peas spilled into the river. The following spring the peas sprouted and began to grow, thus forming the island.
- Delaware is the only state where the legislature can amend the state constitution without voters' approval.

General Reference

- ❑ *Delaware* - Anne Welsbacher
- ❑ *Delaware Facts and Symbols* - Elaine A. Kule
- ❑ *Delaware* – Dottie Brown
- ❑ http://www.state.de.us/gic/kidspage/
- ❑ http://www.statesymbolsusa.org/Delaware/StateSymbolsDelaware.html

Geography

- ❑ Delaware Bay

History & Biographies

- ❑ Henry Heimlich
- ❑ Howard Pyle (author of The Merry Adventures of Robin Hood)
- ❑ Annie Jump Cannon

Science

- ❑ blue hen chicken (state bird)
  - www.daniellesplace.com/html/birdcrafts.html
- ❑ American holly (state tree)
- ❑ peach blossom (state flower)
- ❑ sillimanite (state mineral)
- ❑ chemicals
  - *Chemicals & Reactions* – Jon Richards
  - *Experiments with Chemistry* – Helen J. Challand
  - *I Can Be a Chemist* – Paul Sipiera
- ❑ ladybug (state insect)
  - *Ladybug* - Robert McClung
  - *Ladybugs* - James Rowan
  - *My Ladybug* - Herbert Wong and Matthew Vessel
  - http://www.enchantedlearning.com/subjects/insects/ladybug/Ladybug.shtml
  - http://www.enchantedlearning.com/subjects/insects/ladybug/label/
  - http://www.earthsbirthday.org/butterflies/ladybugs/anatomy.htm
  - http://www.coloring.ws/ladybugs1.htm
  - www.daniellesplace.com/html/ladybugcrafts.html

Literature

- ❑ *The Merry Adventures of Robin Hood* – Howard Pyle (Book-on-tape or abridged children's version. Jim Weiss of Greathall Productions has an audio abridged children's version.)
- ❑ *Bubba and Trixie* – Lisa Ernst
- ❑ *The Grouchy Ladybug* – Eric Carle
- ❑ *Pea Patch Island* – Polly Curren

Language Arts

Preamble to the State Constitution:

Through Divine goodness, all men have by nature the rights of worshiping and serving their Creator according to the dictates of their consciences, of enjoying and defending life and liberty, of acquiring and protecting reputation and property, and in general of obtaining objects suitable to their condition, without injury by one to another; and as these rights are essential to their welfare, for due exercise thereof, power is inherent in them; and therefore all just authority in the institutions of political society is derived from the people, and established with their consent, to advance their happiness; and they may for this end, as circumstances require, from time to time, alter their Constitution of government.

1. Refer to Language Arts Guide starting on page 8.
2. Write a story about landing on Pea Patch Island.

Character

The **original** motto for Delaware - *Liberty and Independence* - was adopted in 1847. It was added to the state seal to acknowledge the ideals of American government. The people of Delaware are proud that they were the first state in the Union, and the motto signifies two of their most important ideals.

The original colonists and statesmen of Delaware were extremely **efficient** in joining the independence movement and becoming the first state. They were **determined** to support and defend the rights of its people.

- **Efficiency** - The act of producing effects; causing to be or exist; active competent power; doing things quickly and accurately.
- **Determination** - Being settled, resolved; a firm or fixed purpose or a firm resolution.

  We should encourage our children to be determined and fixed in their purposes. Determination in a child has to be directed towards the correct goals. We should to teach our children that being determined is good as long as that determination is not in rebellion. Having a fixed purpose was what kept our forefathers focused on achieving freedom and liberty.

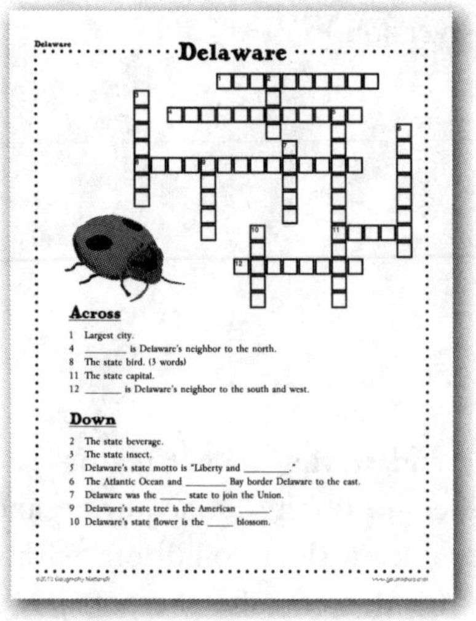

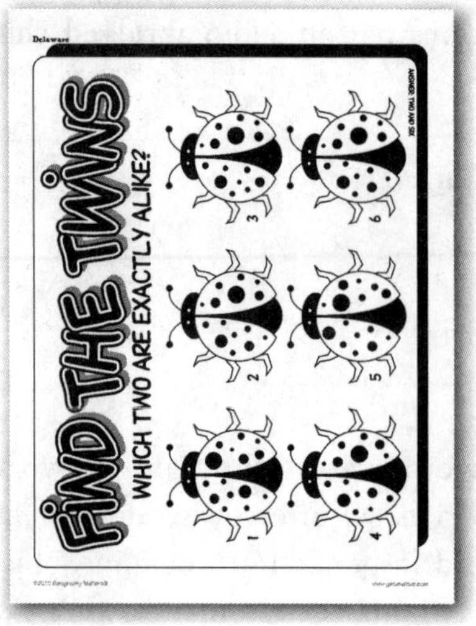

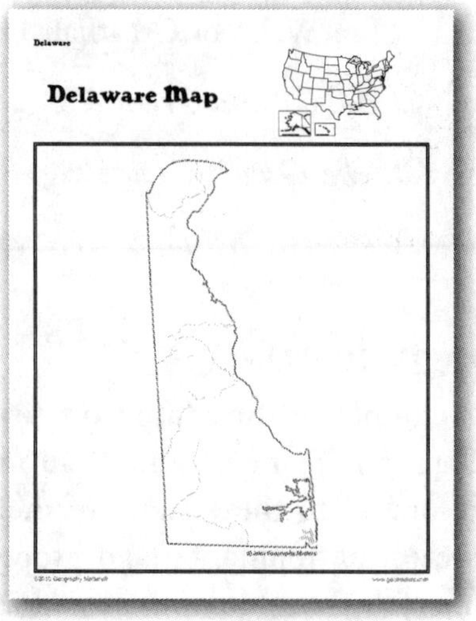

Activities

1. Color or label a map of Delaware.
2. Label Delaware Bay on a map of the United States.
3. Locate the Delmarva Peninsula on a map of the United States.
4. Go to http://www.kidzone.ws/geography/usa/ for printable flag and state symbol coloring pages.
5. Prepare a meal in *Eat Your Way Through the U.S.A.* from the state of Delaware.
6. If studying Henry Heimlich, learn the Heimlich maneuver.
7. Get an early start on Christmas by making holly ornaments.
   - Mix together 2 cups flour, 2 cups salt, and 1 cup water. Knead for 10 minutes.
   - On a floured surface, roll dough out to 1/4-inch thick.
   - Cut dough into shape of holly leaves and berries.
   - Arrange two leaves with a cluster of berries.
   - Make a small hole in the top of each leaf.
   - Place ornament(s) on a cookie sheet and bake at 225° for 2-3 hours. Cool completely.
   - Paint with green and red paints. Allow to dry.
   - String ribbon through the holes in the top of the leaves.
8. If reading *Pea Patch Island*, have peas with lunch or supper.

Florida

The Sunshine State

A land of swaying palm trees and warm ocean breezes, Florida became the 27th state admitted to the Union, on March 3, 1845. Given its name by Juan Ponce de Leon, "Florida" means "full of flowers" or "flowery" in Spanish. Florida is called the Sunshine State because of its abundance of sunny days. The state capital is Tallahassee.

Originally Florida's flag was white with the state seal in the center. In the 1890s Governor Fleming suggested adding a red cross to the background to prevent it from looking like a flag of surrender. This final version was adopted as the official state flag in 1900. The sun represents glory, splendor, and the authority of the state government. The boat symbolizes commerce and growth. The palm tree stands for victory, justice, and honor. The Native American girl strewing flowers, which stand for hope, shows the influence of the different nations on Florida's history.

Located in the far southeast corner of the United States, Florida is a peninsula that juts out almost 400 miles into the Atlantic Ocean. Florida has the lowest average elevation of all 50 states and an extremely warm, mild climate. Hurricanes and strong thunderstorms are the biggest weather threat in the region.

The land in Florida is flat, with one of the largest swamp regions in the world. A vast watery wilderness, the Florida Everglades is a unique wetland ecosystem. Most of this marshland is covered with saw grass so thick that the only way to navigate through it is by using natural water lanes. With its beautiful, sandy beaches, Florida has the longest coastline in the continental United States.

Interesting Facts:

- St. Augustine, founded in 1565, is the oldest city in the United States.
- Lake Okeechobee is the second largest natural body of fresh water completely within the United States.
- Fort Myers has thunder and lightning 100 days a year.
- Florida is the longest peninsula in the United States.
- The Florida Keys are a chain of small coral islands that extend 150 miles off the southern tip of Florida.
- The southernmost point in the continental United States is at Key West, Florida.

General Reference

- ❑ *Florida* - Paul Joseph
- ❑ *Florida Facts and Symbols* - Emily McAuliffe
- ❑ http://www.leg.state.fl.us/kids/

Geography

- ❑ Everglades
  - *Everglades* – Peter Lourie
  - *Everglades* – Christine Sotnak Rom (evolution on page 22)
- ❑ peninsula
  - *Geography From A to Z,* page 34
- ❑ key
  - *Geography From A to Z,* page 27
- ❑ reef
  - *Geography From A to Z,* page 37

History & Biographies

- ❑ Seminole
  - *Seminole* - Richard M. Gaines
- ❑ Osceola
  - *Osceola: Young Seminole Indian* – Electa Clark
  - *Osceola: Seminole Leader* – Ronald Syme
  - *Osceola: Seminole War Chief* –Wyatt Blassingame
- ❑ Neil Armstrong
  - *Neil Armstrong* – Carmen Bredeson
  - *Book of Explorers* - Usborne
  - http://search.nasa.gov/search/search.jsp?nasaInclude=armstrong
- ❑ John Glenn
  - http://members.enchantedlearning.com/explorers/page/g/glenncloze.shtml
  - http://search.nasa.gov/search/centersearch.jsp?centername=glenn&nasaInclude=john+glenn&=Glenn

- ❑ Virgil "Gus" Grissom
  - *Virgil I. Grissom: Boy Astronaut* – Carl L. Chappell
  - http://search.nasa.gov/search/search.jsp?nasaInclude=grissom

Science

- ❑ astronauts & space travel
  - *Astronauts* – Carol Greene
  - *Astronauts* – Tami Deedrick
  - *If You Were an Astronaut* – Virginia Schomp
  - *Astronauts: Training for Space* – Michael D. Cole
  - *Kennedy Space Center* – Timothy R. Gaffney
  - *Moon Flights* – Dennis B. Fradin
  - *The International Space Station* – Franklyn M. Branley
  - *The Story of the Challenger Disaster* – Zachary Kent (RA)
  - http://www.nasa.gov/
- ❑ tomatoes
  - *The Tomato and Other Fruit Vegetables* - Millicent E. Selsam
  - *Tomato* – Barrie Watts
  - http://coloringbookfun.com/vegy/index.htm
- ❑ oranges (The blossom is the state flower.)
- ❑ sabal palm (state tree)
  - *Palm Trees* – Marcia S. Freeman
- ❑ agatized coral (state stone)
- ❑ mangroves
- ❑ glossy ibis
- ❑ manatee (state marine mammal)
  - *Manatees* – Kathy Feeney
  - *Sam the Sea Cow* – Francine Jacobs
  - *Mary Manatee* – Suzanne Tate
  - http://pelotes.jea.com/ColoringPage/Mammal/Colmanat.htm
  - *Zoo Guide,* page 61
  - *Aquarium Guide,* page 205

Literature

- ❑ *Dolphin Adventure* – Wayne Grover (RA)
- ❑ *Dolphin Treasure* – Wayne Grover (RA)
- ❑ *Dolphin Freedom* – Wayne Grover (RA)
- ❑ *Strawberry Girl* – Lois Lenski (RA)

Language Arts

Preamble to the State Constitution:
We, the people of the State of Florida, being grateful to Almighty God for our constitutional liberty, in order to secure its benefits, perfect our government, insure domestic tranquility, maintain public order, and guarantee equal civil and political rights to all, do ordain and establish this constitution.

1. Refer to Language Arts Guide starting on page 8.
2. Have the children keep a journal as if they were astronauts in outer space.
3. Write a story about exploring the Everglades.

Character

The first character quality for Florida was derived from its nickname – The Sunshine State. Sunshine is equated with happy and **cheerful** feelings.

- **Cheerfulness** – Liveliness, animated; good spirits; moderate joy.

The next qualities were chosen because of the devastating 2004 hurricane season. The people of Florida needed a **compassionate**, **generous** nation to help after many homes, businesses, and lives were destroyed by these hurricanes.

- **Compassion** – A temper or disposition to pity; inclination to show mercy; mercy; having a heart that is tender and easily moved by the distresses, sufferings, wants, and infirmities of others.
- **Generosity** – Liberality, bounty, giving freely.

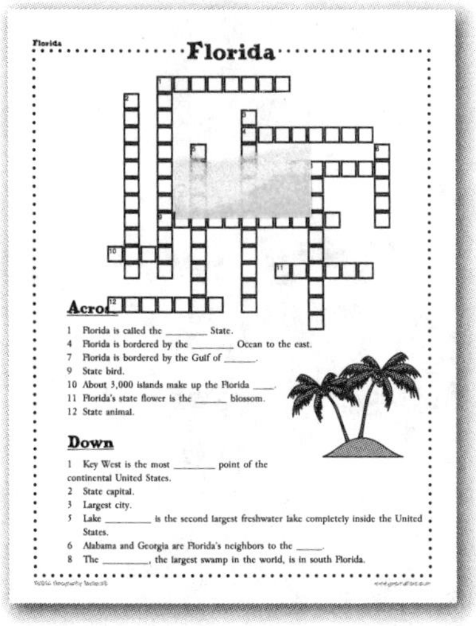

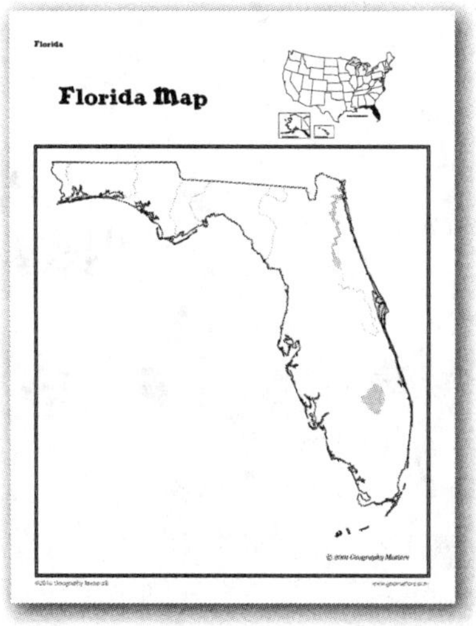

Activities

1. Color or label a map of Florida.
2. Label a map of the United States with the Everglades, Lake Okeechobee, and the Florida Keys.
3. Go to http://www.kidzone.ws/geography/usa/ for printable flag and state symbol coloring pages.
4. Prepare a meal in *Eat Your Way Through the U.S.A.* from the state of Florida.
5. Squeeze oranges for fresh orange juice.
6. Turn a large box into a space ship.
7. Make a magnetic space ship.
   - Decorate a paper plate with a space scene.
   - Cut out a space ship from construction paper.
   - Tape strips of curling ribbon to the space ship to make the fire trail.
   - Tape a paper clip to the back of the space ship.
   - Use a magnet on the underside of the paper plate to move the ship through space.
8. Experiment with growing food in space.
   - Cut the top off a 2-liter bottle where the bottle begins to curve.
   - Fill the bottom portion of the bottle one-fourth full of water.
   - Invert the bottle top into the bottom and secure with tape or hot glue.
   - Cut a length of heavy cotton string so that it will run from the bottom of the bottle into the top with a few inches hanging over the side.
   - Pull apart cotton balls and place in top of bottle.
   - Plant two to three dry beans in the cotton.
   - Keep your space garden in a sunny spot.
   - Add more water to the bottom bottle as needed.
9. Grow a tomato plant.
10. Listen to the state song, "Swanee River."

Georgia

Peach State

Named after King George II of England, Georgia was the 4th state admitted to the Union, on January 2, 1788. Atlanta, one of the largest cities in the South, is the state capital.

After years of controversy, the Confederate emblem was removed from the state flag and the current design was adopted on January 31, 2001. The new flag depicts the state seal in gold surrounded by thirteen stars on a field of blue. The flag also contains small images of three previous state flags as well as the current and a past version of the national flag. Above the small flags are the words "Georgia's History."

Almost the size of all the New England states combined, Georgia is the largest state east of the Mississippi River. Mountains and ridges along the state's northern border slope southward to gently rolling hills. Flat coastal plains extend eastward to the Atlantic Ocean. Southern Georgia is a sunny land of magnolias and moss-draped trees. Pine and hardwood forests cover large portions of the state.

The climate in Georgia varies greatly, with a record high of 113° F and a record low of -17° F. The state also has severe weather such as tornadoes and floods.

Interesting Facts:

- The marble used to build the Lincoln Memorial in Washington, D.C. is from Georgia.
- Atlanta is the most densely wooded city in the U.S.
- Coca-Cola was invented in Georgia in 1886 by James Pemberton.
- Eli Whitney invented the cotton gin near Savannah in 1793.
- The first steamship to cross the Atlantic Ocean sailed from Savannah in 1819.

General Reference

- ❑ *Georgia* – Paul Joseph
- ❑ *Georgia Facts and Symbols* – Emily McAuliffe
- ❑ *Georgia* – Rita C. LaDoux (contains evolution)
- ❑ http://www.legis.state.ga.us/legis/2005_06/house/kids/elemen/elemindex.htm

Geography

- ❑ Stone Mountain
- ❑ Okefenokee Swamp

History & Biographies

- ❑ Eli Whitney
  - *Eli Whitney* – Jean Lee Latham
- ❑ Martha Berry
  - *Martha Berry* – Mary Kay Phelan
- ❑ Martin Luther King, Jr.
  - *Young Martin Luther King, Jr.: I Have a Dream* – Joanne Mattern
  - *Martin Luther King, Jr.* – Patricia and Frederick McKissack
  - *A Picture Book of Martin Luther King, Jr.* – David A. Adler
  - http://members.enchantedlearning.com/history/us/MLK/cloze.shtml
- ❑ Jimmy Carter
  - *Jimmy Carter* – Linda and Charles George
  - *The Carters* – Cass R. Sandak
  - *Jimmy Carter: Beyond the Presidency* – Mellonee Carrigan
  - www.whitehouse.gov/history/presidents/
  - www.presidentialavenue.com/jec.cfm
  - http://www.homeofheroes.com/e-books/presidents/39_carter.html

Science

- ❑ brown thrasher (state bird)
  - http://www.coloring.ws/birds.htm
- ❑ live oak (state tree)
  - *Life Cycle of an Oak Tree* – Angela Royston
- ❑ Cherokee rose (state flower)
- ❑ staurolite (state mineral)
- ❑ kudzu
- ❑ peach (state fruit)
- ❑ peanuts (state crop)
  - *Peanut* – Millicent E. Selsam
  - *Peanuts* – Claire Llewellyn

❑ opossums

- *Opossums* – Emilie U. Lepthien
- *Opossums* – Kazue Mizumura
- http://pelotes.jea.com/ColoringPage/Mammal/colopossu.htm

Literature

❑ *A Net to Catch Time* – Sara Harrell Banks

❑ *The Gift of the Tree* – Alvin Tresselt

❑ *Turn Homeward Hannalee* – Patricia Beatty (RA)

❑ *Be Ever Hopeful Hannalee* – Patricia Beatty (RA)

Language Arts

Preamble to the State Constitution:
To perpetuate the principles of free government, insure justice to all, preserve peace, promote the interest and happiness of the citizen and of the family, and transmit to posterity the enjoyment of liberty, we the people of Georgia, relying upon the protection and guidance of Almighty God, do ordain and establish this Constitution.

1. Refer to Language Arts Guide starting on page 8.

Character

Georgia has never adopted an official state motto; however, the state seal containing the words "Wisdom, Justice and Moderation" was adopted in 1799. "Wisdom, Justice and Moderation" applies to the three branches of government. "Wisdom" is needed by the legislative branch in making the laws. "Justice" applies to the decisions made by the judicial branch. "Moderation" is needed by the executive branch to properly administer the laws. In order to exhibit the qualities mentioned in the motto an individual must have **wisdom**, **justice**, and **temperance**.

- **Wisdom** – Knowledge; the power of discerning and judging correctly, or of discriminating between what is true and what is false, between what is fit and proper, and what is improper.
- **Justice** – Conformity to truth; being exact, proper, accurate.

  Being a just person encompasses many aspects of truth and accuracy. Our children need to be taught to have just thoughts, actions and words. They should be encouraged to treat others justly.
- **Temperance** – Moderation in the indulgence of the appetite and passions; coolness; calmness, without violence.

  Teaching our children to be temperate in a self-gratifying society can be very difficult. We must impress on them the importance of self-control and moderation. They should learn temperance in all things – from eating to watching television.

State Flag Pledge

I pledge allegiance to the Georgia flag and to the principles for which it stands;
wisdom, justice, and moderation.

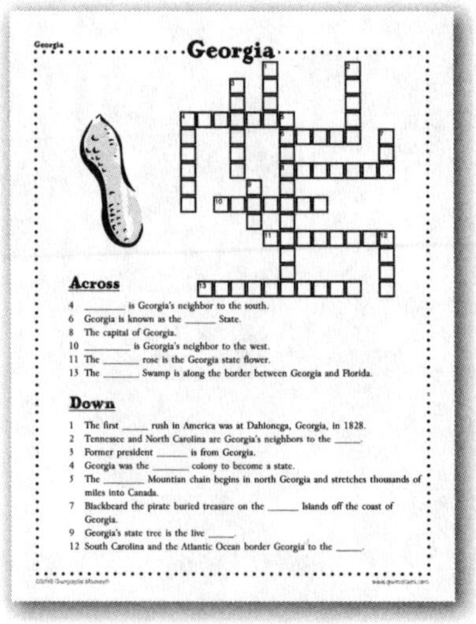

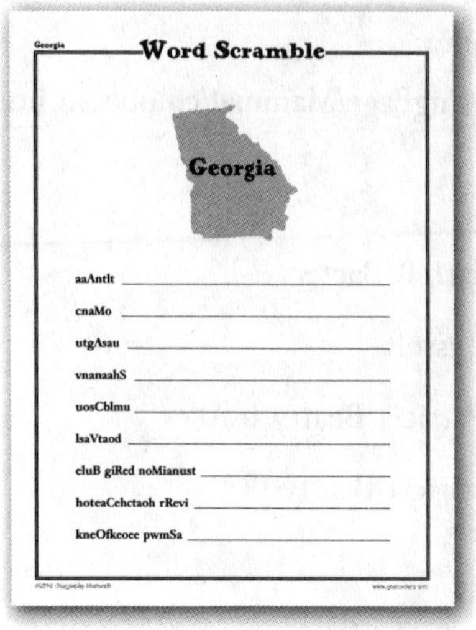

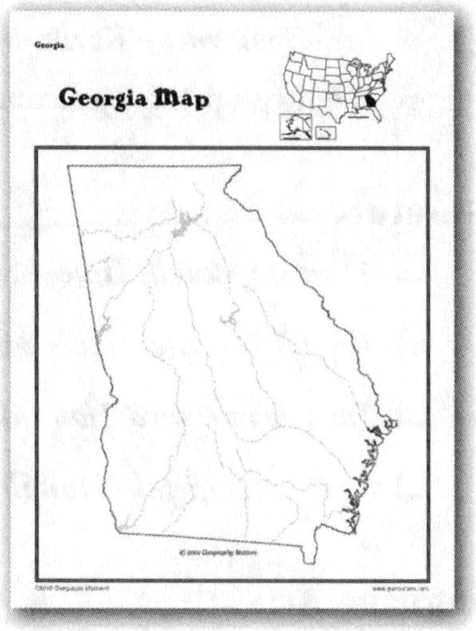

Activities

1. Color or label a map of Georgia.
2. Label the Okefenokee Swamp on a map of the United States.
3. Go to http://www.kidzone.ws/geography/usa/ for printable flag and state symbol coloring pages.
4. Prepare a meal in *Eat Your Way Through the U.S.A.* from the state of Georgia.
5. Make peanut people.
   - Choose several large peanuts in uncracked shells.
   - On each peanut paint eyes, a nose, and a mouth.
   - Spread glue on the bottom half of the peanut.
   - Wrap 1x2-inch strips of fabric around peanut. Press firmly, but gently, into glue.
   - Wrap 3-inch-long pipe cleaners around middle of peanuts for arms.
   - Accessorize peanuts with bow ties and hats from colored paper or fabric.
6. Listen to the state song, "Georgia on My Mind."

Hawaii

Aloha State

The only state made up of islands and located almost entirely in the tropics, Hawaii became the last state admitted to the Union on August 21, 1959. The inhabitants of Hawaii originally called the islands *Ke Ao Nani,* which means "the beautiful world." Hawaii comes from the Polynesian word for homeland, *Hawaiki.* Hawaii is the only state not part of the North American continent. Honolulu, on the island of Oahu, is the state capital.

The state flag was adopted in 1845 and originally represented the independent kingdom. The eight stripes represent the eight major islands. The British flag honors Hawaii's friendship with Britain and remembers the British advisors that once served King Kamehameha when Hawaii was still a monarchy. The flag has remained unchanged through the kingdom, republic, territory, and statehood of Hawaii.

The 132 islands that make up the Hawaiian chain are actually peaks of huge volcanoes. Most of these volcanoes are inactive, but the ones that are active draw hundreds of tourists every year. Only seven of the islands are inhabited: Hawaii, Maui, Molokai, Lanai, Oahu, Kauai, and Niihau.

Cool Pacific winds give Hawaii an extremely mild and pleasant climate. The temperature remains 74°F - 85°F year round, although the mountain tops can go below freezing at night. The southwestern side receives most of the sun and remains mostly dry. The northeast receives more rainfall, especially the city of Hilo—the rainiest city in the United States.

Interesting Facts:

- The largest active volcano in the world, Mauna Loa, is on the island of Hawaii.
- Hawaii is the only state that was an independent monarchy.
- Hawaii has two official languages: English and Hawaiian.
- The Hawaiian language has only twelve letters: *a, e, h, i, k, l, m, n, o, p, u,* and *w.*
- Hawaii's tropical climate makes it one of the world's leading producers of pineapples.

General Reference

- ❑ *Hawaii* – Bob Italia
- ❑ *Hawaii Facts and Symbols* – Emily McAuliffe

Geography

- ❑ island
  - *Geography From A to Z,* page 24
- ❑ archipelago
  - *Geography From A to Z,* pages 6-7
- ❑ Polynesia

History & Biographies

- ❑ King Kamehameha
  - http://www.tammyyee.com/colorkamehameha.html
- ❑ Liliuokalani
  - *Liliuokalani* – Mary Malone
- ❑ attack on Pearl Harbor
  - *The Story of the USS Arizona* – R. Conrad Stein

Science

- ❑ Hawaiian goose (state bird)
  - www.enchantedlearning.com/painting/birds.shtml
- ❑ candlenut tree (state tree)
- ❑ hibiscus (state flower)
- ❑ black coral (state gemstone)
- ❑ pineapple
- ❑ volcanoes
  - *Geography From A to Z,* page 44
  - *Volcanoes! Mountains of Fire* – Eric Arnold
  - *Volcanoes* – Jacqueline Dineen
  - *Volcanoes* – Franklyn M. Branley (makes reference to millions of years)
  - *Volcanoes* – Helen J. Challand (makes reference to millions of years)
  - *Earthquake Games* – Matthys Levy
  - http://members.enchantedlearning.com/subjects/volcano/cloze/general.shtml
  - *Earth Science for Every Kid,* Experiments #37–38

Literature

- ❑ *The Boxcar Children: The Black Pearl Mystery* – Gertrude Chandler Warner (RA)
- ❑ *Dumpling Soup* – Jama Kim Rattigan

Language Arts

Preamble to Constitution:

We, the people of Hawaii, grateful for Divine Guidance, and mindful of our Hawaiian heritage and uniqueness as an island State, dedicate our efforts to fulfill the philosophy decreed by the Hawaii State motto, "*Ua mau ke ea o ka aina i ka pono.*"

We reserve the right to control our destiny, to nurture the integrity of our people and culture, and to preserve the quality of life that we desire.

We reaffirm our belief in a government of the people, by the people and for the people, and with an understanding and compassionate heart toward all the peoples of the earth, do hereby ordain and establish this constitution for the State of Hawaii.

1. Refer to Language Arts Guide starting on page 8.
2. Write a story about exploring Hawaii.
3. Write the Hawaiian alphabet.

Character

The Hawaiian state motto - *The Life of the Land Is Perpetuated in Righteousness* - was adopted on July 31, 1843. The motto originated in an address by King Kamehameha III after the British returned the kingdom to him. The kingdom had been unlawfully ceded to England by an English sea captain.

- **Righteousness** – Purity of heart and rectitude of life; conformity of heart and life to the divine law, comprehending holy principles and affections of heart.
- **Reliability** – Dependableness, trustworthiness, as applied to a person or thing that can be counted upon to do what is expected or required.

  Righteous individuals are reliable individuals. Our children should be taught to be righteous and reliable in everyday living.

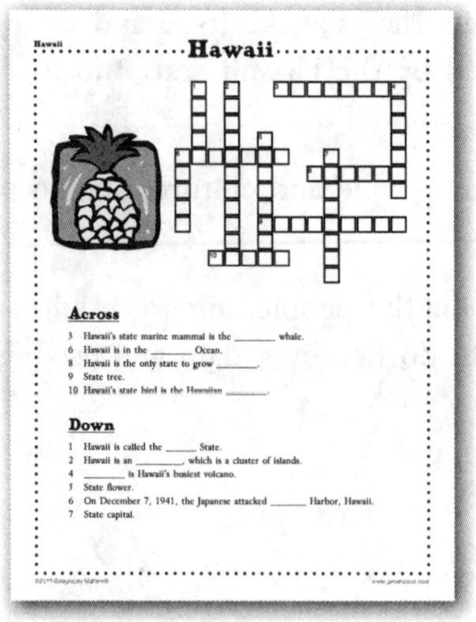

Activities

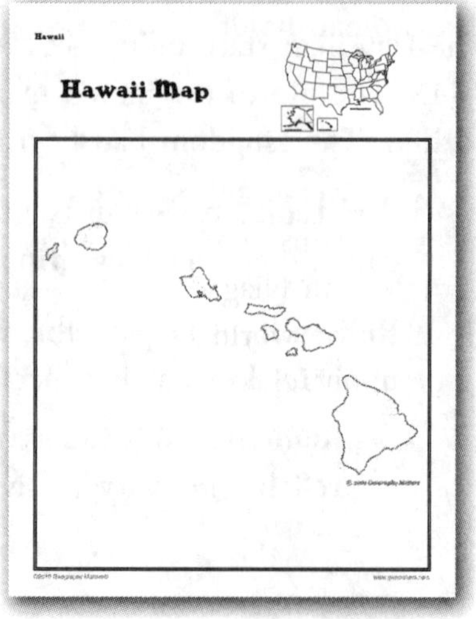

1. Color or label a map of Hawaii.
2. Label Polynesia on a map of the Pacific Rim.
3. Go to http://www.kidzone.ws/geography/usa/ for printable flag and state symbol coloring pages.
4. Go to http://www.state.hi.us/dlnr/dofaw/kids/endgrbk/index.html for coloring pages of Hawaiian animals.
5. Prepare a meal in *Eat Your Way Through the U.S.A.* from the state of Hawaii.
6. Make a lei.
   - Cut a 45-inch piece of heavy thread or dental floss. A finished lei for an adult will be about 36 inches, so this will give you plenty of extra.
   - Thread string onto a large needle.
   - Carefully string flowers (fresh or silk) through the center from front to back.
   - Slide flowers two at a time down string to desired length.
   - Tie securely.

Idaho

Gem State

On July 3, 1890, Idaho became the 43rd state admitted to the Union, The name "Idaho" was originally suggested for Colorado but was rejected because it was not of Native American origin. It was later chosen for the Idaho Territory. The capital of Idaho is Boise.

The state flag was adopted in 1927 and was patterned after the battle flag used by the First Idaho Infantry in 1898 during the Spanish-American War. The flag has a reproduction of the state seal on a field of blue. The woman holding the scales and a spear symbolizes freedom and equality. The miner represents the state's mineral resources. The trees and river stand for Idaho's natural beauty. The elk head represents wildlife, and agriculture is symbolized by the horns of plenty and sheaves of grain.

Idaho's diverse geography has towering, snow-capped mountains, swirling white rapids, peaceful lakes, and steep canyons. The Snake River churns through Hells Canyon, which is deeper than the Grand Canyon. Higher than Niagara Falls, Shoshone Falls plunges down steep, rugged cliffs. One of the most beautiful lakes in the world, Coeur d'Alene Lake, is nestled in the Rocky Mountain region of the state. The terrain of central Idaho is so rugged that it can only be navigated by pack-horses.

The climate in Idaho is equally diverse, with precipitation ranging from less than 10 inches annually in some areas to over 50 inches in other areas.

Interesting Facts:

- Idaho's state seal is the only one in the United States designed by a woman.
- Nuclear energy was first used to produce electricity near Idaho Falls in 1951.
- Idaho Territory was established in 1863 and included present-day Idaho, Montana, and almost all of Wyoming. Montana became a separate territory in 1864. Wyoming followed in 1868.

General Reference

- ❑ *Idaho* – Paul Joseph
- ❑ *Idaho Facts and Symbols* – Elaine A. Kule
- ❑ http://www.statesymbolsusa.org/Idaho/IdahoStateSymbols.html

Geography

- ❑ rapids
    - *Geography From A to Z,* page 37
- ❑ Snake River

History & Biographies

- ❑ Sacajawea
    - *Profiles from History* - Volume 1, pages 147-154
    - *Munford Meets Lewis & Clark,* The Adventures of Munford series - Jamie Aramini
    - *Sacajawea: Wilderness Guide* – Kate Jassem
    - *Sacajawea: Shoshone Trailblazer* – Diane Shaughnessy
    - *Sacajawea: The Journey West* – Elaine Raphael & Don Bolognese
- ❑ Nez Perce
    - *Nez Perce* – Richard M. Gaines
- ❑ Chief Joseph
    - *Chief Joseph: Leader of Destiny* – Kate Jassem

Science

- ❑ mountain bluebird (state bird)
- ❑ western white pine (state tree)
- ❑ syringa (state flower)
- ❑ star garnet (state gem)
- ❑ potato (state vegetable)
    - *More Potatoes!* – Millicent E. Selsam

Literature

- ❑ *Little Bird* – Saviour Pirotta
- ❑ *Bonanza Girl* – Patricia Beatty (RA)

Language Arts

Preamble to Constitution:

We, the people of the state of Idaho, grateful to Almighty God for our freedom, to secure its blessings and promote our common welfare do establish this Constitution.

1. Refer to Language Arts Guide starting on page 8.

Character

The state motto - *Esto Perpetua* - translated as "Let It Be Perpetual," was adopted on March 14, 1891. The motto was first applied to the Republic of Venice in 1623 by Pietro Sarpi, a theologian and mathematician. "Perpetual" means never ceasing, continuing forever in future time, destined to be eternal. We cannot know exactly what was intended by the motto when chosen in 1891. For our heritage to remain perpetual on this earth, we must be **diligent** and **consistent**.

- **Diligence** – Steadiness in application to business; constancy in effort or exertion to accomplish what is undertaken; assiduousness; attentiveness, without idleness.
- **Consistency** – A standing together, as the parts of a system, or of conduct; agreement or harmony of all parts of a complex thing among themselves, or of the same thing with itself at different times; congruity, uniformity.

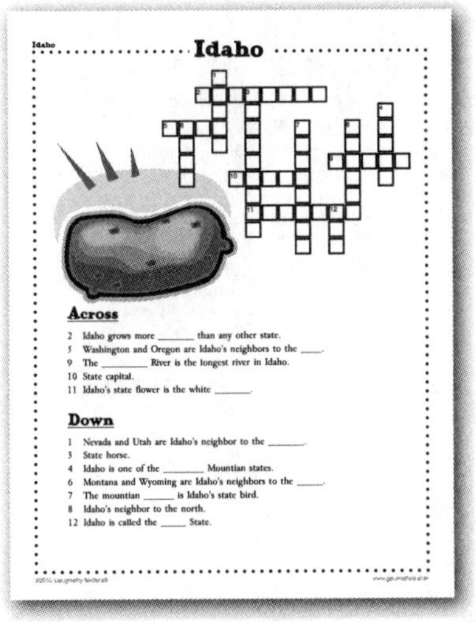

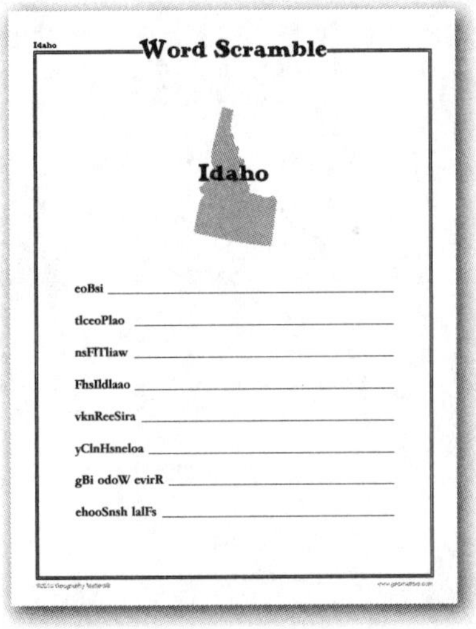

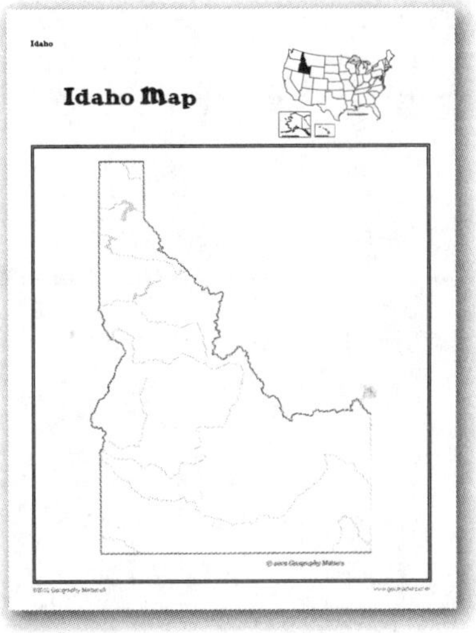

Activities

1. Color or label a map of Idaho.
2. Label the Snake River on a map of the United States.
3. Go to http://www.kidzone.ws/geography/usa/ for printable flag and state symbol coloring pages.
4. Prepare a meal in *Eat Your Way Through the U.S.A.* from the state of Idaho.
5. Do potato stamping. For instructions go to http://www.kid-craft-central.com/potato-stamp.html.
6. Make a potato maze. Go to http://pbskids.org/zoom/activities/sci/potatomaze.html for instructions.

Illinois

Prairie State

The most populous state in the Midwest, Illinois became the 21st state on December 3, 1818. The region was named by French settlers after the Illini people. *Illini* is an Algonquin word meaning "warrior." Illinois is located in the upper Midwest, and its capital is Springfield.

Adopted in 1915, the Illinois state flag shows the state seal on a white background. The eagle holding a shield with stars and stripes represents the original thirteen states. The olive branch stands for peace, and the prairie and rising sun symbolize the plains of Illinois. The dates on the rock are the year that Illinois became a state (1818) and the year the state seal was adopted (1868). The state name was added to the flag in 1970.

An important agricultural state, Illinois contains vast prairies and fertile land. The Mississippi River forms the state's western border and Lake Michigan forms the northeastern border. The largest city is Chicago. The state's temperate climate is sometimes interrupted by severe weather. Illinois has the highest tornado-related death toll in the nation.

Interesting Facts:

- George Pullman built the first railroad sleeping car in Bloomington, Illinois.
- The first metal skyscraper was built in Chicago in 1884–1885. It was ten stories high.
- The first controlled nuclear chain reaction occurred in 1942 at the University of Chicago.

General Reference

- ❑ *Illinois* – Paul Joseph
- ❑ *Illinois Facts and Symbols* – Emily McAuliffe
- ❑ http://www.state.il.us/kids/

Geography

- ❑ tributary
- ❑ Illinois River

History & Biographies

- ❑ Sauk
- ❑ Black Hawk
  - *Black Hawk: Frontier Warrior* – Joanne Oppenheim
  - *Black Hawk: Young Sauk Warrior* – Catherine S. Cleven
- ❑ George Pullman
  - *George Pullman: Young Sleeping Car Builder* – Elisabeth P. Myers
- ❑ D. L. Moody
  - *Hero Tales, Volume 1* – Dave and Neta Jackson
- ❑ Chicago Fire
  - *The Story of the Chicago Fire* – R. Conrad Stein
- ❑ John Deere
  - *John Deere: Blacksmith Boy* – Margaret Bare
  - *Pioneer Plowmaker* – David R. Collins
- ❑ Ronald Reagan
  - *Ronald Reagan: Young Politician* – Montrew Dunham
  - *The Picture Life of Ronald Reagan* – Don Lawson
  - www.whitehouse.gov/history/presidents/
  - www.presidentialavenue.com/rr.cfm
  - http://www.homeofheroes.com/e-books/presidents/40_reagan.html
- ❑ Barack Obama

Science

- ❑ weeping willow
- ❑ cardinal (state bird)
  - *Cardinals* – Lynn Stone
  - www.enchantedlearning.com/painting/birds.shtml
  - http://www.coloring.ws/birds.htm
- ❑ violet (state flower)
- ❑ flourite (state mineral)

❑ skyscrapers

- *Girders and Cranes: A Skyscraper Is Built* – Lee Balterman
- *Up Goes the Skyscraper* – Gail Gibbons
- *A Skyscraper Story* – Charlotte Wilcox
- *Skyscrapers* – Anne and Scott MacGregor
- *Skyscrapers* – Andrew Dunn
- *Into the Sky* – Ryan Ann Hunter

Literature

❑ *Cardinal and Sunflower* – James Preller

❑ *Danger on the Flying Trapeze* – Dave & Neta Jackson (story of D. L. Moody) (RA)

❑ *Abandoned on the Wild Frontier* – Dave & Neta Jackson (RA)

❑ *The Journey* – Sarah Stewert

Language Arts

Preamble to the State Constitution:

We, the People of the State of Illinois – grateful to Almighty God for the civil, political and religious liberty which He has permitted us to enjoy and seeking His blessing upon our endeavors – in order to provide for the health, safety and welfare of the people; maintain a representative and orderly government; eliminate poverty and inequality; assure legal, social and economic justice; provide opportunity for the fullest development of the individual; insure domestic tranquility; provide for the common defense; and secure the blessings of freedom and liberty to ourselves and our posterity – do ordain and establish this Constitution for the State of Illinois.

1. Refer to Language Arts Guide starting on page 8.
2. Have the child write a news article as if he were a reporter covering the Chicago Fire.
3. Ronald Reagan was a great storyteller. Have the children practice this art.
4. If you read *The Journey*, write a poem about the city.
5. If you read *The Journey*, write a diary or journal for a week.

Character

The current motto - *State Sovereignty, National Union* - was adopted in 1818. Until 1868, the motto on the state seal reversed the statements, placing National Union above State Sovereignty. In 1867, the State Senate voted on the official seal, restoring the original placement of the phrases. The motto represents a national debate which has existed since the founding of our country. The issue of state rights is often debated and decided upon by our Supreme Court. The character traits chosen for this state reflect the importance of rectifying this issue in order to prosper our nation. We must be **loyal** to our founding fathers' original intent while promoting **unity** among our citizens. These traits can be studied in light of these issues, or studied as an important part of personal relationships.

- **Loyalty** - Faithfulness to the constituted authority of one's country; faithfulness to those persons or ideals that one is under obligation to defend or support.
- **Unity** – The state of being one; oneness; oneness of sentiment, affection, or behavior.

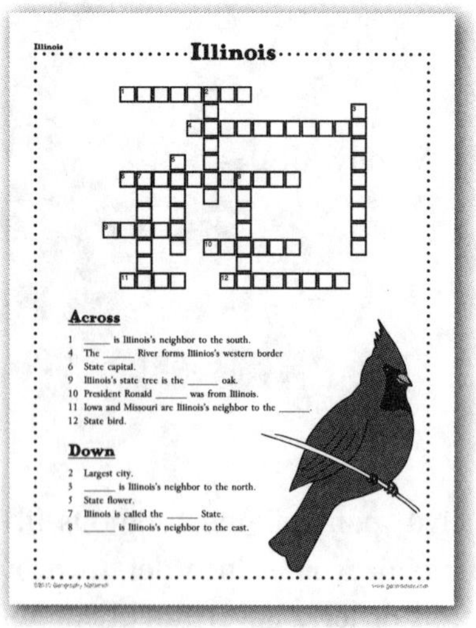

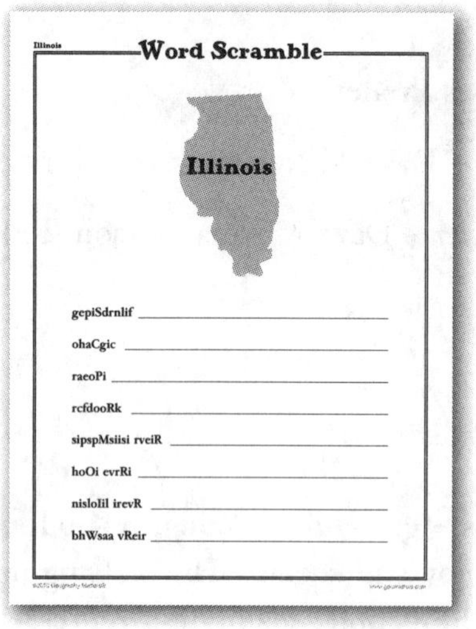

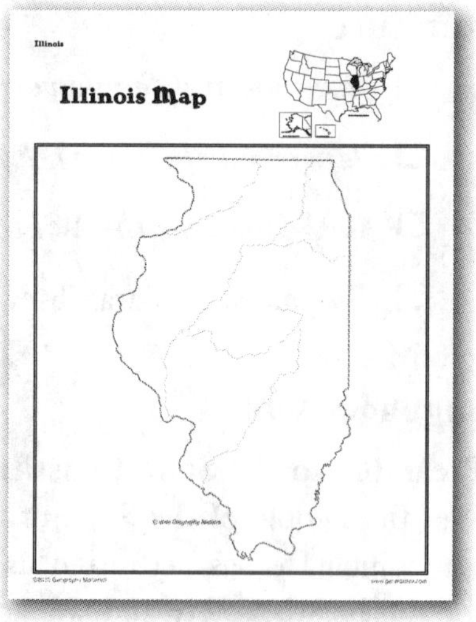

Activities

1. Color or label a map of Illinois.
2. Label the Illinois River on a map of the United States.
3. Go to http://www.kidzone.ws/geography/usa/ for printable flag and state symbol coloring pages.
4. Prepare a meal in *Eat Your Way Through the U.S.A.* from the state of Illinois.
5. Make cardinal bead craft. Go to www.craftsforkids.com/projects/cardinal_tile.htm for instructions.
6. Learn how building foundations work. A fun project for this is found on page 12 of *Skyscrapers* by Andrew Dunn.
7. Build a skyscraper. Use Legos or building blocks or follow the instructions in *Skyscrapers* by Anne and Scott MacGregor.
8. Make a paper model of Wrigley Field. Go to http://papertoys.com/wrigley-field.htm for a template.
9. If you read *The Journey*, go to a city and visit a library, cathedral, or art museum. While you are there, eat hot dogs or feed the pigeons.
10. If you read *The Journey*, label or make a map with all of the oceans.

Indiana

Hoosier State

Indiana, the smallest Midwestern state, became the 19th state admitted to the Union, on December 11, 1816. The name Indiana comes from the word "Indian." The capital is Indianapolis.

The flag of Indiana was adopted in 1917. The flag was the winning entry of a design competition held in 1916 to celebrate Indiana's centennial. The torch on the flag represents freedom and knowledge; the rays stand for their far-reaching effects. The thirteen stars forming the outer circle represent the original thirteen states; the five stars in the inner semicircle represent the next five states; the large star is Indiana, the 19th state.

Indiana is a beautiful, flat land with an abundance of lakes and streams and many underground caves and caverns. The region experiences many "lake effect" snows, but temperatures remain relatively mild. Spring in Indiana brings tornadoes and flooding, with a dry spell at the end of the summer. Fertile plains make Indiana one of the country's top farming states.

Interesting Facts:

- The first professional baseball game was played in Fort Wayne in 1871.
- In 1914, the first Raggedy Ann doll was made in Indianapolis.
- More interstates intersect in Indianapolis than any other city in the U.S.
- The first city to be lit by electricity was Wabash, Indiana.

General Reference

- ❑ *Indiana* – Anne Welsbacher
- ❑ *Indiana Facts and Symbols* – Bill McAuliffe
- ❑ http://www.statesymbolsusa.org/Indiana/StateSymbolsIndiana.html
- ❑ http://www.in.gov/kids_info.htm

Geography

- ❑ Wabash River

History & Biographies

- ❑ Amish
  - *An Amish Year* – Richard Ammon
  - *An Amish Wedding* – Richard Ammon
  - *An Amish Christmas* – Richard Ammon
  - *Raising Yoder's Barn* – Jane Yolen
  - *Amish Home* – Raymond Bial
- ❑ James Whitcomb Riley
- ❑ George Rogers Clark

Science

- ❑ blue jays
  - *Jays* – Lynn Stone
  - www.enchantedlearning.com/painting/birds.shtml
  - http://www.coloring.ws/birds.htm
- ❑ tulip poplar (state tree)
- ❑ peony (state flower)
- ❑ gypsum
- ❑ squirrels
  - *Squirrels and Chipmunks* – Allan Fowler
  - *The Squirrel* – Margaret Lane
  - *Squirrels* – Lee Jacobs
  - *Squirrels* – Emilie U. Lepthien
  - http://www.coloring.ws/squirrel.htm
  - www.daniellesplace.com/html/animal_crafts.html

Literature

- ❑ Read poems by James Whitcomb Riley. Selections can be found online.
- ❑ *Just Plain Fancy* – Patricia Polacco
- ❑ *Adventures of Chatterer the Red Squirrel* – Thornton W. Burgess
- ❑ *The Floating House* – Scott Russell Sanders
- ❑ *Raggedy Ann* – Johnny Gruelle

Language Arts

Preamble to the State Constitution:

To the end, that justice be established, public order maintained, and liberty perpetuated; WE, the People of the State of Indiana, grateful to ALMIGHTY GOD for the free exercise of the right to choose our own form of government, do ordain this Constitution.

1. Refer to Language Arts Guide starting on page 8.
2. If you do activity #6, write about what it was like not to have electricity for a day.
3. Copy a poem by James Whitcomb Riley.

Character

The state motto - *The Crossroads of America* - was adopted by the Indiana General Assembly in 1937. Indiana's railways, waterways, ports, and highways provide access for transporting goods. When this motto was adopted, the center of the United States was located in Indiana. Many routes which have been important since pioneer times intersect in Indiana. This is a great opportunity to discuss choices with your children. When you come to a crossroads, a choice must be made. As parents we should teach our children how to make good choices. We need to be **deliberate** when weighing the consequences of those choices. Children should also have a **teachable** spirit, which will enable them to analyze and benefit from others' wisdom when faced with difficult choices.

- **Deliberation** – Weighing facts and arguments with a view to a choice or decision; carefully considering the probable consequences of a step; circumspect.
- **Teachability** – Readiness to be taught, aptness to learn; readily receiving instruction.

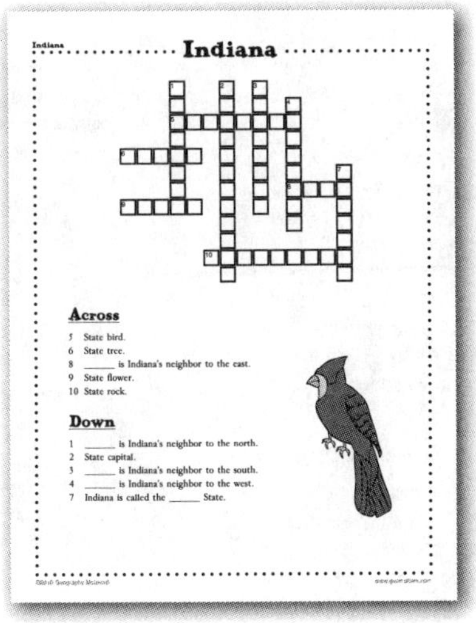

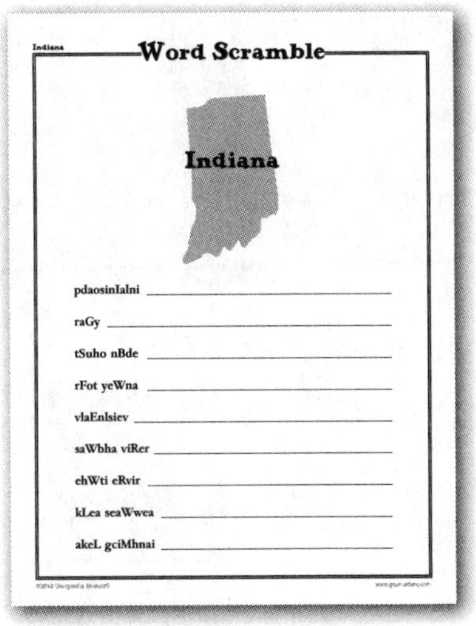

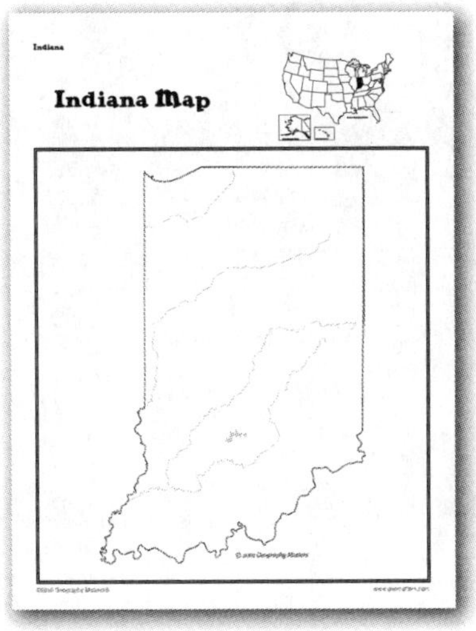

Activities

1. Color or label a map of Indiana.
2. Label the Wabash River on a map of the United States.
3. Go to http://www.kidzone.ws/geography/usa/ for printable flag and state symbol coloring pages.
4. Prepare a meal in *Eat Your Way Through the U.S.A.* from the state of Indiana.
5. Play baseball.
6. Build a squirrel feeder. Check your local home improvement store for a precut kit or go to http://familyfun.go.com/decorating-ideas/gardening/feature/famf0602_proj_squirl/ for instructions.
7. If studying the Amish, do not use electricity for a day. Mom will need to use the stove to prepare meals, but have children help with the prep work without electrical appliances.

Iowa

Hawkeye State

Known as "the land where tall corn grows," Iowa became the 29th state admitted to the Union, on December 28, 1846. The name Iowa is a Dakota word which means "beautiful land." The capital of Iowa is Des Moines.

The state flag was adopted in 1921. Dixie Gebhardt developed the design with three vertical bars: blue representing loyalty, justice, and truth; white for purity; and red representing courage. The colors also stand for French Louisiana, of which Iowa was once a part. Taken from the state seal, an eagle carrying a banner with the state motto is in the center.

Covered with rich, fertile soil, Iowa has some of the best farmland in the nation. Farms cover about 95% of the state's land, and approximately 10% of the population lives on farms. Iowa has a diverse climate that changes rapidly, resulting in destructive tornadoes. The region has hot, muggy summers and harsh, cold winters.

Interesting Facts:

- The first bridge across the Mississippi River was built in Davenport, Iowa, in 1856.
- Iowa has the highest literacy rate in the nation – over 98%.
- Throughout the history of the state, schools were always one of the first buildings to be built in a new town.

General Reference

- ❑ *Iowa* – Anne Welsbacher
- ❑ *Iowa Facts and Symbols* – Elaine A. Kule
- ❑ http://www.statesymbolsusa.org/Iowa/StateSymbolsIowa.html
- ❑ http://www.iowa.gov/state/main/kidsfacts.html

Geography

- ❑ Des Moines River

History & Biographies

- ❑ Herbert Hoover
  - www.whitehouse.gov/history/presidents/
  - http://www.homeofheroes.com/e-books/presidents/31_hoover.html
  - http://www.hoover.nara.gov/
- ❑ Glenn L. Martin
  - *Glenn L. Martin: Boy Conqueror of the Air* – Ruth W. Harley
- ❑ Amelia Earhart
  - *Amelia Earhart: A Dream to Fly* – Sarah Alcott
  - *Amelia Earhart: Adventure in the Sky* – Francene Sabin
- ❑ E. B. White
  - *To the Point* – David R. Collins
  - *Meet E. B. White* – S. Ward

Science

- ❑ box elder
- ❑ hawk
  - www.enchantedlearning.com/painting/birds.shtml
- ❑ wild rose (state flower)
- ❑ geode (state rock)
- ❑ pigs
  - *Pigs* – Gail Gibbons
  - *Life on a Pig Farm* – Judy Wolfman
  - www.coloring.ws/animals.html

Literature

- ❑ *If You Give a Pig a Pancake* – Laura Numeroff
- ❑ *Charlotte's Web* – E. B. White (R/A)
- ❑ *The Three Little Pigs* – retold by Harriet Ziefert
- ❑ *The True Story of the Three Little Pigs* – Jon Scieszka
- ❑ *Kate Shelley and the Midnight Express* – Margaret K. Wetterer
- ❑ *Kate Shelley: Bound for Legend* – Robert SanSouci (RA)

Language Arts

Preamble to the State Constitution:

WE, THE PEOPLE OF THE STATE OF IOWA, grateful to the Supreme Being for the blessings hitherto enjoyed, and feeling our dependence on Him for a continuance of those blessings, do ordain and establish a free and independent government, by the name of the STATE OF IOWA, the boundaries whereof shall be as follows...

1. Refer to Language Arts Guide starting on page 8.
2. If studying Glenn Martin or Amelia Earhart, write a story about a pilot.

Character

The state motto - *Our liberties we prize and our rights we will maintain* - was adopted by the state General Assembly in 1847. The motto reflected the feelings of Iowans as they entered the Union in 1846. As parents we should teach our children to prize our national liberties, but they also need to learn to prize their personal liberty. Our children should learn that with freedom comes responsibility and that in order to obtain more freedom as they get older, they must exhibit responsibility. In order to gain more freedom, a child must be **trustworthy** and **obedient**.

- **Trustworthiness** – Worthy of trust; dependability; reliability.
- **Obedience** - Submission to authority; compliance with commands, orders or injunctions; performing what is required or abstaining from what is forbidden.

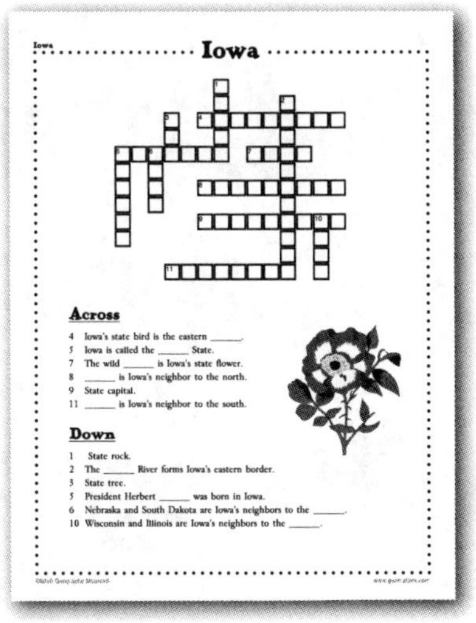

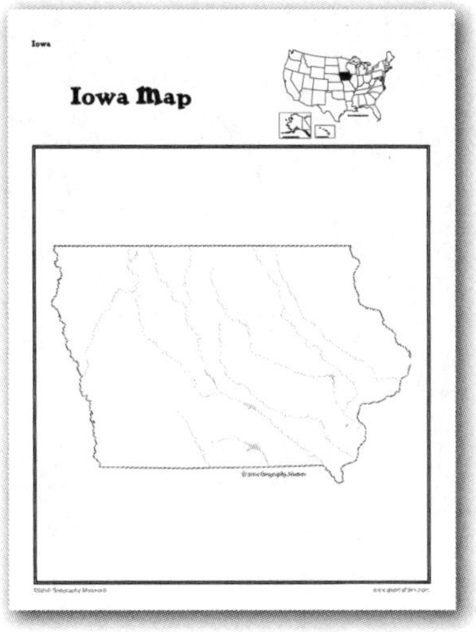

Activities

1. Color or label a map of Iowa.
2. Label the Des Moines River on a map of the United States.
3. Go to http://www.kidzone.ws/geography/usa/ for printable flag and state symbol coloring pages.
4. Prepare a meal in *Eat Your Way Through the U.S.A.* from the state of Iowa.
5. Iowa's state rock is the geode. Break one open and examine it.
6. Map Amelia Earhart's final journey. Information can be found at www.americaslibrary.gov.
7 Fix pigs in a blanket.
8 Pig craft idea.
   - Cut an egg cup from an egg carton and glue onto the back side of a paper plate.
   - Paint the plate and the egg cup pink. Allow to dry.
   - To make the ears, cut a 2-inch square from pink construction paper. Cut the square in half to form two triangles. Staple the ears to the paper plate.
   - Draw eyes with a black marker.
   - Cut a pink pipe cleaner in half. Curl one end of the pipe cleaner around a pencil. Staple the straight end of the pipe cleaner to the front side of the plate at about 8 o'clock.
9. Make a pig cake.
   - Bake a 9-inch round layer cake. Cool completely and frost pink.
   - For snout, put two brown M&Ms on a pink Snowball snack cake and position on cake.
   - For eyes, place green or blue M&Ms on pink Necco Wafers, secure with frosting, and position on cake.
   - For ears, cut a pink Snowball snack cake in half. Take one half and cut in half again. Frost edges pink and position on cake.

Kansas

Sunflower State

Kansas became the 34th state admitted to the Union, on January 29, 1861. The state was named for the Native American tribe, Kansa. The name means "wind people." Kansas is located in the middle of the United States, and its capital is Topeka.

The state flag which depicts the state seal and name was adopted in 1927. The rising sun represents the east, from which most Kansas settlers came. The buffalo, log cabin, riverboat, wagons, and farmer all depict the region's early history. Above the seal is a wreath and sunflower. The wreath represents the Louisiana Purchase. The sunflower symbolizes the prairie and Kansas's future. The original flag did not contain the state name; it was added in 1961.

The geographic center of the continental United States is located in Lebanon, Kansas. The flat terrain contains fertile prairies with deep, rich soil. Sometimes called "America's Breadbasket," Kansas leads all other states in wheat production.

The elevation rises in the western part of the state leading into the Rocky Mountains. The state has three distinct climates. The eastern part of the state has greater rainfall, high humidity, and limited sunshine. The central part of the state, with a higher elevation, has less rain, more wind, and less humidity. The western part of the state is the driest and sunniest area. Kansas also has a high number of tornadoes.

Interesting Facts:

- The first academically qualified female dentist, Lucy Hobbs Taylor, practiced in Kansas in 1867.
- In 1887, Susan Salter was elected mayor of Argonia, Kansas. She was the first woman mayor in the United States.
- The only Pony Express Station maintained in its original condition is located near Topeka, Kansas.

General Reference

- ❑ *Kansas* – Anne Welsbacher
- ❑ *Kansas Facts and Symbols* – Kathleen W. Deedy
- ❑ *Kansas* – Charles Fredeen
- ❑ http://www.statesymbolsusa.org/Kansas/Kansas_symbols.html
- ❑ http://www.kssos.org/resources/kansas_kids.html

Geography

- ❑ prairie
  - *Geography From A to Z*, pages 21 & 35
  - *Prairies and Grasslands* – James P. Rowan
  - *America's Prairies and Grasslands* – Marianne D. Wallace
  - *A Sea of Grass* – David Dvorak, Jr.

History & Biographies

- ❑ Walter Chrysler
  - *Walter Chrysler: Boy Machinist* – Ethel H. Weddle
- ❑ Dwight D. Eisenhower
  - *Dwight D. Eisenhower: Young Military Leader* – Wilma J. Hudson
  - *A Picture Book of Dwight David Eisenhower* – David A. Adler
  - www.whitehouse.gov/history/presidents/
  - www.presidentialavenue.com/de.cfm
- ❑ Russell Stover
- ❑ Omar Knedlik
  - http://en.wikipedia.org/wiki/Omar_Knedlik
  - http://www.kssos.org/resources/kansas_kids.html

Science

- ❑ western meadowlark (state bird)
  - www.enchantedlearning.com/painting/birds.shtml
  - http://www.coloring.ws/birds.htm
- ❑ cottonwood (state tree)
- ❑ sunflower (state flower)
  - *Sunflowers* – Mary Ann McDonald
  - http://members.enchantedlearning.com/colorbynumber/sunflower/
- ❑ calcite
- ❑ salamander (state amphibian)
- ❑ wheat
  - *Wheat: The Golden Harvest* – Dorothy Hinshaw Patent
  - *Winter Wheat* – Brenda Z. Guiberson

Literature

- ❑ *Wagon Wheels* – Barbara Brenner
- ❑ *Three Names* – Patricia Maclachlan
- ❑ *This Is the Sunflower* – Lola M. Schaefer
- ❑ *Prairie Primer A to Z* – Caroline Stutson
- ❑ *Little House on the Prairie* – Laura Ingalls Wilder (RA)
- ❑ *Prairie Day* – adapted from the Little House Books by Laura Ingalls Wilder
- ❑ *Hard Times on the Prairie* – A Little House Chapter Book
- ❑ *Sarah, Plain & Tall* – Patricia MacLachlan
- ❑ *Pioneer Summer* – Deborah Hopkinson

Language Arts

Preamble to the State Constitution:
We, the people of Kansas, grateful to Almighty God for our civil and religious privileges, in order to insure the full enjoyment of our rights as American citizens, do ordain and establish this constitution of the state of Kansas, with the following boundaries, to wit...

1. Refer to Language Arts Guide starting on page 8.

Character

The state motto - *To the stars through difficulties* - was adopted in 1861. The motto was introduced by John J. Ingalls, a United States Senator. According to Mr. Ingalls, the motto refers to the pioneering spirit of the early settlers and the seven-year struggle to achieve statehood. This motto can be used to emphasize satisfaction during difficult times. We should teach our children that difficult times will come, but more importantly teach them how to keep their sanity during those times. It is important to model to our children **contentment** and **joy** in the most trying times.

- **Contentment** – Literally being held, contained within limits; hence being quiet, not disturbed; having a mind at peace; being easy; satisfaction.
- **Joy** – Fondness; rejoicing; a glorious and triumphant state.

Activities

1. Color or label a map of Kansas.
2. Shade in the Great Plains on a map of the United States.
3. Locate and label the geographical center of the United States on a map.
4. Go to http://www.kidzone.ws/geography/usa/ for printable flag and state symbol coloring pages.
5. Prepare a meal in *Eat Your Way Through the U.S.A.* from the state of Kansas.
6. If studying Russell Stover, eat Russell Stover candy.

7. Make a sunflower.
    - Color or paint a paper plate yellow. OR Cut yellow paper into petals and glue onto a paper plate. Allow to dry.
    - Glue sunflower seeds (in the hull) in a circle in the center of the plate.
8. Listen to the state song, "Home on the Range."

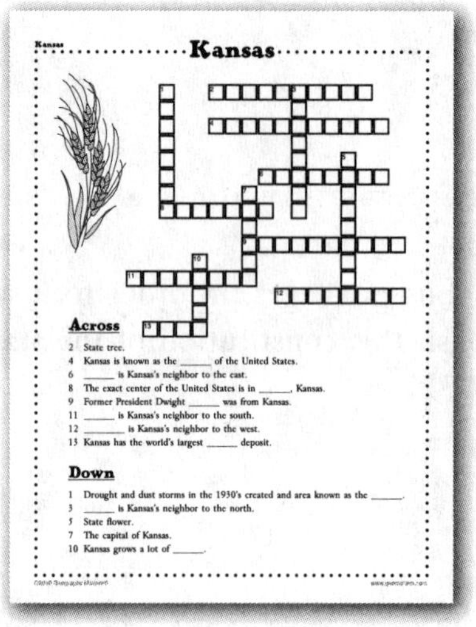

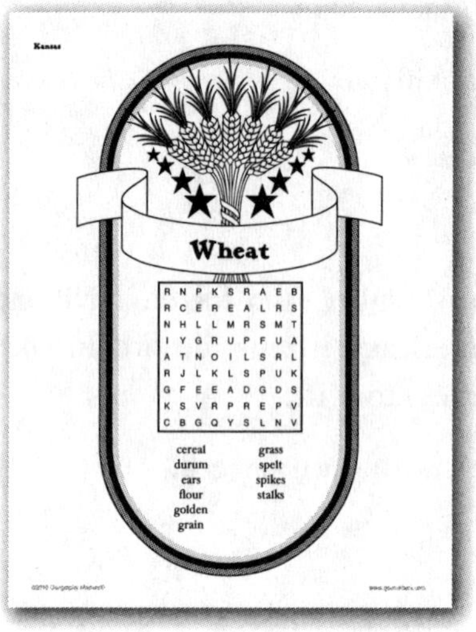

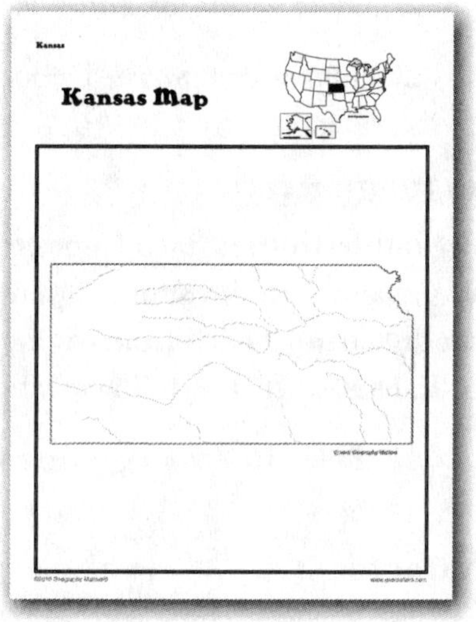

Kentucky

Bluegrass State

A border state between North and South, Kentucky became the 15th state on June 1, 1792. Kentucky, a largely rural state, gets its name from the Wyandot word Kentake, which means "meadowland." Frankfort is the state capital.

In 1918 it was determined that Kentucky should have a state flag, but specifications could not be met to the satisfaction of all concerned for 10 years, and it was not until 1962 that the state legislature officially recognized the design. Kentucky's flag shows the state seal, the state name, and a wreath of goldenrod on a background of blue. The two men greeting each other and the state motto - ***United we stand, divided we fall*** - symbolize brotherhood.

Kentucky's entire northern border is formed by the Ohio River, one of the traditional boundaries between Northern and Southern states. Eastern Kentucky contains the beautiful forested mountains, valleys, rivers, and streams of the Appalachian Mountains. North-central Kentucky is made up of rolling fields, which give the state its nickname. Kentucky has a warm, rainy climate with generally warm summers and cool winters.

Interesting Facts:

- The gold depository at Fort Knox contains more than $6 billion in gold bullion.
- The Corvette was invented in Bowling Green.
- "Happy Birthday to You" was written by two sisters, Mildred and Patty Hill, from Louisville in 1893.
- A moonbow, a type of rainbow that can only be seen at night, is only visible at Cumberland Falls.
- At one time it was illegal in Kentucky for a married woman to rearrange the family's furniture without permission from her husband.

General Reference

- ❑ *Kentucky* - Paul Joseph
- ❑ *Kentucky Facts and Symbols* – Kathleen W. Deady
- ❑ *Growing Up in a Holler in the Mountains* – Karen Gravelle

Geography

- ☐ cave
  - *Geography From A to Z,* page 12
  - *Caves* – Roma Gans
  - *Cave* – Donald M. Silver
  - *Caves and Caverns* – Gail Gibbons (makes reference to millions of years)
- ☐ Mammoth Cave National Park
- ☐ Cumberland Gap
- ☐ Wilderness Trail
  - www.danielboonetrail.com

History & Biographies

- ☐ Daniel Boone
  - *Daniel Boone: Man of the Forests* – Carol Greene
  - *Daniel Boone* – Marianne Johnston
  - *Daniel Boone: Young Hunter and Tracker* – Augusta Stevenson
  - *Daniel Boone and the Wilderness Road* – Catherine E. Chambers
  - *Daniel Boone* – Tom Streissguth
- ☐ Henry Clay
  - *Henry Clay: Young Kentucky Orator* – Helen Albee Monsell
- ☐ Nancy Hanks
  - *Nancy Hanks: Kentucky Girl* – Augusta Stevenson
- ☐ Abraham Lincoln
  - *Abraham Lincoln* – Lola M. Schaefer
  - *Young Abraham Lincoln* – Andrew Woods
  - *Abraham Lincoln* – Sam Wellman
  - *Abe Lincoln's Hat* – Martha Brenner
  - www.whitehouse.gov/history/presidents/
- ☐ Mary Todd Lincoln
  - *Mary Todd Lincoln* – LaVere Anderson
  - *Mary Todd Lincoln: Girl of the Bluegrass* – Katharine E. Wilkie
- ☐ Colonel Harland Sanders
- ☐ Fort Knox

Science

- ❑ hummingbirds
  - *Marvels of Creation, Magnificent Mammals* - Buddy and Kay Davis
  - *Hummingbirds* – Lynn Stone
  - *A Hummingbird's Life* – John Himmelman
  - www.enchantedlearning.com/painting/birds.shtml
- ❑ goldenrod (state flower)
- ❑ Kentucky Coffeetree
- ❑ Kentucky agate (state rock)
- ❑ horses
  - *Horses, Horses, Horses* – Allan Fowler
  - *Album of Horses* – Marguerite Henry
  - *Horses* – Elwyn Hartley Edwards (contains evolution)
  - *Horses* – Elsa Posell
  - www.coloring.ws/animals.html
- ❑ bats
  - *Bats* – Gail Gibbons
  - *A First Look At Bats* – Millicent E. Selsam
  - *Squeaking Bats* – Ruth Berman
  - http://members.enchantedlearning.com/connectdots/bat/
  - www.coloring.ws/animals.html
  - *Zoo Guide*, page 21

Literature

- ❑ *Grace's Letter to Lincoln* – Peter and Connie Roop
- ❑ *Barney's Horse* – Syd Hoff
- ❑ *Billy and Blaze* – C. W. Anderson
- ❑ *Blaze and the Gray Spotted Pony* – C. W. Anderson
- ❑ *Mary on Horseback* – Rosemary Wells (RA)
- ❑ *The Hungry Hummingbird* – April Pulley Sayre
- ❑ *Hummingbird Nest: A Journal of Poems* – Kristine O'Connell George
- ❑ *Somebody Loves You Mr. Hatch* – Eileen Spinelli (†)
- ❑ *Peter's Chair* – Ezra Jack Keats (†)

Language Arts

Preamble to the State Constitution:

We, the people of the Commonwealth of Kentucky, grateful to Almighty God for the civil, political and religious liberties we enjoy, and invoking the continuance of these blessings, do ordain and establish this Constitution.

1. Refer to Language Arts Guide starting on page 8.
2. Write an adventure story about exploring a cave.
3. Keep a journal about heading west on the Wilderness Trail.
4. Make a list of required steps for grooming a horse.
5. Memorize all or part of Lincoln's Gettysburg Address.
6. If you read *The Hungry Hummingbird,* make a list of red things.
7. If you read *Hummingbird Nest,* write or copy a poem about a hummingbird.

Character

The Kentucky state motto - *United we stand, divided we fall* - was adopted in 1792. Isaac Shelby, the state's first governor, is believed to have inspired the motto. He was a hero of the Revolutionary War and enjoyed the "The Liberty Song" written by John Dickinson in 1768. The chorus of that song contains the words, "by uniting we stand, by dividing we fall." In order for a people to be united for a cause, they must be **unselfish** and **considerate**.

- **Unselfishness** – Opposite of selfishness; no undue attachment to one's own interest; thinking and caring about others before oneself.

  Our nation has become a "me first" society. Our citizens are told to "look out for number one." This attitude is opposite of what this motto teaches. Our children need to learn to put others first and themselves last.

- **Consideration** – Respect, regard, and thoughtfulness for another person's feelings; kindness.

  Consideration is another character trait that was once prevalent in our society but is now often ignored. Our children must be taught to realize when someone is in need and to be willing to help. Being considerate can be a kind word for an upset friend or a hot meal for a homeless person. Little deeds mean a lot.

State Flag Pledge

I pledge allegiance to the Kentucky flag, and to the Sovereign State for which it stands, one Commonwealth, blessed with diversity, natural wealth, beauty, and grace from on High.

Activities

1. Color or label a map of Kentucky.
2. Label the Cumberland Plateau and the Kentucky River on a map of the United States.
3. Go to http://www.kidzone.ws/geography/usa/ for printable flag and state symbol coloring pages.
4. Prepare a meal in *Eat Your Way Through the U.S.A.* from the state of Kentucky.
5. If possible, go horseback riding.
6. Listen to the state song, "My Old Kentucky Home."
7. If you read *The Hungry Hummingbird*, look at pictures of a trumpet vine and paint a picture of them.
8. If you read *The Hungry Hummingbird* or *Hummingbird Nest*, put out a hummingbird feeder.
9. Make a flying bat.
   - Cut a 4-inch square of black construction paper. Fold it in half and cut off the corners to make a circle.
   - Open circle and cut halfway up the fold to the center. Overlap the cut edges and glue.
   - Place two 2x9-inch pieces of black construction paper on top of each other. Cut off the top corners to make a dome shape. Scallop the opposite end to make the wings.
   - Glue the wings to the back side of the head.
   - Make eyes, nose, mouth, and ears from scraps of construction paper and glue on to bat.
   - Glue, staple, or tape a piece of yarn or string to the back side of the head.

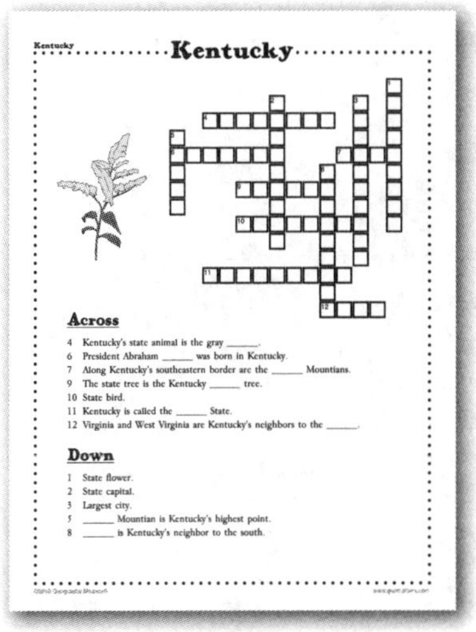
Kentucky

Kentucky

Across

4 Kentucky's state animal is the gray ______.
6 President Abraham ______ was born in Kentucky.
7 Along Kentucky's southeastern border are the ______ Mountians.
9 The state tree is the Kentucky ______ tree.
10 State bird.
11 Kentucky is called the ______ State.
12 Virginia and West Virginia are Kentucky's neighbors to the ______.

Down

1 State flower.
2 State capital.
3 Largest city.
5 ______ Mountian is Kentucky's highest point.
8 ______ is Kentucky's neighbor to the south.

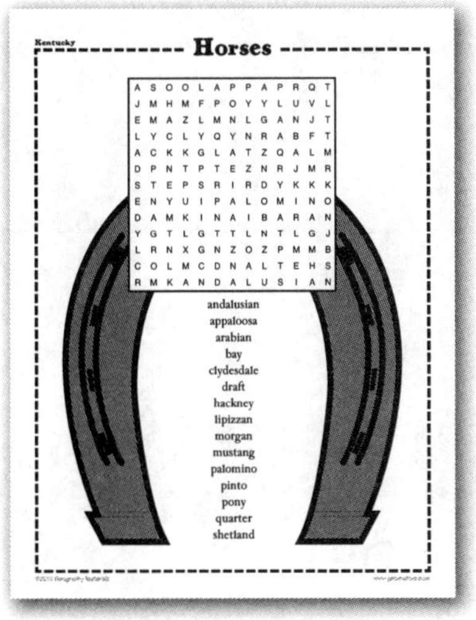
Kentucky

Horses

andalusian
appaloosa
arabian
bay
clydesdale
draft
hackney
lipizzan
morgan
mustang
palomino
pinto
pony
quarter
shetland

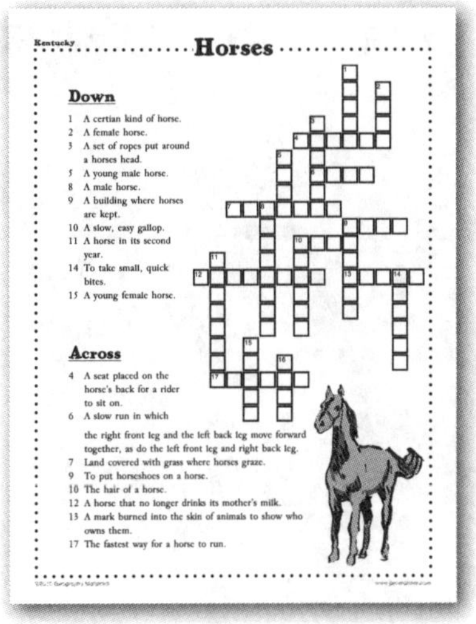
Kentucky

Horses

Down

1 A certian kind of horse.
2 A female horse.
3 A set of ropes put around a horses head.
5 A young male horse.
8 A male horse.
9 A building where horses are kept.
10 A slow, easy gallop.
11 A horse in its second year.
14 To take small, quick bites.
15 A young female horse.

Across

4 A seat placed on the horse's back for a rider to sit on.
6 A slow run in which the right front leg and the left back leg move forward together, as do the left front leg and right back leg.
7 Land covered with grass where horses graze.
9 To put horseshoes on a horse.
10 The hair of a horse.
12 A horse that no longer drinks its mother's milk.
13 A mark burned into the skin of animals to show who owns them.
17 The fastest way for a horse to run.

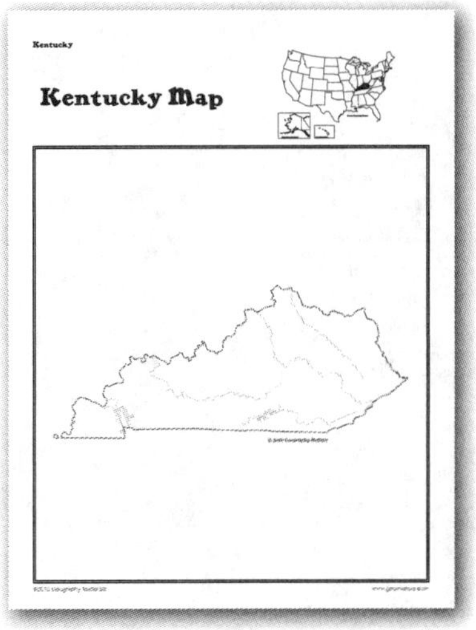
Kentucky

Kentucky Map

Louisiana

Pelican State

Louisiana, with its rich blend of Spanish and French cultures, became the 18th state on April 30, 1812. Explorer Robert Cavelier, Sieur de la Salle named the region in honor of King Louis XIV of France. Baton Rouge is the state capital.

The official flag of Louisiana consists of a solid blue field with the coat-of-arms of the state, the pelican feeding its young, in white in the center, with a ribbon beneath, also in white, containing in blue the motto of the state, *Union, Justice and Confidence.* It was adopted by an act of the legislature in 1912. The pelican represents self-sacrifice and the state's role as protector.

Louisiana has been important throughout the history of the United States because it is home to the mouth of the Mississippi River. Along the Gulf of Mexico, much of the land is below sea level and must be protected by a series of dikes and levees. Louisiana's general coastline along the Gulf of Mexico is 397 miles long, but because the marshy coast has been made extremely uneven from silt deposits, the tidal shoreline is 7,721 miles long. The tidal shoreline includes bays, offshore islands, and river mouths. Only Alaska and Florida have longer tidal shorelines.

Interesting Facts;

- Avery Island has the oldest salt mine in the western hemisphere.
- It was once illegal in Louisiana to whistle on Sunday.
- Built in 1716, St. Louis Cathedral in New Orleans is the oldest cathedral in continuous use in the United States.
- Louisiana has the tallest state capitol building in the United States; the building is 450 feet tall with 34 floors.
- The town of Jean Lafitte was once a hideaway for pirates.

General Reference

- ❑ *Louisiana* – Anne Welsbacher
- ❑ *Louisiana Facts and Symbols* – Emily McAuliffe
- ❑ http://www.statesymbolsusa.org/Louisiana/Louisianastatesymbols.html
- ❑ http://house.louisiana.gov/pubinfo/Kids.htm

Geography

- ❑ mouth of a river
  - *Geography From A to Z,* page 32
- ❑ delta
  - *Geography From A to Z,* page 17
- ❑ swamp
  - *Geography From A to Z,* page 42
  - *Explore a Spooky Swamp* – Wendy W. Cortesi
  - *Wetlands* – Ronald Rood
  - *Marshes and Swamps* – Lynn Stone, pages 31-44
- ❑ bayou

History & Biographies

- ❑ Cajuns
  - *Cajun Home* – Raymond Bial
- ❑ Louis Armstrong
  - *Louis Armstrong* – Genie Iverson
- ❑ Ruby Bridges
  - *The Story of Ruby Bridges* – Robert Coles
  - *Through My Eyes* – Ruby Bridges (RA)

Science

- ❑ pelican (state bird)
  - *Marvels of Creation, Breathtaking Birds* - Buddy and Kay Davis
  - *That Wonderful Pelican* – Jack Denton Scott (Contains evolution, but if your library has a copy, check it out for the photographs on pages 29-39.)
  - www.enchantedlearning.com/painting/birds.shtml
  - http://www.coloring.ws/birds.htm
- ❑ bald cypress (state tree)
- ❑ gardenia
- ❑ agate (state gemstone)
- ❑ frogs
  - *Frogs* – Gail Gibbons
  - *From Tadpole to Frog* – Wendy Pfeffer
  - http://coloringbookfun.com/frog/index.htm
  - http://members.enchantedlearning.com/subjects/amphibians/cloze/froglifecycle.shtml
  - http://www.coloring.ws/frog1.htm

- ❑ alligators (state reptile)
  - *Alligators and Crocodiles* – Lynn M. Stone
  - *Alligators: A Success Story* – Patricia Lauber (Contains evolution; may want to skip first chapter.)
  - *Zoo Guide*, page 189
  - www.coloring.ws/animals.html
- ❑ sugar (Sugarcane is one of Louisiana's main crops.)
  1. Go to the grocery store or look on your pantry shelves and make a list of 20 items that have sugar in them.
  2. Put 1 tablespoon of sugar in a disposable metal pie tin. Place the tin on a stove burner and turn on low heat. Let the sugar heat until smoke stops coming off. Most of what is left is carbon. What color is it?

Literature

- ❑ *Petite Rouge: A Cajun Red Riding Hood* – Mike Artell
- ❑ *Bayou Lullaby* – Kathi Appelt
- ❑ *Adventures of Grandfather Frog* – Thornton W. Burgess
- ❑ *Toby Belfer Visits Ellis Island* – Gloria Teles Pushker
- ❑ "America, We the People," the official state judicial poem, written by Sylvia Davidson Lott Buckley:

America,
We the people
Justice, the word most sought by all, seek God to bless the courts with truth,
for through His wisdom we rise or fall.

America,
We the people
Do honor this great lady fair, who with her mighty arms still holds,
the scales of Justice for all to share.

America,
We the people
Do offer threads of hope to all, for Justice covers everyone;
she does not measure, short or tall.

America,
We the people
Boldly make this pledge to thee, that Justice will, in mind and heart,
guide each destiny.

America,
We the people

Language Arts

Preamble to the State Constitution:

We, the people of Louisiana, grateful to Almighty God for the civil, political, economic, and religious liberties we enjoy, and desiring to protect individual rights to life, liberty, and property; afford opportunity for the fullest development of the individual; assure equality of rights; promote the health, safety, education, and welfare of the people; maintain a representative and orderly government; ensure domestic tranquility; provide for the common defense; and secure the blessings of freedom and justice to ourselves and our posterity, do ordain and establish this constitution.

1. Refer to Language Arts Guide starting on page 8.
2. Write a story about living on a bayou.
3. Copy "America, We the People."

Character

The origin of the Louisiana motto - *Union, Justice and Confidence* - is unclear. The motto was adopted in 1902 as part of the state seal. The character traits to emphasize are **confidence** and **fairness**.

- **Confidence** – Trust, or reliance; an assurance of mind or belief in the integrity, stability, or veracity of oneself or another, or in the truth and reality of a fact.
- **Fairness** – Openness, frankness, honesty; hence equality; just equitableness.

  Life isn't always fair, but we should strive to be fair in our dealings with others. Children need to learn to treat others fairly and be considerate of others. We are not to judge people based on outward appearance; this is especially important to instill in our children.

State Flag Pledge

I pledge allegiance to the flag of the state of Louisiana
and to the motto for which it stands:
A state, under God, united in purpose and ideals,
confident that justice shall prevail for all of those abiding here.

Activities

1. Color or label a map of Louisiana.
2. Label the Red River, Lake Pontchartrain, and the Mississippi Delta on a map of the United States.
3. Go to http://www.kidzone.ws/geography/usa/ for printable flag and state symbol coloring pages.
4. Go to http://lacoast.gov/education/kids/coloringbooks/Coastal/index.htm for a state coloring page.
5. Prepare a meal in *Eat Your Way Through the U.S.A.* from the state of Louisiana.
6. Listen to the state song, "You are My Sunshine."
7. Make a swamp diorama.
8. Make an alligator box.
    - Paint the outside of a shoebox and lid green and the inside and underside red.
    - Cut teeth from white paper; glue them inside the box and lid.
    - Glue two small, black buttons onto two green pom-poms. Glue them on the lid.
    - Glue two small, black buttons on the lid for nostrils.

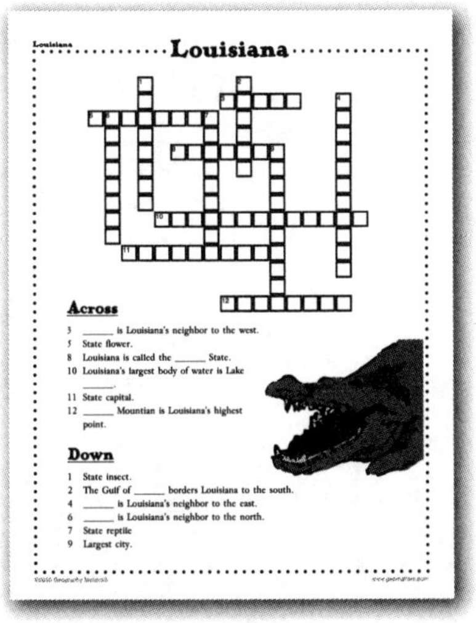

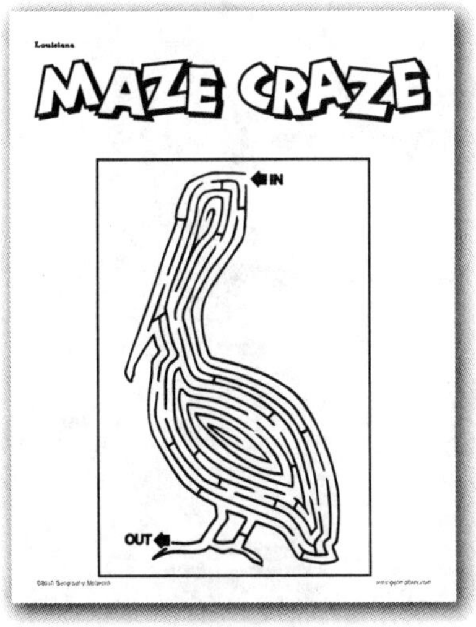

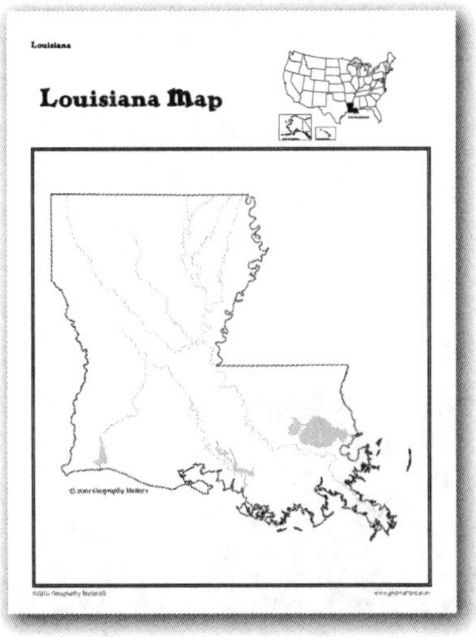

Maine

Pine Tree State

Maine is the largest New England state and forms the northeastern corner of the United States. Maine joined the Union on March 15, 1820, making it the 23rd state. Maine most likely means "mainland." Early explorers used the term "The Main" to differentiate the mainland from the offshore islands. The state capital is Augusta.

The flag of Maine was adopted by the Legislature in 1909. The state coat of arms has a blue field. Representing Maine's agricultural and maritime industries are a farmer on one side of the shield and a seaman on the other. The lower portion of the shield is of water and the upper section sky. The pine tree stands for Maine's forests, which cover 90% of its land. Below the tree lies a moose, the state animal, indigenous to the state and symbolic of Maine's reverence for wildlife. The star and motto depict Maine's northern location.

Maine is probably best known for its beautiful, rugged shoreline featuring jagged rocks and cliffs and thousands of bays and inlets. Inland, the state has sparkling lakes, rushing rivers, thick forests, and towering mountains. Cities and towns lie mostly in southern Maine. Maine is cooler than most of the rest of the country. Arctic air and coastal winds keep the region from being warmed by Gulf Stream air currents, making Maine's winters colder than other places that are just as far north.

Interesting Facts:

- Some parts of Maine are so wild there aren't even roads. The only access is by seaplane or canoe.
- West Quoddy Head, a small peninsula, is the country's easternmost point.
- Maine is the only state that shares its border with only one other state.
- Portland is the birthplace of poet Henry Wadsworth Longfellow.
- Earmuffs were invented by 15-year-old Chester Greenwood of Farmington in 1873.

General Reference

- ❑ *Maine* – Paul Joseph
- ❑ *Maine Facts and Symbols* – Emily McAuliffe
- ❑ http://maine.gov/sos/kids/

Geography

- ❑ cliff
  - *Geography From A to Z,* page 12
- ❑ promontory
  - *Geography From A to Z,* page 36

History & Biographies

- ❑ Abbie Burgess
  - *Keep the Lights Burning, Abbie* – Peter and Connie Roop
- ❑ lighthouses
  - *Beacons of Light: Lighthouses* – Gail Gibbons
- ❑ ships
  - *Ships and Seaports* – Katharine Carter
  - *Boats* – Ken Robbins
- ❑ Milton Bradley

Science

- ❑ black-capped chickadee (state bird)
  - http://www.coloring.ws/birds.htm
- ❑ eastern white pine (state tree & flower)
- ❑ lupine
- ❑ tourmaline (state gemstone)
- ❑ lobster
  - www.state.me.us/sos/kids/fyigames/cllobst.html
- ❑ tidal pool
  - *A Tidal Pool* - Philip Steele
  - *Tide Pool* – Paul Fleisher
- ❑ whales
  - *Finding Out About Whales* – Elin Kelsey
  - http://members.enchantedlearning.com/subjects/whales/cloze/general.shtml
  - http://members.enchantedlearning.com/connectdots/
  - www.coloring.ws/animals.html
- ❑ blueberries (state berry)
  - http://coloringbookfun.com/food/index.htm

Literature

- ❑ Poems by Henry Wadsworth Longfellow
- ❑ *The Lighthouse Children* – Syd Hoff
- ❑ *Little Toot* – Hardie Gramatky
- ❑ *Clipper Ship* – Thomas Lewis
- ❑ *Lighthouse Dog to the Rescue* – Angeli Perrow
- ❑ *Sign of the Beaver* – Elizabeth George Speare (RA)
- ❑ *The Seashore Book* – Charlotte Zolotow
- ❑ *One Morning in Maine* – Robert McCloskey
- ❑ *Birdie's Lighthouse* – Deborah Hopkinson

Language Arts

Preamble to the State Constitution:
We the people of Maine, in order to establish justice, insure tranquility, provide for our mutual defense, promote our common welfare, and secure to our selves and our posterity the blessings of liberty, acknowledging with grateful hearts the goodness of the Sovereign Ruler of the Universe in affording us an opportunity, so favorable to the design; and, imploring His aid and direction in its accomplishment, do agree to form ourselves into a free and independent State, by the style and title of the STATE OF MAINE, and do ordain and establish the following Constitution for the government of the same.

1. Refer to Language Arts Guide starting on page 8.
2. Maine is the only state whose name has only one syllable. Practice breaking words into syllables.
3. Write a story about being a lighthouse keeper.
4. Write a story about being the captain of a ship.
5. Copy all or part of a poem by Henry Wadsworth Longfellow. (Note: *The Song of Hiawatha* will be covered in Minnesota.)

Character

The motto for Maine - *Dirigo* - has been translated as "I direct" or "I guide." It is believed to imply that as a star guides a sailor, the state guides its citizens.

- **Submission** – Yielding to the will or power of another; obedience.
- **Tolerance** – Endurance; indulgent; the power or capacity of enduring.

Activities

1. Color or label a map of Maine.
2. Label the Atlantic Ocean and West Quoddy Head on a map of the United States.
3. Go to http://www.kidzone.ws/geography/usa/ for printable flag and state symbol coloring pages.
4. Go to http://www.state.me.us/sos/kids/fyigames/clchick.htm for a state coloring page.
5. Prepare a meal in *Eat Your Way Through the U.S.A.* from the state of Maine.
6. Make a whale mobile. For instructions go to http://members.enchantedlearning.com/crafts/Whalemobile.shtml.

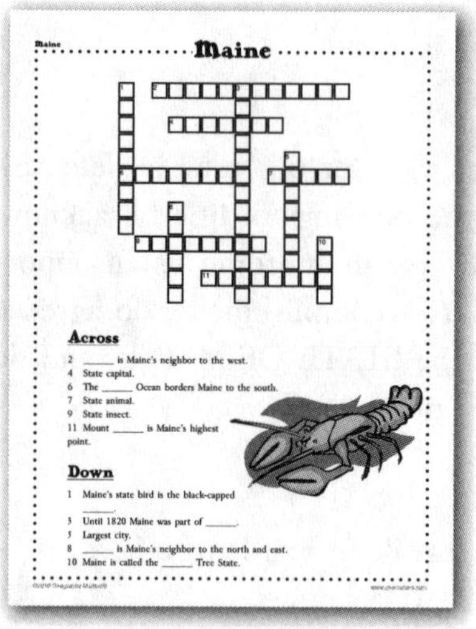

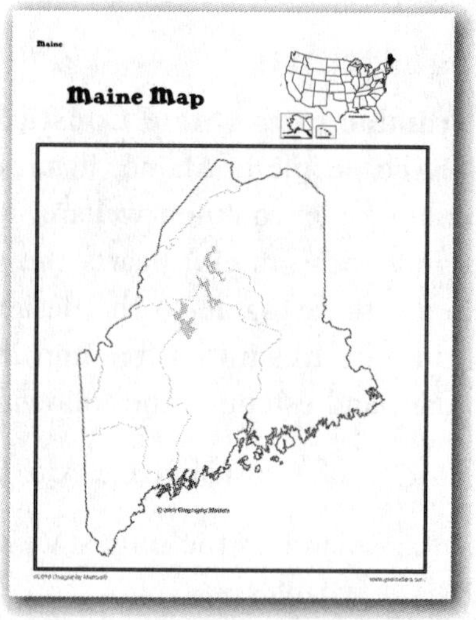

Maryland

Old Line State

One of the original thirteen colonies, Maryland became the 7th to join the Union, on April 28, 1788. Maryland was named for Queen Henrietta Maria, wife of King Charles I of England. Annapolis is the state capital.

Maryland has the only state flag that is a true heraldic banner, reproducing the arms of the family of the Lords Baltimore who ruled Maryland throughout most of its colonial period. Each side of the family, the Calverts and the Crosslands, is represented by two quarters of the flag. The flag was adopted in 1904.

The Chesapeake Bay divides Maryland into two parts – the Eastern Shore and the Western Shore. The Eastern Shore is low and flat and shares the Delmarva Peninsula with parts of Delaware and Virginia. Part of the Western Shore is low and flat, but much of it is rolling plains, hills and valleys, mountains, and plateaus. More than 40% of Maryland is forested. Maryland's coastline along the Atlantic Ocean measures only 31 miles. But the many arms and inlets of the Chesapeake Bay give Maryland a total coastline of 3,190 miles.

Interesting Facts:

- The first telegraph line went from Baltimore to Washington, D.C.
- Maryland has the narrowest section of land; it is only one mile wide.
- The first dental school in the United States opened at the University of Maryland.
- The United States Naval Academy was founded on October 10, 1845 at Annapolis.

General Reference

- ❑ *Maryland* - Paul Joseph
- ❑ *Maryland Facts and Symbols* – Muriel L. Dubois
- ❑ http://www.mdkidspage.org/

Geography

- ❑ bay
  - *Geography From A to Z,* page 10
- ❑ Chesapeake Bay

History & Biographies

- ❑ Johns Hopkins
- ❑ Frederick Douglas
    - *A Picture Book of Frederick Douglass* – David A. Adler
    - *Young Frederick Douglas* – Linda Walvoord Girard
    - http://members.enchantedlearning.com/history/us/aframer/douglass/cloze.shtml
- ❑ Harriet Tubman
    - *Escape North! The Story of Harriet Tubman* – Monica Kulling
    - *Harriet Tubman* – Francene Sabin
- ❑ Thurgood Marshall
    - *Thurgood Marshall: Fight for Justice* – Rae Bains
    - *A Picture Book of Thurgood Marshall* – David A. Adler

Science

- ❑ white ash
- ❑ Baltimore oriole (state bird)
    - *Orioles* – Lynn Stone
    - www.enchantedlearning.com/painting/birds.shtml
    - http://www.coloring.ws/birds.htm
- ❑ black-eyed Susan (state flower)
- ❑ sulfur
- ❑ crabs
    - www.coloring.ws/animals.html

Language Arts

Preamble to the State Constitution:
We, the People of the State of Maryland, grateful to Almighty God for our civil and religious liberty, and taking into our serious consideration the best means of establishing a good Constitution in this State for the sure foundation and more permanent security thereof, declare...

1. Refer to Language Arts Guide starting on page 8.

Character

Maryland has two mottoes which appear on the state seal. The first one reflects the colonial origins of the state: *Manly deeds, Womanly words*. The second reflects the deep religious sentiment of the original colonists: *With favor wilt thou compass us as with a shield.* The latter motto is believed to have been taken from Psalm 5:12.

This would be a great time to discuss the different roles of men and women. We will discuss two predominant traits for each sex. This is not meant to imply these traits are exclusive to that gender; however, the **modesty** and **gentleness** are generally referred to for women and **bravery** and **heroism** are encouraged for men. These are only a few of the qualities desired of men and women; please feel free to expand the list to incorporate those traits you deem important for your children.

- **Modesty** – In females, modesty is used also as synonymous with chastity, or purity of manners. In this sense, modesty results from purity of mind, or from the fear of disgrace and ignominy fortified by education and principle. Unaffected modesty is the sweetest charm of female excellence, the richest gem in the diadem of their honor.
- **Gentleness** – Softness of manners; mildness of temper; sweetness of disposition; meekness; kindness; benevolence.
- **Bravery** – Courage, undaunted spirit; intrepidity; gallantry; fearlessness of danger; often united with generosity or dignity of mind which despises meanness and cruelty, and disdains to take advantage of a vanquished enemy.
- **Heroism** – The qualities of a hero; bravery; courage; intrepidity.

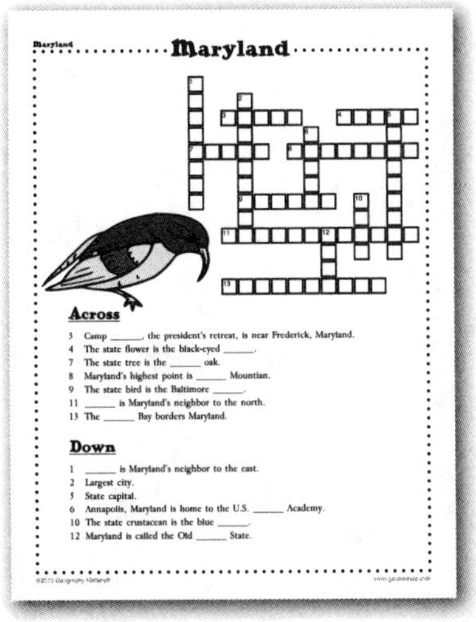
Maryland

Across
3 Camp ______, the president's retreat, is near Frederick, Maryland.
4 The state flower is the black-eyed ______.
7 The state tree is the ______ oak.
8 Maryland's highest point is ______ Mountian.
9 The state bird is the Baltimore ______.
11 ______ is Maryland's neighbor to the north.
13 The ______ Bay borders Maryland.

Down
1 ______ is Maryland's neighbor to the east.
2 Largest city.
5 State capital.
6 Annapolis, Maryland is home to the U.S. ______ Academy.
10 The state crustacean is the blue ______.
12 Maryland is called the Old ______ State.

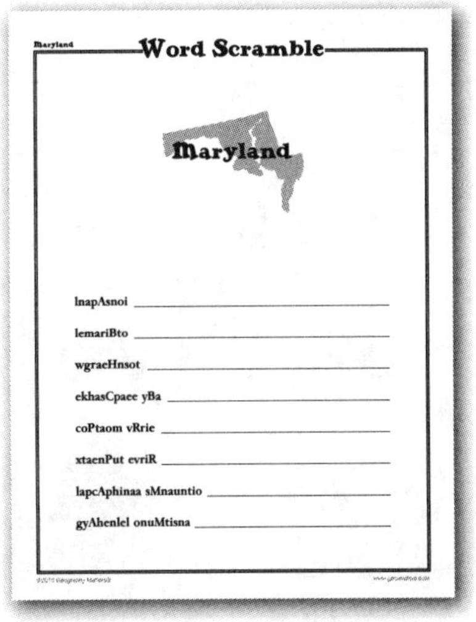
Word Scramble

Maryland

lnapAsnoi ______
lemariBto ______
wgraeHnsot ______
ekhasCpaee yBa ______
coPtaom vRrie ______
xtaenPut evriR ______
lapcAphinaa sMnauntio ______
gyAhenlel onuMtisna ______

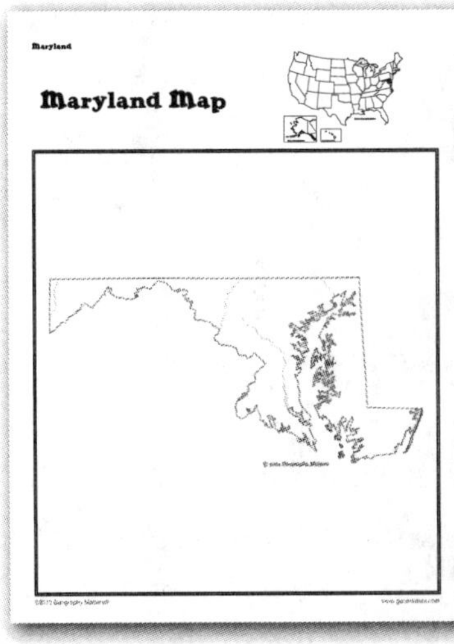
Maryland Map

Activities

1. Color or label a map of Maryland.
2. Label the Chesapeake Bay on a map of the United States.
3. Go to http://www.kidzone.ws/geography/usa/ for printable flag and state symbol coloring pages.
4. Prepare a meal in *Eat Your Way Through the U.S.A.* from the state of Maryland.

5. Make a crab.
    - Punch eight holes around a paper plate.
    - Cut drinking straws into 1-inch pieces. You will need 24 pieces.
    - Thread pipe cleaners through the holes in the paper plate. Twist to secure.
    - Put three pieces of straw on each pipe cleaner to represent the leg segments.
    - Punch two holes close together and put one pipe cleaner through with the ends sticking up for the antennae. Twist to secure. Add a bead to each end for the eyes.
    - Bend legs to look like crab is walking.
    - Paint or color, if desired.
6. Make a Smith Island Cake, the official state cake of Maryland.
   http://www.smithisland.org/cakerecipe.html

Massachusetts

Bay State

Massachusetts, the birthplace of the American Revolution, was the 6th state to join the Union, on February 6, 1788. Massachusetts was named after the Massachuset tribe, which lived near present-day Boston. The name probably means "near the great hill," and historians believe it refers to the Great Blue Hill south of the city. Boston is the capital of Massachusetts.

The flag of Massachusetts was adopted in 1908 and revised in 1971, replacing a pine tree with the coat of arms of the Commonwealth of Massachusetts. The Indian points an arrow downward, symbolizing peace. The star over his shoulder represents Massachusetts as a state. The arm and sword above the shield stand for the state motto.

The landscape of Massachusetts is a series of hills and valleys. From sea level near the ocean, the state reaches an elevation of 3,500 feet near its western border with New York. The Atlantic Ocean on the eastern border makes cities such as Boston and Gloucester important ports and allows for a large fishing industry.

Interesting Facts:

- The first post office in what would become the United States was established in Boston in 1639.
- The Constitution of Massachusetts is the oldest constitution still in use today. It was ratified in 1780.
- Patented in 1876, the telephone was invented in Boston by Alexander Graham Bell.
- Basketball was invented by James Naismith in 1891 in Springfield.
- William Morgan, director of the Holyoke YMCA, invented volleyball in 1895.
- The country's first subway was opened in Boston in 1897.
- In 1903, the first World Series was played in Boston.

General Reference

- ❑ *Massachusetts* - Paul Joseph
- ❑ *Massachusetts Facts and Symbols* – Emily McAuliffe
- ❑ *Massachusetts* – J. F. Warner (contains evolution)
- ❑ http://www.statesymbolsusa.org/Massachusetts/state_symbols.html
- ❑ http://www.sec.state.ma.us/cis/ciskid/kididx.htm

Geography

- ❑ cape
  - *Geography From A to Z,* page 11
- ❑ bogs and marshes
  - *Geography From A to Z,* page 28
  - *Marshes and Swamps* – Lynn Stone, pages 16–30

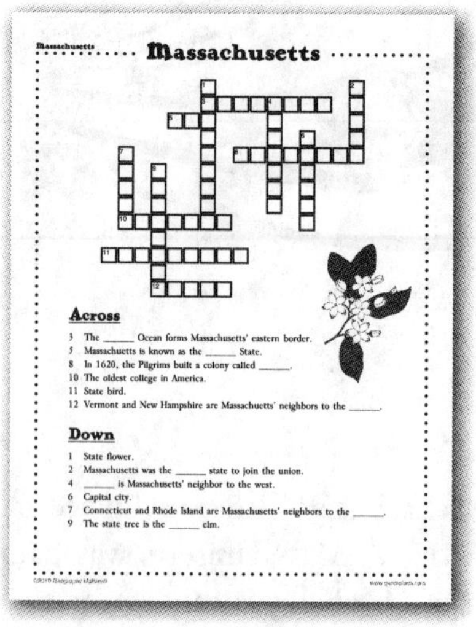

History & Biographies

- ❑ William Bradford
  - *Profiles from History* - Volume 1, pages 79-86
- ❑ Squanto
  - *Profiles from History* - Volume 1, pages 87-96
- ❑ Wampanoag
  - *Tapenum's Day* – Kate Waters
  - *Clambake: A Wampanoag Tradition* – Russell M. Peters
- ❑ John Chapman (a.k.a. Johnny Appleseed) (state folk hero)
  - *The True Tale of Johnny Appleseed* – Margaret Hodges
  - *Johnny Appleseed* – David Harrison
  - http://www.dltk-kids.com/crafts/miscellaneous/mjohnny-poster.html
- ❑ Emily Dickinson
- ❑ Louisa May Alcott
  - *Louisa May Alcott: Young Writer* – Laurence Santrey
- ❑ Alexander Graham Bell
  - *Hello, Alexander Graham Bell Speaking* – Cynthia Copeland Lewis
  - *Book of Inventors* - Usborne, page 29
- ❑ Leonard Bernstein
  - *Leonard Bernstein* – Mike Venezia
- ❑ John F. Kennedy
  - *The Story of the Assassination of John F. Kennedy* – R. Conrad Stein
  - *High Hopes: A Photobiography of John F. Kennedy* – Deborah Heiligman
  - www.whitehouse.gov/history/presidents/
  - www.presidentialavenue.com/jk.cfm
  - http://www.homeofheroes.com/e-books/presidents/35_kennedy.html

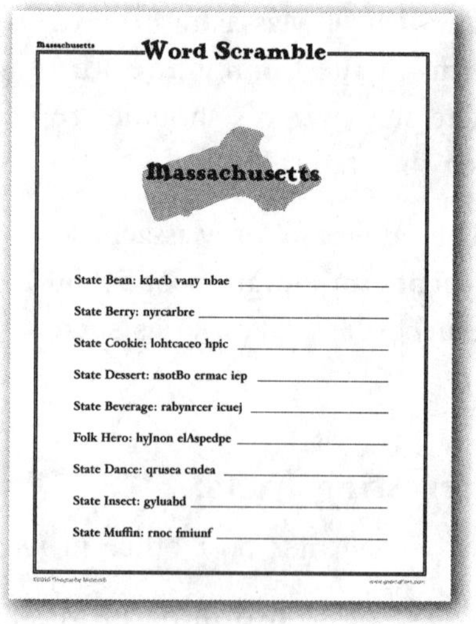

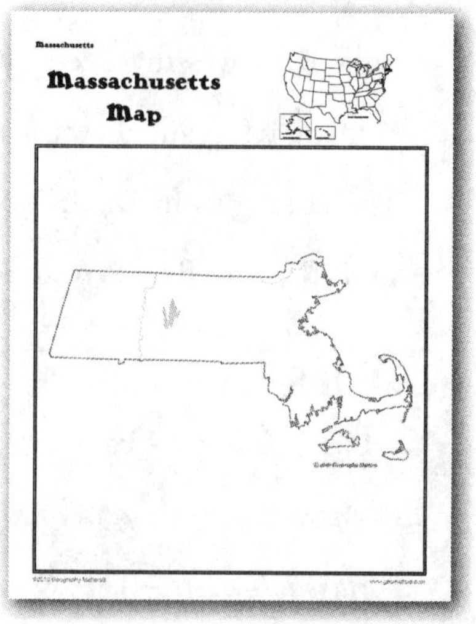

- ❑ George H. W. Bush
  - www.whitehouse.gov/history/presidents/
  - www.presidentialavenue.com/gb.cfm
  - http://www.homeofheroes.com/e-books/presidents/35_kennedy.html
- ❑ Barbara Bush
  - *Barbara Bush: First Lady of Literacy* – June Behrens

Science

- ❑ herons
  - *Marvels of Creation, Breathtaking Birds* - Buddy and Kay Davis
  - *Herons* – Frank Staub
  - *Zoo Guide,* page 127
- ❑ American elm (state tree)
- ❑ mayflower (trailing arbutus) (state flower)
- ❑ rhodonite (state gemstone)
- ❑ cranberry (state berry)
  - *Cranberries* – William Jaspersohn
- ❑ telephone
  - http://pbskids.org/zoom/activities/sci/stringtelephone.html

Literature

- ❑ *The American Revolution,* Adventures of Munford series - Jamie Aramini
- ❑ *An American Army of Two* – Janet Greeson
- ❑ *Peg and the Whale* – Kenneth Oppel
- ❑ *The Adventures of Obadiah* – Brinton Turkle
- ❑ *Island Boy* – Barbara Cooney
- ❑ *Little Women* – Louisa May Alcott (RA) (Abridged children's version or book-on-tape.)
- ❑ Make Way for Ducklings - Robert McCloskey (state book)

Language Arts

Preamble to the State Constitution:

The end of the institution, maintenance, and administration of government, is to secure the existence of the body politic, to protect it, and to furnish the individuals who compose it with the power of enjoying in safety and tranquility their natural rights, and the blessings of life: and whenever these great objects are not obtained, the people have a right to alter the government, and to take measures necessary for their safety, prosperity and happiness.

The body politic is formed by a voluntary association of individuals: it is a social compact, by which the whole people covenants with each citizen, and each citizen with the whole people, that all shall be governed by certain laws for the common good. It is the duty of the people, therefore, in framing a constitution of government, to provide for an equitable mode of making laws, as well as for an impartial interpretation, and a faithful execution of them; that every man may, at all times, find his security in them.

We, therefore, the people of Massachusetts, acknowledging, with grateful hearts, the goodness of the great Legislator of the universe, in affording us, in the course of His providence, an opportunity, deliberately and peaceably, without fraud, violence or surprise, of entering into an original, explicit, and solemn compact with each other; and of forming a new constitution of civil government, for ourselves and posterity; and devoutly imploring His direction in so interesting a design, do agree upon, ordain and establish the following Declaration of Rights, and Frame of Government, as the Constitution of the Commonwealth of Massachusetts.

1. Refer to Language Arts Guide starting on page 8.
2. Read and discuss the poem *Blue Hills of Massachusetts* which can be found at: www.masshome.com/mapoem.html
3. Read and discuss the poetry of Emily Dickinson.

Character

The motto for Massachusetts - *By the sword we seek peace, but peace only under liberty* - is attributed to English political writer Algernon Sydney (1622-1683). In order to defend liberty, our citizens must be **persistent** and **vigilant**.

- **Persistence** – Steadiness in pursuit; not receding from a purpose or undertaking.
- **Vigilance** – Watchfulness, circumspection; attention to discovering and avoiding danger; or providing for safety.

Activities

1. Color or label a map of Massachusetts.
2. Label Cape Cod, Cape Cod Bay, and Nantucket Sound on a map of the United States.
3. Go to http://www.kidzone.ws/geography/usa/ for printable flag and state symbol coloring pages.
4. Prepare a meal in *Eat Your Way Through the U.S.A.* from the state of Massachusetts.
5. Listen to the music of Leonard Bernstein.
6. Play basketball and/or volleyball.

Michigan

Wolverine State

Michigan, in the very heart of the Great Lakes, became the 26th state on January 26, 1837. Michigan is named for Lake Michigan. The Chippewa called the lake *Michigama*, which means "large lake." Lansing is the capital of Michigan.

In 1911, the state's coat of arms, adopted in 1832, was placed on a blue field to make the state flag. The sun rising over water and a man standing in a field, representing peace and the man's ability to defend his rights, appear on a shield supported by an elk and a moose, symbols of Michigan's wealth and resources. An eagle over the shield depicts the jurisdiction of the federal government over state government. The flag has three mottoes, which translate as "One Nation Made Up of Many States" (red ribbon), "I Will Defend" (blue shield), and "If You Seek a Pleasant Peninsula, Look Around" (white ribbon).

Michigan is made up of two peninsulas. The Lower Peninsula is shaped like a big mitten and is home to industry and the vast majority of the state's ten million residents. Almost half of the population lives in or around Detroit. The Upper Peninsula, or U.P., is heavily forested and sparsely inhabited. Four of the five Great Lakes - Superior, Michigan, Huron, and Erie - border Michigan and form the state's 3,200-mile coast, the longest of any inland state.

Interesting Facts:

- Sault Ste. Marie was founded by Father Jacques Marquette in 1668. It is the third oldest remaining settlement in the United States.
- The Mackinac Bridge is one of the longest suspension bridges in the world. Connecting the Upper and Lower Peninsulas of Michigan, it spans 5 miles over the Straits of Mackinac, where Lake Michigan and Lake Huron meet. The Mighty Mac took 3 years to complete and was opened to traffic in 1957.
- Vernor's ginger ale, the first soda pop made in the United States, was created in Detroit. In 1862, pharmacist James Vernor was trying to create a new beverage when he was called away to serve in the Civil War. When he returned 4 years later, the drink, stored in an oak case, had acquired a delicious gingery flavor.
- Standing anywhere in the state, a person is within 85 miles of one of the Great Lakes.
- Michigan was the first state to provide in its Constitution for the establishment of public libraries.

General Reference

- ❑ *Michigan* – Paul Joseph
- ❑ *Michigan Facts and Symbols* – Emily McAuliffe
- ❑ *Michigan* – Karen Sirvaitis (contains evolution)
- ❑ http://www.statesymbolsusa.org/Michigan/MichiganSymbols.html
- ❑ http://www.michigan.gov/mikids

Geography

- ❑ Lake Huron
- ❑ strait
  - *Geography From A-Z,* page 41

History & Biographies

- ❑ Ottawa
- ❑ Pontiac
  - *Pontiac: Young Ottawa Leader* – Howard Peckham
  - *Pontiac: Chief of the Ottawa* – Jane Fleischer
- ❑ Jacques Marquette
- ❑ Henry Ford
  - *Henry Ford* – Haydn Middleton
  - *We'll Race You, Henry* – Barbara Mitchell
  - *Henry Ford: Young Man with Ideas* – Hazel B. Aird
  - *Henry Ford: A Pictorial Biography* – Jeanine M. Head
  - *Book of Inventors* - Usborne, page 13
- ❑ Daniel Gerber
- ❑ Patricia Polacco
  - www.patriciapolacco.com

Science

- ❑ American beech
- ❑ daffodil
- ❑ chlorastrolite (state gemstone)
- ❑ wolverine
  - *Zoo Guide,* page 103
  - *Marvels of Creation, Magnificent Mammals* - Buddy and Kay Davis

- ❑ woodpecker
    - *Zoo Guide,* page 147
    - *Marvels of Creation, Breathtaking Birds* - Buddy and Kay Davis
    - *Woodpeckers* – Lynn Stone
    - *Woodpeckers* – Mary Ann McDonald
    - www.enchantedlearning.com/painting/birds.shtml
    - http://familycrafts.about.com/od/birdprojects/
- ❑ daffodil
- ❑ chlorastrolite (state gemstone)
- ❑ wolverine
    - *Zoo Guide,* page 103
    - *Marvels of Creation, Magnificent Mammals* - Buddy and Kay Davis
- ❑ combustion engines
    - *The Internal Combustion Engine* – Ross R. Olney
- ❑ automobiles
    - *Automobiles* – Sylvia Wilkinson
    - http://members.enchantedlearning.com/connectdots/car/

Literature

- ❑ *Mike Mulligan and His Steam Shovel* – Virginia Lee Burton
- ❑ *Aunt Chip and the Great Triple Creek Dam Affair* – Patricia Polacco
- ❑ *The Keeping Quilt* – Patricia Polacco
- ❑ *Betty Doll* – Patricia Polacco
- ❑ *Thunder Cake* – Patricia Polacco
- ❑ *Meteor!* – Patricia Polacco
- ❑ *Chicken Sunday* – Patricia Polacco

Language Arts

Preamble to the State Constitution:

The People of the State of Michigan do ordain this Constitution. (No further preamble for Michigan)

1. Refer to Language Arts Guide starting on page 8.

Character

The state motto of Michigan - *If you seek a pleasant peninsula look about you* - is believed to have been inspired by a similar phrase inscribed on the door of St. Paul's Cathedral in London. The state motto was adopted in 1835 at the Constitutional Convention. This motto can be applied to several different traits.

Our children should be **observant** of things around them and **appreciative** of their blessings.

- **Observance** – Taking notice; attentively viewing or noticing; careful attention.

  This trait has two different meanings, and both are important. Our children should be observant of the world around them to perceive the needs of others or the wrong thoughts.

- **Appreciation** – Valuing; setting a price or value on; gratitude and thankfulness for items received.

State Flag Pledge

I pledge allegiance to the flag of Michigan,
and to the state for which it stands,
two beautiful peninsulas united by a bridge of steel,
where equal opportunity and justice to all is our ideal.

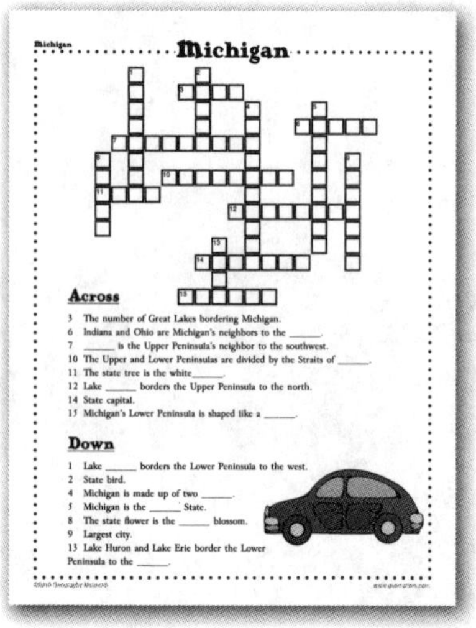

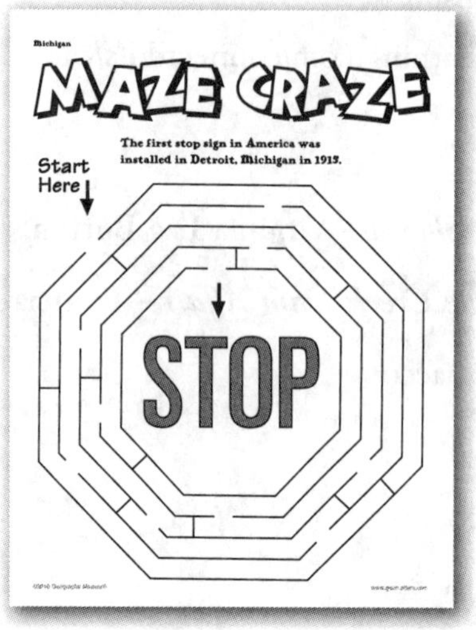

Activities

1. Color or label a map of Michigan.
2. Label Lake Huron and the Straits of Mackinac on a map of the United States and shade blue.
3. Go to http://www.kidzone.ws/geography/usa/ for printable flag and state symbol coloring pages.
4. Prepare a meal in *Eat Your Way Through the U.S.A.* from the state of Michigan.
5. Drink ginger ale.

Minnesota

North Star State

Sometimes called the Land of 10,000 Lakes, Minnesota became the 32nd state on May 11, 1858. In reality, there are more than 15,000 lakes scattered across Minnesota contributing to its natural beauty. The name Minnesota comes from the Sioux words *minni*, meaning "water," and *sotah*, which means "clouded" or "sky-tinted." St. Paul is the state capital.

The Minnesota state flag is royal blue with a gold fringe. In the center of the flag is the state seal. On the seal, the Indian riding into the sunset and the farmer symbolize the white settlers' rise and the Indians' decline in pioneer Minnesota. The waterfall and forest represent the state's natural features. Around the state seal is a wreath of the state flower, the lady slipper. Three dates are woven into the wreath: 1858, the year Minnesota became a state; 1819, the year Fort Snelling was established; and 1893, the year the official flag was adopted. Nineteen stars ring the wreath. The largest star represents Minnesota.

Bordered by Lake Superior, northeastern Minnesota is a land of rocky cliffs and dense forests. Most of the state, though, is covered by gently rolling plains. Minneapolis, the state's largest city, and St. Paul are known as the Twin Cities; they are the industrial and cultural center of Minnesota.

Interesting Facts:

- Lake Itasca, in northwestern Minnesota, is the source or headwater of the Mississippi River. At this point what becomes a mighty river is a stream so narrow that you can step across it.
- The original name of the settlement that became St. Paul was Pig's Eye, named for the French-Canadian whiskey trader Pierre "Pig's Eye" Parrant.
- In 1930, Richard Drew invented cellophane tape in St. Paul.
- Tonka Trucks were developed and continue to be manufactured in Minnetonka.
- The Minneapolis Public Library is said to have started the first children's department in a library. They separated children's books from the rest of the collection in 1889.

General Reference

- ❑ *Minnesota* – Paul Joseph
- ❑ *Minnesota Facts and Symbols* – Bill McAuliffe
- ❑ http://www.sos.state.mn.us/Kids/kidshome.html
- ❑ http://www.leg.state.mn.us/youth/

Geography

- ❑ lake
  - *Geography From A to Z,* page 27
- ❑ Lake Superior

History & Biographies

- ❑ Chippewa
  - *The Chippewa* – Alice Osinski
- ❑ Charles Lindberg
- ❑ Richard Drew
  - *Book of Inventors* - Usborne, page 22
  - http://inventors.about.com/library/inventors/blscotchtape.htm
- ❑ Walter Mondale
- ❑ Charles Schulz
  - *Charles Schulz* – Mae Woods
  - www.schulzmuseum.org/

Science

- ❑ common loon (state bird)
  - *Marvels of Creation, Breathtaking Birds* - Buddy and Kay Davis
  - http://www.friendsacrossamerica.com/colorstatemnbirdflower.html
- ❑ Norway pine (state tree)
- ❑ lady's slipper (state flower)
- ❑ red granite
- ❑ pond and lake ecosystems
  - *Wonders of the Pond* – Francene Sabin
  - *Pond Life* – Lynn M. Stone
  - *Around the Pond: Who's Been Here?* – Lindsay Barrett George
  - *A Freshwater Pond* – Adam Hibbert
  - *Pond* – Gordon Morrison
  - http://mbgnet.mobot.org/fresh/index.htm

Literature

- ❑ *Peanuts* comic strips – Charles Schulz
- ❑ *Ducklings and Pollywogs* – Anne Rockwell
- ❑ *Marven of the Great North Woods* – Kathryn Lasky
- ❑ *On the Banks of Plum Creek* – Laura Ingalls Wilder (RA)
- ❑ *Laura & Nellie* – A Little House Chapter Book
- ❑ *School Days* – A Little House Chapter Book
- ❑ *Klara's New World* – Jeanette Winter

Language Arts

Preamble to the State Constitution:
We, the people of the state of Minnesota, grateful to God for our civil and religious liberty, and desiring to perpetuate its blessings and secure the same to ourselves and our posterity, do ordain and establish this Constitution

1. Refer to Language Arts Guide starting on page 8.
2. If you explore a pond or lake, write about what you saw.
3. Minnehaha Falls on Minnehaha Creek in Minneapolis were made famous by Henry Wadsworth Longfellow's poem *The Song of Hiawatha*. Read and discuss all or part of this poem.

Character

The original motto, chosen by Henry Sibley, was translated from Latin as "I wish to see what is above," but it was incorrectly engraved as "I cover to see what is above." The incorrect motto was adopted in 1849, but then changed in 1858 for the state seal to the current motto – *Star of the North* – which was officially adopted in 1861.

The North Star was often used for geographical purposes and was an accurate and dependable standard of navigation. Our children should learn the importance of **accuracy** and **dependability** in their lives. They have to be accurate and dependable in the little things so it becomes habitual and will transfer to the larger responsibilities they will obtain later in life.

- **Accuracy** – Exact conformity to truth, or to a standard or rule, or to a model.
- **Dependability** – Relying, resting in confidence; trusting or confiding; having full confidence or belief in.

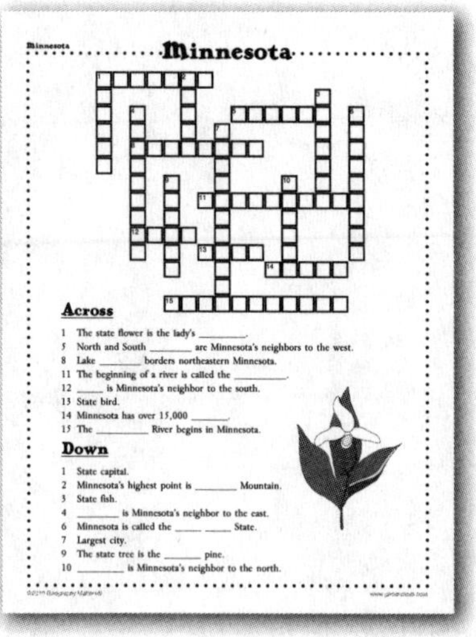

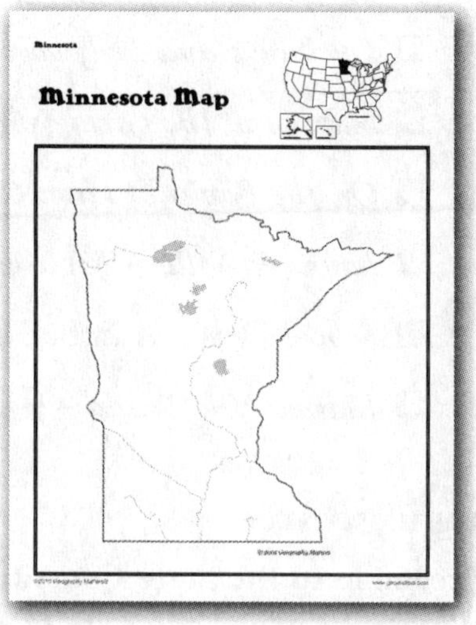

Activities

1. Color or label a map of Minnesota.
2. Label Lake Superior on a map of the United States and shade it blue.
3. Go to http://www.kidzone.ws/geography/usa/ for printable flag and state symbol coloring pages.
4. Prepare a meal in *Eat Your Way Through the U.S.A.* from the state of Minnesota.
5. If studying Charles Schulz, draw a comic strip.
6. Explore a lake or pond in your area.

Mississippi

Magnolia State

Rich in history, Mississippi became the 20th state on December 10, 1817. Mississippi takes its name from the mighty river that forms most of its western border. The name "Mississippi" comes from Native American words that mean "father of water." The state capital is Jackson.

Adopted in 1894, the flag of Mississippi reflects the state's ties to the United States and the Confederacy. The red, white, and blue stripes stand for the national flag; the Confederate battle flag is depicted in the upper left portion. In April 2001, a special statewide vote was taken to decide whether to keep the 1894 design or adopt a new one. Mississippians voted overwhelmingly to continue flying the state banner that prominently displays the Confederate battle flag, bucking a trend toward stripping the racially divisive emblem from public venues in the South.

Farmland and forest-covered hills stretch over most of the state, but the land along the Mississippi River is so low that dams and levees have been built to help control flooding. Even with these efforts, flooding is quite common in the delta region.

Interesting Facts:

- In 1834, Captain Isaac Ross, whose plantation was in Lorman, freed his slaves and arranged for them to be sent to Africa, where they founded the country of Liberia.
- In 1902, while on a hunting expedition in Sharkey County, President Theodore Roosevelt refused to shoot a captured bear. The act resulted in the creation of the world-famous teddy bear.
- Vicksburg businessman Joseph A. Biedenharn was the first to bottle Coca-Cola in 1894.
- Root beer was invented in Biloxi in 1898 by Edward Adolf Barq, Sr.

General Reference

❑ *Mississippi* – Paul Joseph

❑ *Mississippi Facts and Symbols* – Karen Bush Gibson

Geography

❑ Mississippi River

History & Biographies

- ❑ plantations
  - *Life on a Southern Plantation* – Sally Senzell Isaacs
  - *Life on a Plantation* – Bobbie Kalman
  - *Southern Plantation Cooking* – Mary Gunderson (more than just a cookbook)
  - *The Strength of These Arms* – Raymond Bial
  - *Christmas in the Big House, Christmas in the Quarters* – Patricia C. McKissack and Frederick L. McKissack
- ❑ Hiram Revels
- ❑ Jim Henson

Science

- ❑ snipes
  - *Marvels of Creation, Breathtaking Birds* - Buddy and Kay Davis
- ❑ magnolia (state tree and flower)
- ❑ bentonite
- ❑ hurricanes
  - *Hurricanes* – Seymour Simon
  - *Hurricanes* – Arlene Erlbach
  - *Disaster! Hurricane* – Dennis Brindell Fradin
  - *Do Tornadoes Really Twist?* – Melvin and Gilda Berger, pages 24–46
- ❑ cotton
  - *Cotton* – Millicent E. Selsam
  - http://www.agr.state.nc.us/markets/kidstuff/dotf/cotton.htm

Literature

- ❑ *Hurricane* – David Wiesner
- ❑ *Working Cotton* – Sherley Anne Williams
- ❑ *Granddaddy's Gift* – Margaree King Mitchell
- ❑ *Love, Ruby Lavender* – Deborah Wiles

Language Arts

Preamble to the State Constitution:

We, the people of Mississippi in convention assembled, grateful to Almighty God, and involving his blessing on our work, do ordain and establish this Constitution.

1. Refer to Language Arts Guide starting on page 8.
2. Write a story about life on a southern plantation.
3. Use adjectives and adverbs to describe a hurricane.
4. Write a story about living through a hurricane.
5. Make a list of items you would bring if you had to evacuate your home due to a hurricane.

Character

The origin of the Mississippi motto - *By valor and arms* - is unclear. The trait to study in this state is **valor**.

- **Valor** – Strength of mind in regard to danger; that quality which enables a man to encounter danger with firmness; personal bravery; courage; intrepidity; prowess.

State Flag Pledge

I salute the flag of Mississippi
and the sovereign state for which it stands
with pride in her history and achievements
and with confidence in her future
under the guidance of Almighty God.

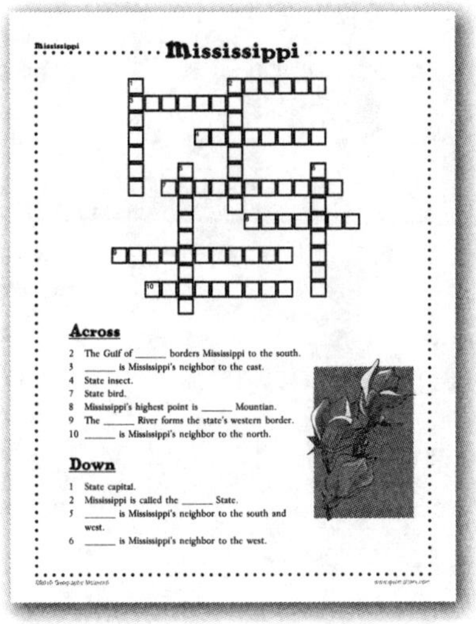
Mississippi

Across

2 The Gulf of ______ borders Mississippi to the south.
3 ______ is Mississippi's neighbor to the east.
4 State insect.
7 State bird.
8 Mississippi's highest point is ______ Mountain.
9 The ______ River forms the state's western border.
10 ______ is Mississippi's neighbor to the north.

Down

1 State capital.
2 Mississippi is called the ______ State.
5 ______ is Mississippi's neighbor to the south and west.
6 ______ is Mississippi's neighbor to the west.

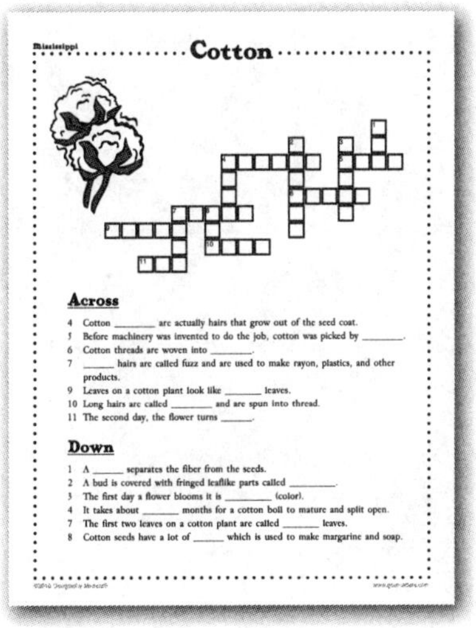
Cotton

Across

4 Cotton ______ are actually hairs that grow out of the seed coat.
5 Before machinery was invented to do the job, cotton was picked by ______.
6 Cotton threads are woven into ______.
7 ______ hairs are called fuzz and are used to make rayon, plastics, and other products.
9 Leaves on a cotton plant look like ______ leaves.
10 Long hairs are called ______ and are spun into thread.
11 The second day, the flower turns ______.

Down

1 A ______ separates the fiber from the seeds.
2 A bud is covered with fringed leaflike parts called ______.
3 The first day a flower blooms it is ______ (color).
4 It takes about ______ months for a cotton boll to mature and split open.
7 The first two leaves on a cotton plant are called ______ leaves.
8 Cotton seeds have a lot of ______ which is used to make margarine and soap.

Mississippi Map

Activities

1. Color or label a map of Mississippi.
2. Label the Mississippi River on a map of the United States.
3. Go to http://www.kidzone.ws/geography/usa/ for printable flag and state symbol coloring pages.
4. Prepare a meal in *Eat Your Way Through the U.S.A.* from the state of Mississippi.
5. If studying Jim Henson, make puppets.
6. For instructions for a cotton ball catapult, go to: http://pbskids.org/zoom/activities/sci/cottonballcatapult.html
7. Drink root beer.

Missouri

Show Me State

On August 10, 1821, Missouri, the Gateway to the West, became the 24th state to join the Union. The name "Missouri" most likely comes from a Native American word meaning "the one who owns canoes." Missouri's nickname, the Show Me State, can be traced to an 1899 speech given by Congressman Willard Vandiver who said, "...frothy eloquence neither convinces nor satisfies me. I am from Missouri. You have got to show me." Jefferson City is the state capital.

Adopted in 1913, the flag of Missouri has three horizontal stripes of red, white, and blue representing valor, purity, vigilance, and justice. In the center of the flag is the state seal. Two grizzly bears hold shields of the United States and Missouri to show that the state supports itself and the Union. The helmet symbolizes enterprise and hardiness. The 24 stars show that Missouri was the 24th state. The Roman numerals give the date that Missouri's first constitution was adopted.

Vast fields of golden grain and green grasses cover rolling plains in northern and western Missouri. Swift streams tumble through the wooded area of southern Missouri known as the Ozarks. The Mississippi River forms Missouri's eastern border, and the wide Missouri River cuts across the state from west to east. Missouri owes much of its commercial importance to these two rivers – the largest rivers in the United States.

Interesting Facts:

- The first ice cream cones were served at the 1904 World's Fair in St. Louis.
- Also at the 1904 World's Fair, Richard Blechyden served tea with ice and invented iced tea.
- The first successful parachute jump to be made from a moving airplane was made by Captain Berry at St. Louis in 1912.
- Bordered by eight states, Missouri ties with Tennessee as the most neighborly state in the union.

General Reference

- ❑ *Missouri* - Anne Welsbacher
- ❑ *Missouri Facts and Symbols* – Emily McAuliffe
- ❑ http://www.sos.mo.gov/kids/

Geography

- ❑ headwater
  - *Geography From A to Z,* page 22
- ❑ Missouri River
- ❑ St. Louis Gateway Arch
  - http://members.enchantedlearning.com/history/us/monuments/stlouisarch/

History & Biographies

- ❑ Lewis and Clark
  - *Profiles from History* - Volume 1, pages 139-146
  - *Munford Meets Lewis & Clark,* The Adventures of Munford series - Jamie Aramini
  - *Lewis & Clark: Hands On* – Sharon Jeffus
- ❑ Samuel Clemens (a.k.a. Mark Twain)
  - *Mark Twain: Author of Tom Sawyer* – Carol Greene
  - *Mark T-W-A-I-N!: A Story about Samuel Clemens* – David R. Collins
  - *Mark Twain: Boy of Old Missouri* – Miriam E. Mason
- ❑ J. C. Penney
  - *J. C. Penney: Golden Rule Boy* – Wilma J. Hudson
- ❑ Harry S. Truman
  - www.whitehouse.gov/history/presidents/
  - www.presidentialavenue.com/ht.cfm
  - http://www.homeofheroes.com/e-books/presidents/33_truman.html

Science

- ❑ bitternut
- ❑ eastern bluebird (state bird)
  - http://familycrafts.about.com/od/birdprojects/ (click on birds color page)
  - www.enchantedlearning.com/painting/birds.shtml
- ❑ hawthorn (state flower)
- ❑ mozarkite (state rock)
- ❑ mules (state animal)
  - www.first-school.ws/t/cpmule.htm
- ❑ rivers
  - *Rivers* – Norman and Madelyn Carlisle
  - *Mississippi River* – Peter Lourie

- *Rivers* – Andrew Haslam (has many hands-on projects)
- www.enchantedlearning.com/usa/rivers/
- *Earth Science for Every Kid,* Experiment #46

Literature

- ❑ *Riding the Pony Express* – Clyde Bulla (RA)
- ❑ *Tom Sawyer* – Mark Twain (RA abridged children's version or book-on-tape)
- ❑ *Grandpa Was a Cowboy* – Silky Sullivan
- ❑ *Simply Delicious* – Margaret Mahy
- ❑ *Duke the Dairy Delight Dog* – Lisa Campbell Ernst
- ❑ *Scoop After Scoop: A History of Ice Cream* – Stephen Krensky

Language Arts

Preamble to the State Constitution:
We the people of Missouri, with profound reverence for the Supreme Ruler of the Universe, and grateful for His goodness, do establish this constitution for the better government of the state.

1. Refer to Language Arts Guide starting on page 8.

Character

The motto for Missouri - *The welfare of the people shall be the supreme law* - can be found in Cicero's De Legibus, Book III, but it is unclear when it was officially adopted as the state motto. Welfare is generally thought of as the state helping the less fortunate; however, as Americans we are to be concerned about the welfare of others. Our children should learn to be **helpful** and **polite** toward others.

- **Helpfulness** – Helping, aiding, or assisting; furnishing or administering a remedy.
- **Polite** – Polish or elegance of manners; ease and gracefulness of manners, united with a desire to please others and a careful attention to their wants and wishes.

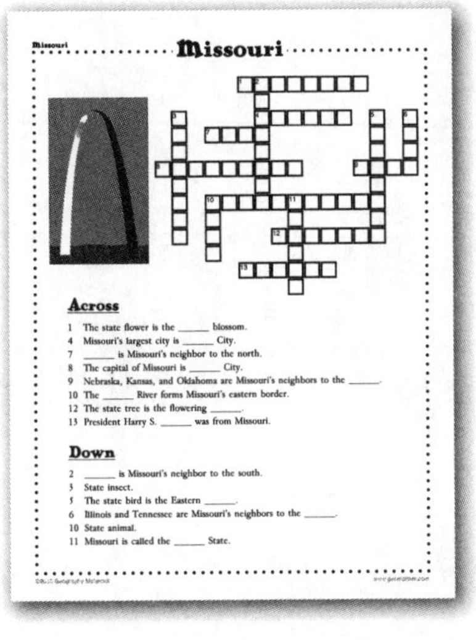

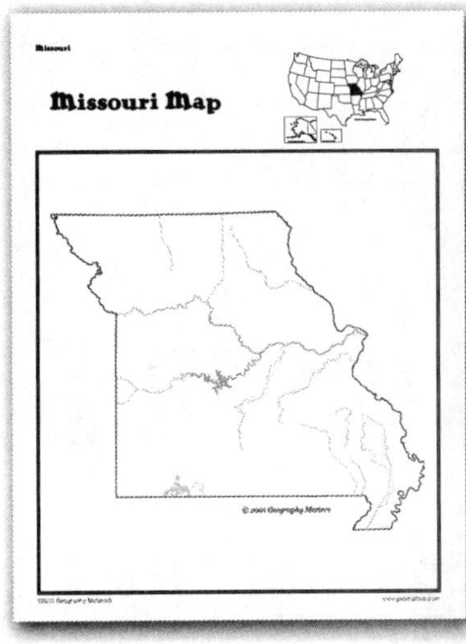

Activities

1. Color or label a map of Missouri.
2. Label the Missouri River on a map of the United States.
3. Using a map of the United States, find the headwaters of the Missouri River.
4. Go to http://www.kidzone.ws/geography/usa/ for printable flag and state symbol coloring pages.
5. Prepare a meal in *Eat Your Way Through the U.S.A.* from the state of Missouri.
6. Take a virtual tour of the governor's mansion at http://www.missourimansion.org/tour/.
7. Make a river diorama.
8. Build an arch. Go to http://pbskids.org/zoom/activities/sci/arch.html for instructions.
9. Eat an ice cream cone.
10. Drink iced tea.

Montana

Big Sky Country

During the glory days of the Wild West, Montana became the 41st state on November 8, 1889. The name "Montana" comes from a Spanish word meaning "mountainous." Early explorers, who saw the sun glistening on snow-capped peaks, called the area The Land of Shining Mountains. Gold and silver were discovered in those mountains, which gave the state another nickname, the Treasure State. Montana's capital is Helena.

The flag of Montana was adopted in 1905 and revised in 1981 to add the state name. The plow, pick, and shovel rest on the soil to show Montana's agricultural and mineral industries. The waterfall and mountain scenery represent the natural resources and beauty of the state. The state motto - *Gold and Silver* - appears on a ribbon.

Montana, the 4th largest state, is a land of tall, rugged mountains in the west and vast, sweeping plains in the east. Montana is the only state that has a triple divide. This allows Montana's rivers to empty into the Gulf of Mexico, Hudson Bay, and the Pacific Ocean.

Interesting Facts:

- More sapphires are found in Montana than any other state.
- The Montana Yogo Sapphire is the only North American gem to be included in the Crown Jewels of England.
- Montana has the largest grizzly bear population in the lower 48 states.
- The highest point in the state is Granite Peak at 12,799 feet.

General Reference

- ❑ *Montana* – Paul Joseph
- ❑ *Montana Facts and Symbols* – Shelley Swanson Sateren
- ❑ http://montanakids.com/

Geography

❑ Continental Divide

- *Geography From A to Z,* page 13

History & Biographies

- ❑ Cheyenne
  - *Cheyenne* – Richard M. Gaines
  - *The Cheyenne* – Dennis B. Fradin
- ❑ Crow
  - *The Crow* – Ruth Hagman
  - *Buffalo Days* – Diane Hoyt-Goldsmith

Science

- ❑ osprey
  - *Marvels of Creation, Breathtaking Birds* - Buddy and Kay Davis
  - *Zoo Guide*, page 139
  - http://www.coloring.ws/birds.htm
  - http://pelotes.jea.com/ColoringPage/Birds/Colospre.htm
- ❑ ponderosa pine (state tree)
- ❑ bitterroot (state flower)
- ❑ sapphire (state gemstone)
- ❑ grizzly bear (state animal)
  - *Marvels of Creation, Magnificent Mammals* - Buddy and Kay Davis
  - *Grizzly Bear* – Jason and Jody Stone
  - *The Grizzly Bear Family Book* – Michio Hoshino
  - *Grizzly Bear* – Berniece Freschet
  - *Grizzlies* – Lynn M. Stone
  - www.coloring.ws/animals.html

Literature

- ❑ *The Biggest Bear* – Lynd Ward
- ❑ *Ask Mr. Bear* – Marjorie Flack
- ❑ *Once We Had a Horse* – Glen Rounds
- ❑ *The Blind Colt* – Glen Rounds (RA)
- ❑ *When the Circus Came to Town* – Laurence Yep (RA)
- ❑ *Petunia Beware* – Roger Duvoisin (†)

Language Arts

Preamble to the State Constitution:

We the people of Montana grateful to God for the quiet beauty of our state, the grandeur of our mountains, the vastness of our rolling plains, and desiring to improve the quality of life, equality of opportunity and to secure the blessings of liberty for this and future generations do ordain and establish this constitution.

1. Refer to Language Arts Guide starting on page 8.
2. Write a story about crossing the Continental Divide.
3. Research and narrate how to mine for sapphires.

Character

The origin of the Montana motto - *Gold and silver* - is unknown.

This is a great opportunity to discuss wealth and money. Being **thrifty**, yet **giving** with our finances is a healthy way to view money. It is important to teach our children to be frugal with their money, not greedy or careless.

- **Thriftiness** – Frugality; using economy and good management of property.
- **Giving** – Bestowing, conferring; imparting, granting, delivering.

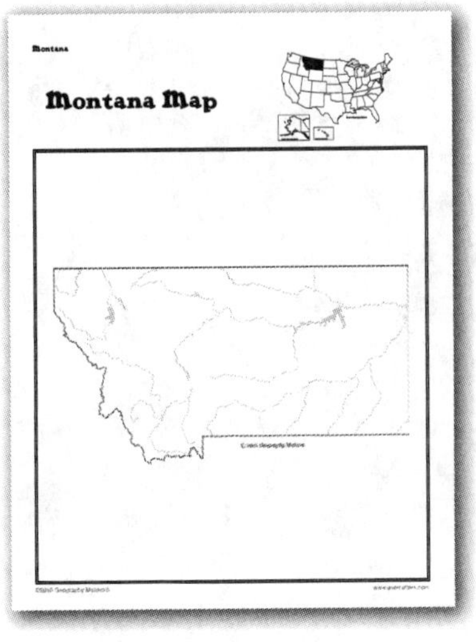

Activities

1. Color or label a map of Montana.
2. Label a map of the United States with the Continental Divide.
3. Using a map of the United States, follow Montana's rivers and see which ones empty into the Gulf of Mexico, which ones empty into Hudson Bay, and which ones empty into the Pacific Ocean.
4. Go to http://www.kidzone.ws/geography/usa/ for printable flag and state symbol coloring pages.
5. Prepare a meal in *Eat Your Way Through the U.S.A.* from the state of Montana.
6. For bear craft ideas go to http://familycrafts.about.com/od/bearcrafts/.

Nebraska

Cornhusker State

A leading farm state, Nebraska joined the Union on March 1, 1867, making it the 37th state. The name "Nebraska" comes from the Native American word ***nebrathka,*** which means "spreading water" and was the Oto name for the Platte River. The capital of Nebraska is Lincoln.

Nebraska's state flag, adopted in 1925, bears a silver and gold version of the state seal centered on a field of dark blue. The settler's cabin, the growing corn, and the shocks of grain stand for agriculture. The steamboat and train represent transportation. The smith stands for the mechanical arts.

Pioneers once described Nebraska as the "Great American Desert" because they thought if trees wouldn't grow there, neither would crops. Were they ever wrong! With their determined spirit, the people of Nebraska made the state a land of ranches and farms. They built irrigation systems and practiced scientific farming. Where crops wouldn't grow, Nebraskans grazed cattle.

Strong determination also helps Nebraskans combat the elements. Nebraska's climate ranges from extremely hot in the summer to extremely cold in the winter. The weather can changed suddenly and, at times, violently – sparking thunderstorms, tornadoes, blizzards, and hailstorms.

Interesting Facts:

- Nebraska has more miles of river than any other state.
- The 911 emergency system was developed and first used in Lincoln, Nebraska.
- In Blue Hill, Nebraska, no female wearing a "hat that would scare a timid person" can be seen eating onions in public.

General Reference

- ❑ *Nebraska* – Anne Welsbacher
- ❑ *Nebraska Facts and Symbols* – Emily McAuliffe
- ❑ *Nebraska* – Kathleen Thompson

Geography

- ❑ Platte River

History & Biographies

- ❑ William Jennings Bryan
- ❑ John J. Pershing
- ❑ Gerald Ford
  - www.whitehouse.gov/history/presidents/
  - http://www.ford.utexas.edu/
  - www.presidentialavenue.com/gf.cfm

Science

- ❑ hackberry
- ❑ crow
  - *Crows! Strange and Wonderful* – Laurence Pringle
  - www.enchantedlearning.com/painting/birds.shtml
- ❑ daisy
- ❑ prairie agate (state rock)
- ❑ corn
  - *Corn: What It Is, What It Does* – Cynthia Kellogg
  - *Corn Is Maize* – Aliki
  - *Corn Belt Harvest* – Raymond Bial
  - http://coloringbookfun.com/vegy/index.htm

Literature

- ❑ *Black Crow, Black Crow* – Ginger Foglesong Guy
- ❑ *Sod Houses on the Great Plains* – Glen Rounds
- ❑ *Dandelions* – Eve Bunting

Language Arts

Preamble to the State Constitution:
We, the people, grateful to Almighty God for our freedom, do ordain and establish the following declaration of rights and frame of government, as the Constitution of the State of Nebraska.

1. Refer to Language Arts Guide starting on page 8.

Character

The origin and adoption of the motto - *Equality before the law* - is unverifiable.

In order to be perceived as equal towards others, one must be **fair** and **prudent**.

- **Fairness** – Frankness; honesty; justice; lack of disguise; fraud, or prevarication.
- **Prudence** – Wisdom applied to practice; caution; circumspection; practical wisdom; carefulness of the consequences of enterprises, measures, or actions.

Activities

1. Color or label a map of Nebraska.
2. Label the Platte River on a map of United States.
3. Go to http://www.kidzone.ws/geography/usa/ for printable flag and state symbol coloring pages.
4. Prepare a meal in *Eat Your Way Through the U.S.A.* from the state of Nebraska.
5. Make a potted daisy.
    - Cut two 3-inch circles from white poster board. Set aside.
    - Fold six doilies in half, then pleat by 1/2-inch folds to make a fan.
    - Make doily flower by arranging the six fans like petals and gluing them onto the center point of one of the white poster board circles.
    - Wrap a lollipop or craft stick with green floral tape.
    - Glue stick to back of doily flower. Glue remaining white poster board circle over stick as a backing.
    - Cut two leaves from green poster board or heavy construction paper.
    - Wrap two short lengths of floral wire with green floral tape. Glue onto the back side of the leaves. (You may want to use hot glue.)
    - Attach leaves to flower "stem" with floral tape.
    - Glue a yellow pom-pom or picture of child to center of flower.
    - Fill 4-inch flower pot with floral Styrofoam. Insert flower. Cover Styrofoam with moss.
6. Corn cob painting.
    - Pour tempera paint of varying colors on paper plates.
    - Dip or roll corn cobs in paint.
    - Make designs on manila paper.

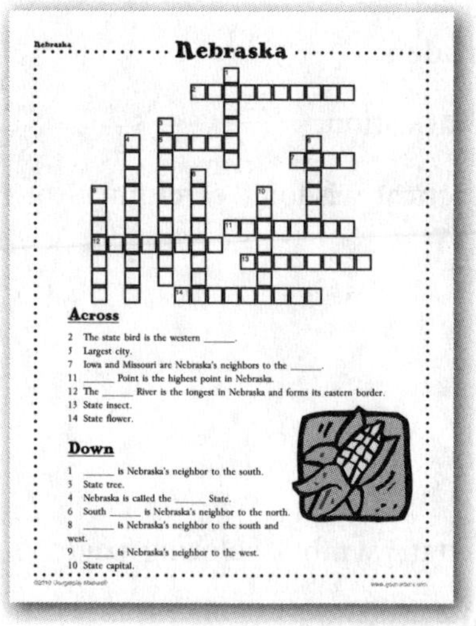

Nebraska

Nebraska

Across

2 The state bird is the western ______.
5 Largest city.
7 Iowa and Missouri are Nebraska's neighbors to the ______.
11 ______ Point is the highest point in Nebraska.
12 The ______ River is the longest in Nebraska and forms its eastern border.
13 State insect.
14 State flower.

Down

1 ______ is Nebraska's neighbor to the south.
3 State tree.
4 Nebraska is called the ______ State.
6 South ______ is Nebraska's neighbor to the north.
8 ______ is Nebraska's neighbor to the south and west.
9 ______ is Nebraska's neighbor to the west.
10 State capital.

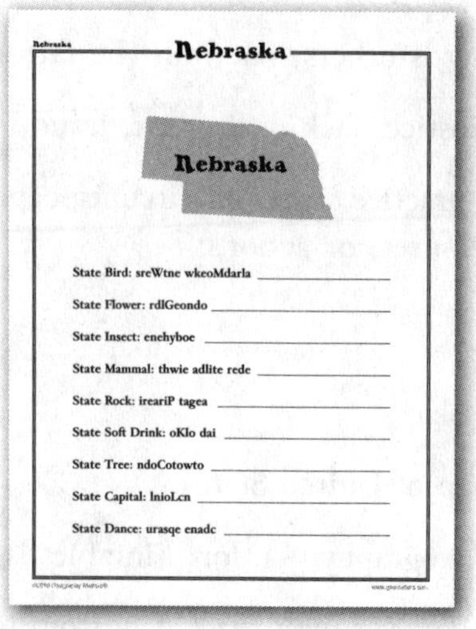

Nebraska

Nebraska

State Bird: sreWtne wkeoMdarla ____________
State Flower: rdlGeondo ____________
State Insect: enehyboe ____________
State Mammal: thwie adlite rede ____________
State Rock: ireariP tagea ____________
State Soft Drink: oKlo dai ____________
State Tree: ndoCotowto ____________
State Capital: lnioLcn ____________
State Dance: urasqe enadc ____________

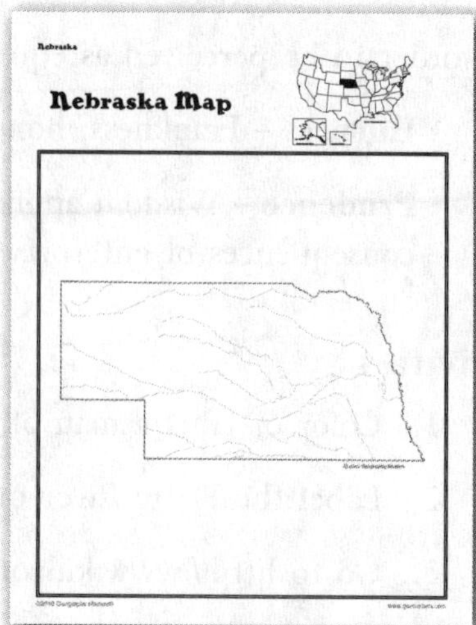

Nebraska

Nebraska Map

Nevada

Sagebrush State

On October 31, 1864, Nevada became the 36th state to join the Union. The name "Nevada" comes from the Spanish word for "snow-covered." Carson City is the state capital.

The flag of Nevada came from a design competition and was adopted by the state legislature in 1929. It was revised in 1991, and the state name was placed underneath the star that represents the state. The boughs of sagebrush show the state flower. The words "Battle Born" recall that Nevada gained statehood during the Civil War.

A land of rugged snow-capped mountains, grassy valleys, and sandy deserts, Nevada has great extremes in climate and terrain. Pine forests cover many mountain slopes, and clear streams flow through steep, rocky canyons. The Sierra Nevada mountain range, with majestic Lake Tahoe, cuts across the southwest corner of the state. Nevada lies almost entirely within the Great Basin.

Interesting Facts:

- In Death Valley, the kangaroo rat can live its entire life without drinking a drop of liquid.
- The only Nevada lake with an outlet to the sea is man-made Lake Mead.
- The federal government owns about 85% of Nevada's land.

General Reference

- ❑ *Nevada* – Paul Joseph
- ❑ *Nevada Facts and Symbols* – Karen Bush Gibson
- ❑ http://www.nv.gov/new_KidsHomework.htm

Geography

- ❑ Great Basin
- ❑ Hoover Dam
  - *The Hoover Dam* – Patra McSharry Sevastiades
  - *Hoover Dam* – Elizabeth Mann

History & Biographies

- ❑ Shoshoni
    - *The Shoshoni* – Dennis B. Fradin
- ❑ The Comstock Lode

Science

- ❑ single-leaf pinyon (state tree)
- ❑ sagebrush (state flower)
- ❑ vulture
    - *Zoo Guide,* page 111
    - *Marvels of Creation, Breathtaking Birds* - Buddy and Kay Davis
    - www.enchantedlearning.com/painting/birds.shtml
- ❑ black fire opal (state gemstone)
- ❑ porcupine
    - *Zoo Guide,* page 71
    - *Marvels of Creation, Magnificent Mammals* - Buddy and Kay Davis
    - *Lucky Porcupine* – Miriam Schlein
    - *Porcupines* – Wyatt Blassingame
- ❑ kangaroo rat
    - http://www.enchantedlearning.com/subjects/mammals/rodent/Kangarooratprintout.shtml
- ❑ dams
    - *Dams* – Cass R. Sandak
    - *Dams Give Us Power* – Lee Sullivan Hill

Literature

- ❑ *Brave as a Mountain Lion* – Ann Herbert Scott

Language Arts

Preamble to the State Constitution:
We the people of the State of Nevada grateful to Almighty God for our freedom in order to secure its blessings, insure domestic tranquility, and form a more perfect Government, do establish this CONSTITUTION.

1. Refer to Language Arts Guide starting on page 8.

Character

There is no known documentation detailing the origin of the motto - *All for our country* - however, it is believed to have summarized the patriotic spirit that existed at the Constitutional Convention held in Carson City on July 4, 1864. The country was in the midst of a civil war, and the Union needed more states to lend support, so Nevada was granted statehood. In 1866, the state legislature adopted an official state seal. The motto was to be part of the engraved seal. In light of the spirit of the convention our traits for this state are **eagerness** and **conscientiousness**. The delegates who were present at that first constitutional convention in Nevada were conscientious of the dire situation our country was facing, yet they were eager to be involved in the affairs of the nation. Our children should learn to be conscientious in regard to the issues our nation faces today. If they learn to be influenced by their conscience while they are young, it will be easier for them to make wise decisions later in life.

- **Eagerness** – Ardent desire to do, pursue, or obtain anything; animated zeal; vehement longing; ardor of inclination.
- **Conscientiousness** – Being influenced by conscience; being governed by a strict regard for the dictates of conscience, or by the known or supposed rules of right and wrong.

Activities

1. Color or label a map of Nevada.
2. Label the Great Basin on a map of the United States.
3. Go to http://www.kidzone.ws/geography/usa/ for printable flag and state symbol coloring pages.
4. Prepare a meal in *Eat Your Way Through the U.S.A.* from the state of Nevada.
5. Build a dam. Go to http://pbskids.org/zoom/activities/sci/buildadam.html for instructions.

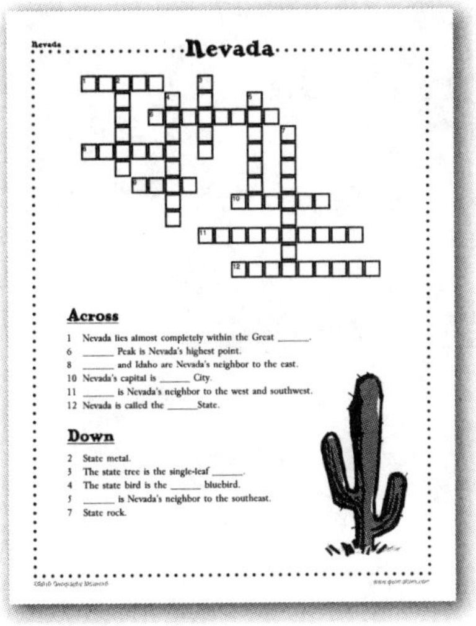

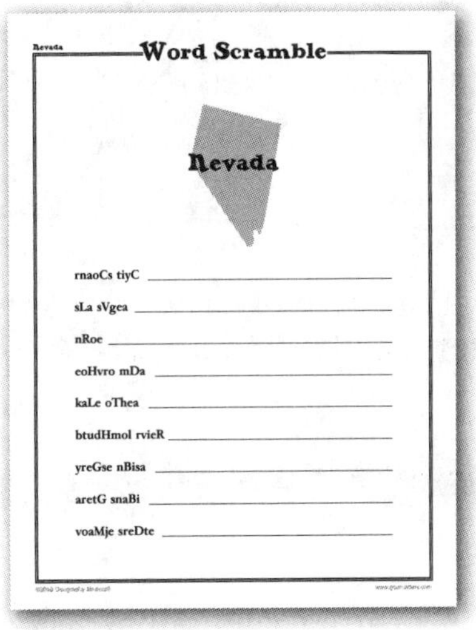

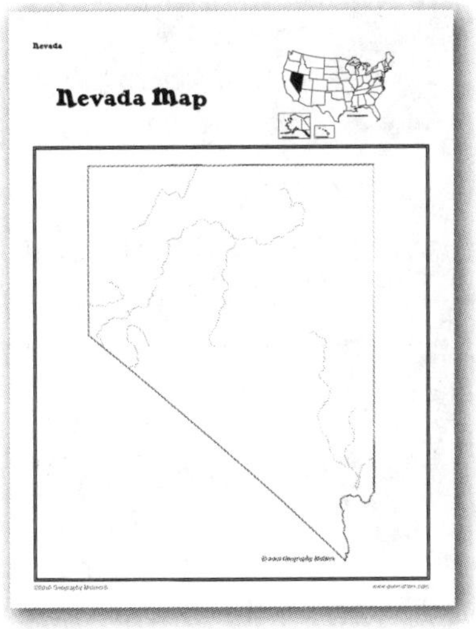

New Hampshire

Granite State

The first colony to secede from Great Britain, New Hampshire was the 9th state to ratify the Constitution, on June 21, 1788. New Hampshire was named in 1629 for the county of Hampshire, England. Concord is the state capital.

The state flag, which shows the state seal surrounded by nine stars in a laurel wreath on a blue field, was adopted in 1909. The seal depicts a ship, the *Raleigh*, being built at the town of Portsmouth during the Revolutionary War. The laurel wreath around the ship symbolizes victory. The date 1776 is the year the state adopted its first constitution. The nine stars represent New Hampshire as the 9th state.

Along New Hampshire's northern border are the White Mountains. At 6,288 feet above sea level, Mount Washington is the highest point in the northeast and is one of the windiest and coldest places on earth. A wind gust of 231 miles per hour was recorded there on April 12, 1934. The Connecticut River forms the state's western border. More than 80% of New Hampshire is covered with forest. Lake Winnipesaukee, New Hampshire's largest lake, covers 72 square miles.

Interesting Facts:

- In 1833 the first free public library in the United States was established in Peterborough.
- Levi Hutchins of Concord invented the first alarm clock in 1787.
- New Hampshire's State House is the oldest state capitol in which a legislature still meets in its original chambers.
- The granite profile "Old Man of the Mountain" was once one of the most famous natural landmarks in the state. The Old Man's head measured 40 feet from chin to forehead and was made up of five ledges. The natural sculpture above Echo Lake slid off the mountain in May 2003 and no longer graces the landscape of New Hampshire.

General Reference

- ❑ *New Hampshire* – Anne Welsbacher
- ❑ *New Hampshire Facts and Symbols* – Muriel L. Dubois
- ❑ *New Hampshire* – Dottie Brown (contains evolution)
- ❑ http://www.nh.gov/nhfacts/index.html

Geography

- ❑ White Mountains

History & Biographies

- ❑ Franklin Pierce
  - www.whitehouse.gov/history/presidents/
- ❑ Alan Shepard, Jr.
- ❑ Sarah Josepha Hale
- ❑ Eleanor Porter
- ❑ Robert Frost
  - *Robert Frost: Boy with Promises to Keep* – Ellen Wilson
  - *Robert Frost* – edited by Gary D. Schmidt (This is a compilation of poetry with a short biographical sketch at the beginning of the book.)

Science

- ❑ purple finch (state bird)
  - http://www.coloring.ws/birds.htm
- ❑ white birch (state tree)
- ❑ purple lilac (state flower)
- ❑ granite (state rock)
- ❑ whitetail deer (state animal)
  - http://www.coloring.ws/deer.htm

Literature

- ❑ *Lucy's Summer* – Donald Hall
- ❑ *A Gathering of Days* – Joan Blos (RA)
- ❑ *Pollyanna* – Eleanor Porter (RA)
- ❑ *Mary Had a Little Lamb* – Sarah Josepha Hale
- ❑ *Robert Frost* – edited by Gary D. Schmidt
- ❑ *Ox-Cart Man* – Donald Hall
- ❑ *Shaker Boy* – Mary Lyn Ray
- ❑ *Old Home Day* – Donald Hall

Language Arts

New Hampshire's constitution has no preamble.

1. Refer to Language Arts Guide starting on page 8.
2. Discuss the poetry of Robert Frost.

Character

The motto - *Live Free or Die* - was adopted in 1945 by the state legislature. The statement is attributed to General John Stark, a hero of the Revolutionary War. His original statement - 'Live free or die; death is not the worst of evils' - was sent as a toast to his comrades in 1809 when he declined the invitation to direct a reunion of the 1777 Battle of Bennington due to his declining health. The sentiment expressed by General Stark was a common view during his lifetime. As time has passed, the idea of freedom has come to be taken for granted. It is important for our children to appreciate the price of our freedom and understand its origin. They must be willing and able to defend that freedom if it is ever threatened. They need to be **independent** thinkers and **inquisitive** citizens in order to preserve our freedoms.

- **Independence** – Opposite of dependence; not being subject to the control of others; not relying on others; not being influenced by others.
- **Inquisitiveness** – Asking questions; addiction to inquiry; inclination to seek information by questions; inclination to seek knowledge by discussion, investigation, or observation; being given to research.

Activities

1. Color or label a map of New Hampshire.
2. Label the White Mountains on a map of the United States.
3. Go to http://www.kidzone.ws/geography/usa/ for printable flag and state symbol coloring pages.
4. Prepare a meal in *Eat Your Way Through the U.S.A.* from the state of New Hampshire.

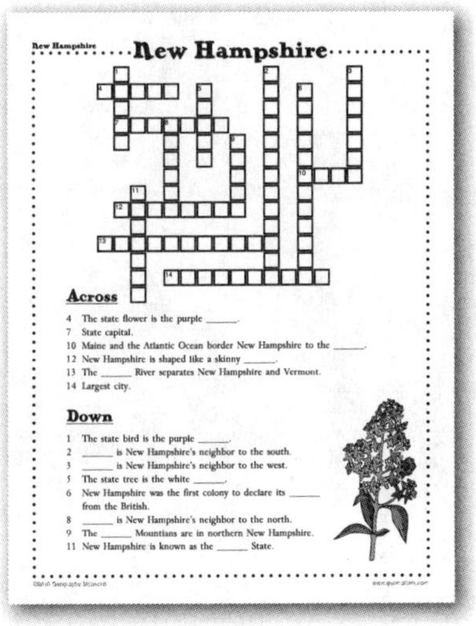

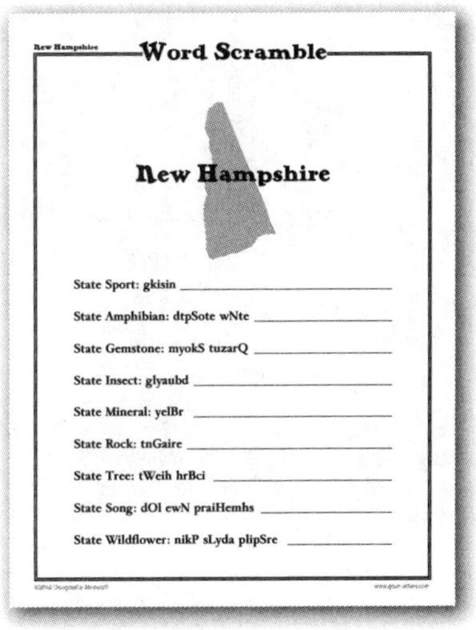

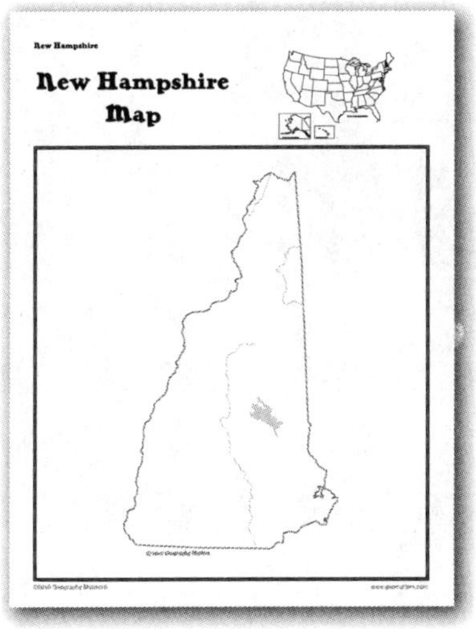

New Jersey

Garden State

Earning the nickname Cockpit of the Revolution because of all the battles fought on its soil during the American Revolution, New Jersey became the 3rd state on December 18, 1787. New Jersey was named after England's Isle of Jersey. The capital of New Jersey is Trenton.

The flag of New Jersey was adopted in 1896. The buff-colored field recalls the uniforms worn by New Jersey troops during the Revolution. The three plows, the horse's head, and the goddess Ceres holding a horn of plenty signify the agricultural importance of New Jersey. Liberty stands on the left. 1776 was the year New Jersey signed the Declaration of Independence.

Except for the 50-mile border shared with New York, New Jersey is completely surrounded by water. The Delaware River forms New Jersey's western border and flows into Delaware Bay. The Hudson River separates New Jersey from New York and empties into the Atlantic Ocean. In southern New Jersey, the rich soil of the Atlantic Coastal Plain enables the state to be a chief grower of fruits and vegetables.

Interesting Facts:

- Thomas Edison invented electric lights at his Menlo Park laboratory in 1879.
- New Jersey has the highest population density in the United States – an average of 1,030 people per square mile, which is thirteen times the national average.
- New Jersey has the highest percent of urban population in the country, with about 90% of the people living in urban areas.
- New Jersey is the only state in which all counties are classified as metropolitan areas.

General Reference

- ❑ *New Jersey* – Anne Welsbacher
- ❑ *New Jersey Facts and Symbols* – Shelley Swanson Sateren
- ❑ http://www.state.nj.us/hangout_nj/
- ❑ http://www.njleg.state.nj.us/kids/index.asp

Geography

- ❑ Delaware River

History & Biographies

- ❑ James Fenimore Cooper
  - *James Fenimore Cooper: Leatherstocking Boy* – Gertrude Hecker Winders
  - *Great Lives: American Literature* – Doris Faber
- ❑ Thomas Edison
  - *Thomas Edison* – Haydn Middleton
  - *Young Thomas Edison* – Claire Nemes
  - *Tom Edison: Young Inventor* – Sue Guthridge
  - *Book of Inventors* - Usborne
  - www.nps.gov/edis/home.htm
- ❑ Grover Cleveland
  - www.whitehouse.gov/history/presidents/
  - http://www.homeofheroes.com/e-books/presidents/22_cleveland_first.html

Science

- ❑ American goldfinch (state bird)
  - www.enchantedlearning.com/painting/birds.shtml
  - http://www.coloring.ws/birds.htm
- ❑ northern red oak (state tree)
- ❑ morning glory
- ❑ willemite
- ❑ bridges
  - *Cross a Bridge* – Ryan Ann Hunter
  - *Bridges Are to Cross* – Philemon Sturges
  - *Bridges Connect* – Lee Sullivan Hill
  - *Bridges! Amazing Structures to Design, Build & Test* – Carol A. Johmann
- ❑ electricity
  - *How Electricity Is Made* – C. L. Boltz
  - *Switch On, Switch Off* – Melvin Berger
  - *Experiments with Electricity* – Helen J. Challand
  - *Science Book of Electricity* – Neil Ardley

Literature

- ❑ *The Last of the Mohicans* – James Fenimore Cooper (RA) (abridged children's version or book-on-tape)
- ❑ *My Little Artist* – Donna Green
- ❑ *The Little Red Lighthouse and the Great Gray Bridge* – Hildegarde Swift and Lynd Ward
- ❑ *The Gardener* – Sarah Stewart
- ❑ *The Quiltmaker's Gift* – Jeff Brumbeau
- ❑ *Albert, the Dog Who Liked to Ride in Taxis* – Cynthia Zarin

Language Arts

Preamble to the State Constitution:
We, the people of the State of New Jersey, grateful to Almighty God for the civil and religious liberty which He hath so long permitted us to enjoy, and looking to Him for a blessing upon our endeavors to secure and transmit the same unimpaired to succeeding generations, do ordain and establish this Constitution.

1. Refer to Language Arts Guide starting on page 8.
2. If you read *The Gardener*, write a letter to a relative.
3. If you read *The Gardener*, write names of flowers in Latin.

Character

There is no known documentation to prove the origin of the motto - *Liberty and prosperity.* When individuals (or nations) are prosperous, they should use those resources to be **kind** towards others. We should also use our vast resources to create **inventive** solutions to share with other nations, thus improving their lifestyles.

- **Kindness** – Disposition to do good to others, and to make them happy by granting their requests, supplying their wants or assisting them in distress; benevolence towards others.
- **Inventiveness** – Ability to invent; skill in making something that did not exist before; the act of thinking or planning in the mind.

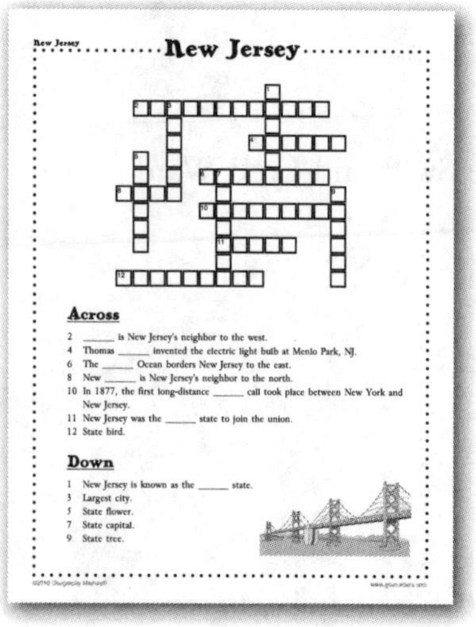

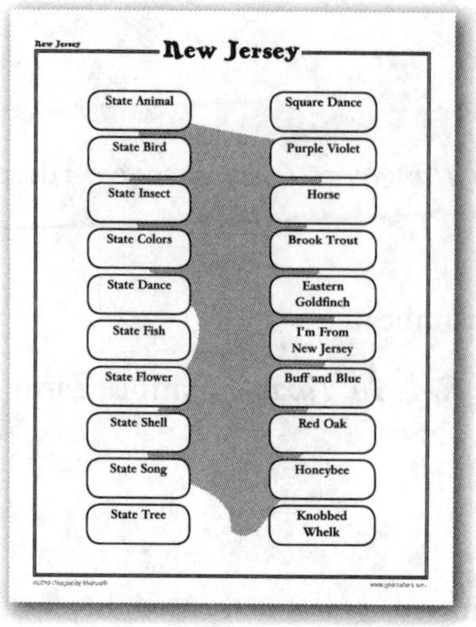

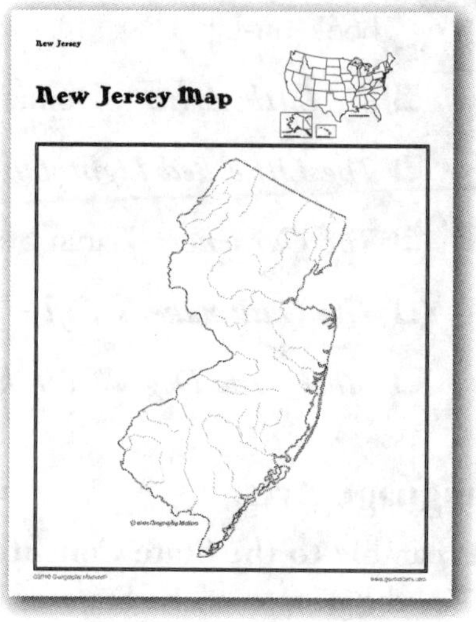

Activities

1. Color or label a map of New Jersey.
2. Label the Delaware River on a map of the United States.
3. Go to http://www.kidzone.ws/geography/usa/ for printable flag and state symbol coloring pages.
4. Prepare a meal in *Eat Your Way Through the U.S.A.* from the state of New Jersey.
5. New Jersey is the leading grower of green beans. Go to http://coloringbookfun.com/vegy/index.htm for vegetable coloring pages.
6. Design and build a bridge. (Legos or K'Nex work great for this.)
7. For instructions for an experiment with electrical circuits, go to http://pbskids.org/zoom/activities/sci/electricalmessages.html.
8. If you read *The Gardener*, plant some bulbs or seeds in a window box.
9. If you read *The Gardener*, make bread or a cake with flowers on it.

New Mexico

Land of Enchantment

Steeped in history and tradition, New Mexico became the 47th state on January 6, 1912. The Spanish named New Mexico for Mexico, which takes its name from an Aztec war god. Santa Fe, the country's oldest seat of government, was the capital of a Spanish province in 1610 and is the capital of New Mexico today.

The distinctive flag of New Mexico was adopted in 1925. The flag depicts the sun symbol of the Zia Pueblo in red on a field of yellow. The colors represent the Spanish flag, a reminder that New Mexico was once a Spanish territory.

New Mexico is a diverse land of mountains, canyons, deserts, caves, plateaus, and flat-topped mesas. The eastern third of the state is covered with rolling plains. The majestic Rocky Mountains extend into north central New Mexico. South and west of the Rockies, scattered mountain ranges are separated by deserts. Northwestern New Mexico is composed of plains, canyons, cliffs, and mesas.

Interesting Facts:

- New Mexico has the oldest road made by Europeans in the United States, the El Camino Real (the Royal Road). It has been in use since 1581.
- Santa Fe is the highest capital city in the United States at 7,000 feet above sea level.
- Each October Albuquerque hosts the world's largest international hot air balloon fiesta.
- The Palace of Governors in Santa Fe, built in 1610, is one of the oldest public buildings in America.
- Lakes and rivers make up only .002% of the state's total surface area, the lowest water-to-land ratio of all 50 states. Most of New Mexico's lakes are man-made reservoirs. A dam on the Rio Grande formed the Elephant Butte Reservoir, the state's largest lake.
- Since New Mexico's climate is so dry, three-fourths of the roads are left unpaved. The roads don't wash away.

General Reference

- ❑ *New Mexico* – Paul Joseph
- ❑ *New Mexico Facts and Symbols* – Shelley Swanson Sateren
- ❑ www.governor.state.nm.us/kidscorner.php

Geography

- ❑ gulch
  - *Geography From A to Z,* page 21
- ❑ Guadalupe Mountains

History & Biographies

- ❑ Apache
  - *Apache* – Richard M. Gaines
  - *Apache Rodeo* – Diane Hoyt-Goldsmith
- ❑ Cochise
- ❑ Geronimo
  - *Geronimo: Boy Warrior* – George Edward Stanley
  - *Geronimo: Apache Warrior* – James Rothaus
- ❑ Kit Carson
  - *Kit Carson* – Nardi Reeder Campion
  - *Kit Carson: Boy Trapper* – Augusta Stevenson
  - *Kit Carson: Frontier Scout* – Carl Green
- ❑ John Simpson Chisum
- ❑ Georgia O'Keefe
  - *My Name Is Georgia* – Jeanette Winter

Science

- ❑ greater roadrunner (state bird)
  - *Marvels of Creation, Breathtaking Birds* - Buddy and Kay Davis
  - *Zoo Guide,* page 131
  - www.enchantedlearning.com/painting/birds.shtml
  - http://www.coloring.ws/birds.htm
- ❑ pinyon (state tree)
- ❑ yucca (state flower)
- ❑ sandstone

- ❑ hot air balloons (state aircraft)
  - *A Rainbow Balloon* – Ann Lenssen
  - *Ballooning* – Carole S. Briggs
  - *Full of Hot Air* – Gary Paulsen
  - *Jean Felix Piccard: Boy Balloonist* – Lena Young de Grummond (This biography is mostly set in Switzerland, so we put it under hot air balloons rather than History & Biographies.)

Literature

- ❑ *Wild Horses* – Glen Rounds
- ❑ *Where the Buffalo Roam* – Jacqueline Geis
- ❑ *The Amazing Air Balloon* – Jean Van Leeuwen

Language Arts

Preamble to the State Constitution:
We, the people of New Mexico, grateful to Almighty God for the blessings of liberty, in order to secure the advantages of a state government, do ordain and establish this Constitution.

1. Refer to Language Arts Guide starting on page 8.
2. Write a story about taking a hot air balloon ride.

Character

The motto for New Mexico - *It grows as it goes* - originates in Lucretius's *De Rerum Natura*, Book VI. It is unclear why the motto was chosen, and it could have numerous meanings. For this state we will focus on a few personality traits that impact others in a positive way. When someone is **enthusiastic** and **loving**, it "grows" on others. We want our children to be enthusiastic and make others feel special. We also want them to have a genuine love towards others and apply the "golden rule" in their lives.

- **Enthusiasm** – High excitment; warmth and ardor; zeal in pursuit of an object; elevation.
- **Love** – Strong affection; fondness; kindness.

State Flag Pledge

I salute the flag of the state of New Mexico
and the Zia symbol of perfect friendship among united cultures.

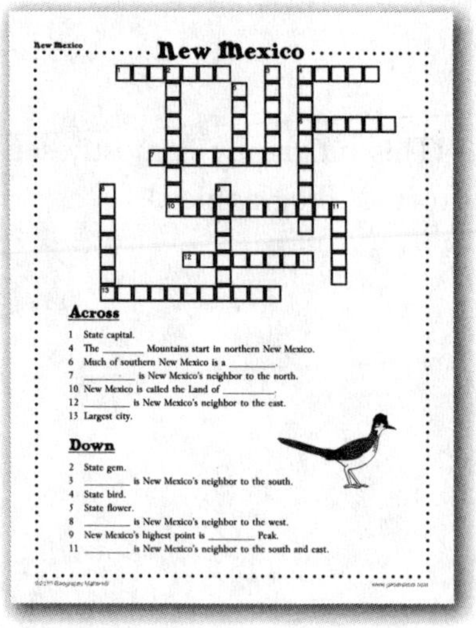

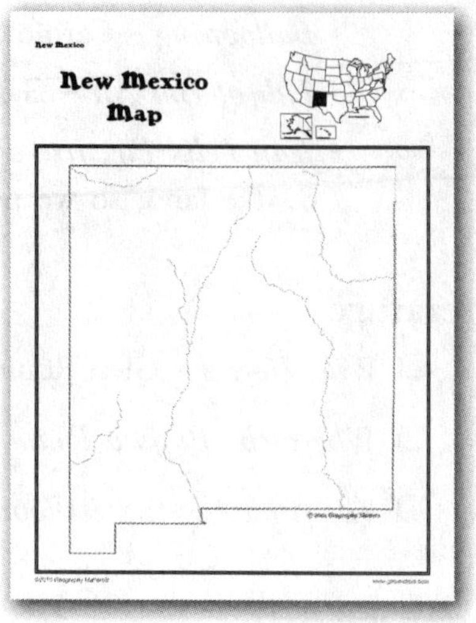

Activities

1. Color or label a map of New Mexico.
2. Label the Guadalupe Mountains on a map of the United States.
3. Go to http://www.kidzone.ws/geography/usa/ for printable flag and state symbol coloring pages.
4. Prepare a meal in *Eat Your Way Through the U.S.A.* from the state of New Mexico.
5. Go to http://pbskids.org/zoom/activities/sci/hotairballoon.html for instructions on a hot air balloon experiment.
6. Paint a picture in the style of Georgia O'Keefe.

New York

Empire State

Named after the Duke of York of England, New York became the 11th state on July 26, 1788. Historians believe that New York's nickname, the Empire State, came from a remark made by George Washington. When Washington visited New York in 1783, he predicted that it would become the seat of a new empire.

Adopted in 1909, the flag of New York depicts the state seal on a blue field. The two women symbolize Liberty and Justice. The crown at the feet of Liberty signifies that she has rejected kings and monarchies.

New York City, the largest city in the United States, is the financial and business center of the nation. New York is so much more than just the city, however. Its landscape is covered with wooded hills and sparkling lakes. The Adirondacks cover much of northern New York. Out of the Adirondacks, the Hudson River flows more than 300 miles to the Atlantic Ocean. South of the Adirondacks, the Appalachian Plateau spreads over half the state; within this region are the Catskills.

Interesting Facts:

- European settlers who brought seeds to New York introduced apples in the 1600s.
- The first capital of the United States was New York City. In 1789, George Washington took his oath as president on the balcony at Federal Hall.
- The first railroad in America ran a distance of eleven miles between Albany and Schenectady.
- Joseph C. Gayetty of New York City invented toilet paper in 1857.
- The Genesee River is one of the few rivers in the world that flows south to north.
- Gennaro Lombardi opened the first United States pizzeria in 1895 in New York City.

General Reference

- ❑ *New York* – Anne Welsbacher
- ❑ *New York Facts and Symbols* – Emily McAuliffe
- ❑ http://www.statesymbolsusa.org/New_York/NewYorkStateSymbols.html
- ❑ http://www.iloveny.com/kids/
- ❑ http://www.dos.state.ny.us/kids_room/

Geography

- ☐ Lake Ontario
- ☐ Erie Canal
  - *The Amazing Impossible Erie Canal* – Cheryl Harness
- ☐ Niagara Falls
  - *Niagara Falls* – Leonard Everett Fisher
  - *Geography From A to Z,* page 45
- ☐ Adirondack Mountains
- ☐ New York City
  - *Under New York* – Linda Oatman High
  - *My New York* – Kathy Jakobsen
- ☐ Statue of Liberty
  - *The Statue of Liberty* – Marc Tyler Nobleman
  - *The Story of the Statue of Liberty* – Betsy & Giulio Maestro
  - *The Statue of Liberty* – Craig A. Doherty
  - http://members.enchantedlearning.com/history/us/monuments/sol/
- ☐ Ellis Island
  - *If Your Name Was Changed at Ellis Island* – Ellen Levine
  - *Ellis Island* – Steven Kroll
  - *Ellis Island* – Patricia Ryon Quiri
- ☐ Empire State Building
  - *The Story of the Empire State Building* – Patrick Clinton
  - *Joe and the Skyscraper* – Dietrich Neumann
- ☐ Brooklyn Bridge
  - *Brooklyn Bridge* – Lynn Curlee

History & Biographies

- ☐ Iroquois (The Iroquois consists of five tribes – the Mohawk, Oneida, Seneca, Onondaga, and Cayuga.)
  - *The Mohawk* – Jill Duvall
  - *The Seneca* – Jill Duvall
- ☐ Sojourner Truth
- ☐ William Fargo
  - *William Fargo: Boy Mail Carrier* – Katharine E. Wilkie
- ☐ George Eastman

- ❑ Theodore Roosevelt
  - *Young Teddy Roosevelt* – Cheryl Harness
  - *Teddy Roosevelt: Rough Rider* – Louis Sabin
  - *Don't You Shoot that Bear: A Life of Theodore Roosevelt* – Robert Quackenbush (RA)
  - www.whitehouse.gov/history/presidents/
  - *Click! A Story about George Eastman* – Barbara Mitchell
  - *George Eastman: Young Photographer* – Joanne Landers Henry
- ❑ F. W. Woolworth
  - *F. W. Woolworth: Five and Ten Boy* – Elisabeth P. Myers

Science

- ❑ larch
- ❑ pigeons
  - *Pigeons* – Bernice Kohn Hunt
  - www.enchantedlearning.com/painting/birds.shtml
- ❑ rose (state flower)
- ❑ shale
- ❑ photography
  - *Book of Inventors* - Usborne, pages 30-31
  - *Photography* – Tony Freeman

Literature

- ❑ *Teddy Bear, Teddy Bear* – Michael Hague
- ❑ *Fire at the Triangle Factory* – Holly Littlefield
- ❑ *Peter and the Pigeons* – Charlotte Zolotow
- ❑ *The Memory Coat* – Elvira Woodruff
- ❑ *All of a Kind Family* – Sidney Taylor (RA)
- ❑ *Toby Belfer Visits Ellis Island* – Gloria Teles Pushker
- ❑ *Winter on the Farm* – adapted from the Little House Books by Laura Ingalls Wilder
- ❑ *Farmer Boy Days* – A Little House Chapter Book
- ❑ *Farmer Boy* – Laura Ingalls Wilder (RA)
- ❑ *White Snow, Bright Snow* – Alvin Tresselt
- ❑ *Radio Rescue* – Lynne Barasch
- ❑ *Fireboat: The Heroic Adventures of the John J. Harvey* – Maira Kalman

Language Arts

Preamble to the State Constitution:
WE, THE PEOPLE of the State of New York, grateful to Almighty God for our freedom, in order to secure its blessings, DO ESTABLISH THIS CONSTITUTION.

1. Refer to Language Arts Guide starting on page 8.
2. Write a story of an explorer discovering Niagara Falls.
3. Write a story of an immigrant arriving in America through Ellis Island.
4. Tell a story or give step-by-step instructions with photographs.

Character

The New York motto - *Ever Upward* - was first used with reference to physical progress but has evolved to include spiritual, mental, and social aspects as well.

In order to continue to make forward progress in any endeavor, one must be **disciplined** and **orderly**. These traits come easily for some and are a constant struggle for others. If we can instill in our children the importance of discipline and order, it will be of great benefit as they mature into adults. It is important to maintain a balance in these traits and not become so rigid and demanding that it stifles their individuality and creativity.

- **Discipline** – Instruction, education, subjection to rules and regulations; admonition; good behavior; self-government.
- **Orderliness** – Observance of order or method; being well-regulated; not being tumultuous.

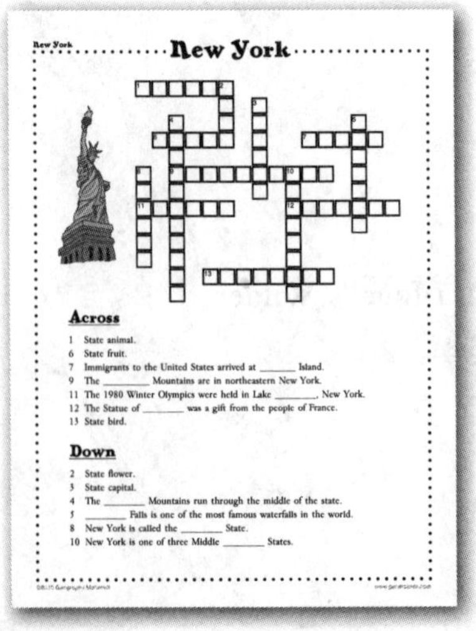

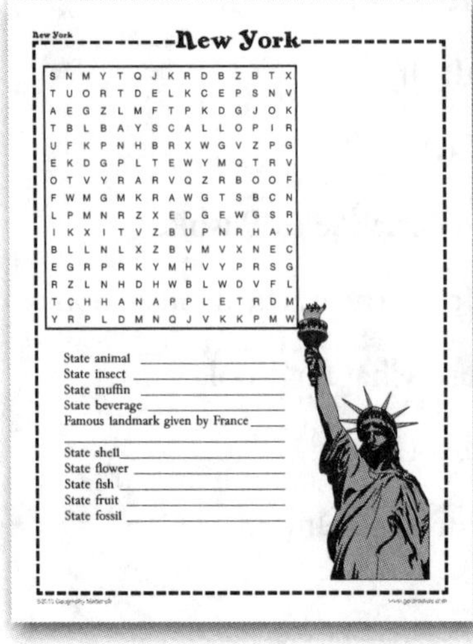

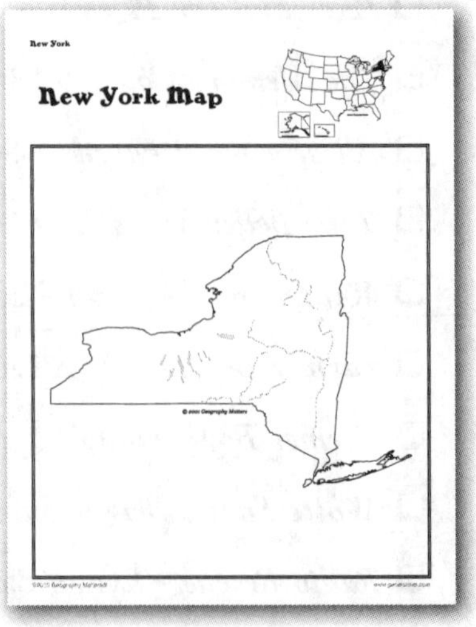

Activities

1. Color or label a map of New York.
2. Label Lake Ontario and the Adirondack Mountains on a map of the United States.
3. Go to http://www.kidzone.ws/geography/usa/ for printable flag and state symbol coloring pages.
4. Prepare a meal in *Eat Your Way Through the U.S.A.* from the state of New York.
5. The apple muffin is the state muffin of New York. Go to http://assembly.state.ny.us/kids/?body=colorpic&pic=muffin for a muffin coloring page.
6. Make a paper model of the Empire State Building. Go to http://papertoys.com/empire-building.htm for a template.
7. Make a paper model of the Statue of Liberty. Go to http://papertoys.com/statue.htm for a template.
8. Listen to the song "New York, New York."
9. Learn photography.

North Carolina

Tar Heel State

Named for King Charles I of England, North Carolina joined the Union as the 12th state on November 21, 1789. More than ten Civil War battles were fought on North Carolina soil. According to legend, Confederate soldiers retreated during one particularly fierce battle, leaving North Carolina troops to fight alone. After the battle, the surviving North Carolinians threatened to put tar on the heels of the retreating soldiers so that they would "stick better in the next fight." From that time on, North Carolina has been known as the Tar Heel State.

The flag of North Carolina was adopted in 1885. The flag, two horizontal stripes of red and white and a vertical stripe of blue, contains the initials of the state and two dates: May 20, 1775 and April 12, 1776. These are the dates of the two North Carolina Declarations of Independence that were made before the national Declaration on July 4, 1776.

North Carolina is a southern state with a long coastline on the Atlantic Ocean. Islands, reefs, and sandbars make its shores some of the most treacherous in the world. Many ships have wrecked near Cape Hatteras in an area called the "Graveyard of the Atlantic" due to rough seas and difficult currents. Moving westward across the state, fertile plains rise to rolling, wooded hills. In the far western portion of North Carolina, the Blue Ridge, Great Smoky, and Appalachian Mountains provide spectacular beauty.

Interesting Facts:

- The first English child born in America was born in Roanoke in 1587. Her name was Virginia Dare.
- The phrase "that's a bunch of bunk" came about when a lawmaker from Buncombe County, North Carolina, made a speech that had no point and made the man look like an idiot because he didn't know what he was talking about. The phrase started out as "that's a bunch of buncombe," and over the years it shortened to just plain "bunk."
- In 1903, the Wright Brothers made the first successful flight powered by man at Kill Devil Hill near Kitty Hawk.
- Whitewater Falls in Transylvania County is the highest waterfall in the eastern United States.
- Mount Mitchell in the Blue Ridge Mountains is the highest peak east of the Mississippi. It towers 6,684 feet above sea level.
- The Biltmore Estate in Asheville is America's largest home; it includes a 255-room chateau and extensive gardens.
- Beech Mountain is highest town in the eastern United States at 5,506 feet above sea level.

General Reference

- ❑ *North Carolina Facts and Symbols* – Shelley Swanson Sateren
- ❑ *North Carolina* – Paul Joseph
- ❑ http://www.secretary.state.nc.us/kidspg/
- ❑ http://www.governor.state.nc.us/Highlights/NCkids/index.html
- ❑ http://www.agr.state.nc.us/markets/kidstuff/
- ❑ http://www.aoc.state.nc.us/www/homecourt/index.html

Geography

❑ sound

- *Geography From A to Z,* page 41

History & Biographies

❑ Cherokee

- *The Cherokee* – Andrew Santella
- *The Cherokee* – Emilie U. Lepthien
- *Cherokee* – Richard M. Gaines
- *The Trail of Tears* – R. Conrad Stein

❑ Sequoyah

- *Sequoyah: Cherokee Hero* – Joanne Oppenheim
- *Sequoya* – Ruby L. Radford

❑ first flight

- (North Carolina and Ohio both claim the rights to the first flight. The Wright Brothers were from Ohio, but the first flight took place in North Carolina. We chose to put this topic under North Carolina, but it certainly can be studied under Ohio.)
- *Wilbur and Orville Wright: The Flight to Adventure* – Louis Sabin
- *Young Wilbur and Orville Wright: First to Fly* – Andrew Woods
- *Wilbur and Orville Wright: Boys with Wings* – Augusta Stevenson
- *Book of Inventors* - Usborne, page 19
- http://members.enchantedlearning.com/inventors/page/w/wrightcloze.shtml
- http://members.enchantedlearning.com/connectdots/airplane/

❑ Billy Graham

Science

- ❑ great egret
  - www.enchantedlearning.com/painting/birds.shtml
- ❑ Fraser fir (state Christmas tree)
- ❑ Queen Anne's lace
- ❑ emerald (state gemstone)
- ❑ turtles
  - *All About Turtles* – Jim Arnosky
  - Zoo Guide, page 197
  - www.coloring.ws/animals.html
  - www.daniellesplace.com/html/animal_crafts.html
- ❑ horseshoe crab
  - *Horseshoe Crab* – Robert M. McClung
  - *Aquarium Guide*, page 145
- ❑ airplanes & flight
  - *Amazing Aircraft* – Seymour Simon
  - *Take Off!* – Ryan Ann Hunter
  - *The Jet Alphabet Book* – Jerry Pallotta
  - *How Do Airplanes Fly?* – Isaac Asimov and Elizabeth Kaplan

Literature

- ❑ *My Great-Aunt Arizona* – Gloria Houston
- ❑ *First Flight* – George Shea
- ❑ *Blue Ridge Billy* – Lois Lenski (RA)
- ❑ *The Three Little Pigs and the Fox* – William H. Hooks

Language Arts

Preamble to the State Constitution:
We, the people of the State of North Carolina, grateful to Almighty God, the Sovereign Ruler of Nations, for the preservation of the American Union and the existence of our civil, political and religious liberties, and acknowledging our dependence upon Him for the continuance of those blessings to us and our posterity, do, for the more certain security thereof and for the better government of this State, ordain and establish this Constitution.

1. Refer to Language Arts Guide starting on page 8.
2. Write a newspaper article about the first flight.
3. Write the Cherokee alphabet. See http://www.native-languages.org/cherokee_alphabet.htm

Character

The state motto – *To Be Rather than To Seem* - was adopted in 1893. The motto, which originated in Latin, can be found in Cicero's De Amicitia. The original meaning of the phrase has been changed from a negative connotation to a positive. Cicero implied that not so many people wish to be endowed with virtue as wish to seem to be endowed with virtue. The modern version implies that it is better to be virtuous than to seem virtuous.

The character qualities implied by this motto are **virtue** and **honesty**. In a society full of citizens wanting to portray themselves as something they aren't, it is imperative that we teach our children to be honest and sincere with themselves and others.

- **Virtue** – Moral goodness; conformity to the moral law; practicing the moral duties and abstaining from vice; chastity.
- **Honesty** – Uprightness; justce; fairness; freedom from trickishness and fraud; acting and having the disposition to act at all times according to justice or correct principles; sincerity.

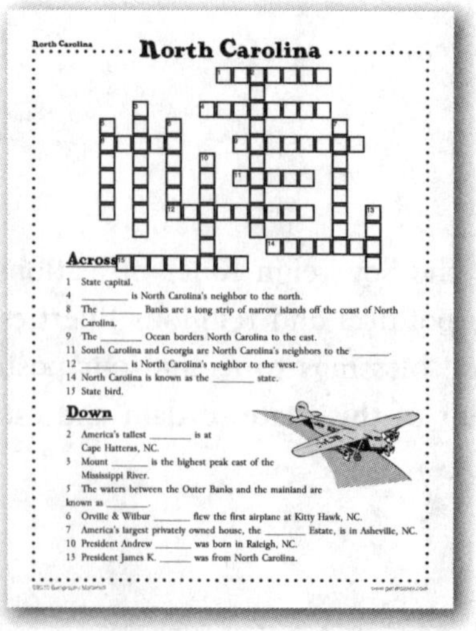

North Carolina

North Carolina

Across

1 State capital.
4 ________ is North Carolina's neighbor to the north.
8 The ________ Banks are a long strip of narrow islands off the coast of North Carolina.
9 The ________ Ocean borders North Carolina to the east.
11 South Carolina and Georgia are North Carolina's neighbors to the ________.
12 ________ is North Carolina's neighbor to the west.
14 North Carolina is known as the ________ state.
15 State bird.

Down

2 America's tallest ________ is at Cape Hatteras, NC.
3 Mount ________ is the highest peak east of the Mississippi River.
5 The waters between the Outer Banks and the mainland are known as ________.
6 Orville & Wilbur ________ flew the first airplane at Kitty Hawk, NC.
7 America's largest privately owned house, the ________ Estate, is in Asheville, NC.
10 President Andrew ________ was born in Raleigh, NC.
13 President James K. ________ was from North Carolina.

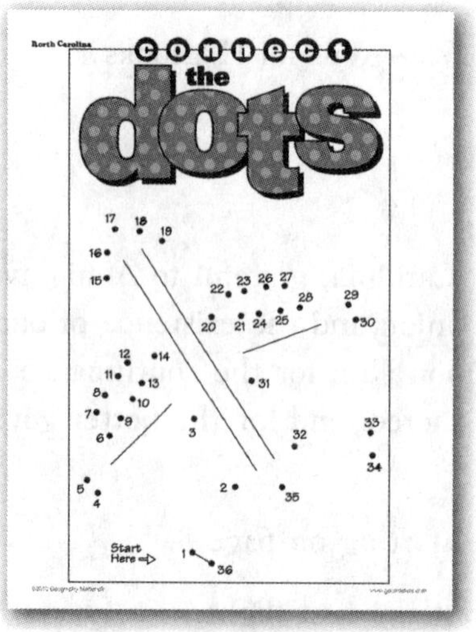

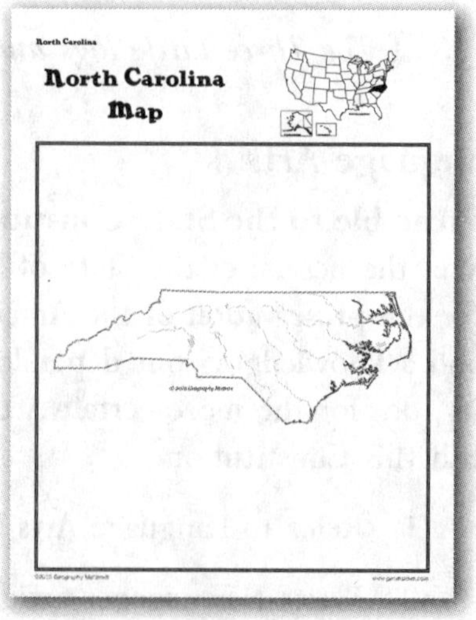

Activities

1. Color or label a map of North Carolina.
2. Label Pamlico Sound on a map of the United States.
3. Go to http://www.kidzone.ws/geography/usa/ for printable flag and state symbol coloring pages.
4. Prepare a meal in *Eat Your Way Through the U.S.A.* from the state of North Carolina.
5. Make a paper or model airplane.
6. For instructions on an experiment with flight, go to http://pbskids.org/zoom/activities/sci/deltawing-flyer.html.
7. The first miniature golf course was built in Fayetteville. Play miniature golf.
8. Krispy Kreme Doughnuts was founded in Winston-Salem. If you have a Krispy Kreme in your area, enjoy one of these tasty treats.

North Dakota

Peace Garden State

One of the last regions of the American frontier to be settled, North Dakota became the 39th state on November 2, 1889. North Dakota was named for the Dakota Sioux. The word "Dakota" means "friends" or "allies." The state capital is Bismarck.

Originally the regimental flag of the First North Dakota Infantry, the flag of North Dakota was adopted in 1911 almost without alteration. In the center of the flag is a modified version of the national coat of arms.

Endless prairie dominates the eastern half of North Dakota. In fact, it is so flat that you can see the 19-story capitol building in Bismarck for miles. The land gradually rises to high plateaus in the western part of the state. The Badlands of the Little Missouri River lie in the southwest. This rough, scenic region features rock masses and hills that have been carved by wind and water into striking formations.

Interesting Facts:

- The geographic center of North America is near Rugby. A rock obelisk, about fifteen feet tall, flanked by poles flying the United States and Canadian flags, marks the location.
- In North Dakota, it is illegal to lie down and fall asleep with your shoes on.
- In Fargo, one may be jailed for wearing a hat while dancing, or even for wearing a hat to a function where dancing is taking place.

General Reference

❑ *North Dakota* – Anne Welsbacher

❑ *North Dakota Facts and Symbols* – Karen Bush Gibson

Geography

❑ Lake Sakakawea and Garrison Dam

History & Biographies

❑ Pierre de la Verendrye

- *Fur Trader of the North* – Ronald Syme

Science

- ❑ peachleaf willow
- ❑ barn swallow
  - *Swallows in the Birdhouse* – Stephen R. Swinburne
- ❑ wild prairie rose (state flower)
- ❑ lignite
- ❑ blizzards
  - *Wild Weather: Blizzards!* – Lorraine Jean Hopping
  - *Disaster! Blizzards and Winter Weather* – Dennis Brindell Fradin
  - *Blizzards* – Steven Otfinoski

Literature

- ❑ *The Blizzard* – Betty Ren Wright
- ❑ *Dakota Dugout* – Ann Turner

Language Arts

Preamble to the State Constitution:
We, the people of North Dakota, grateful to Almighty God for the blessings of civil and religious liberty, do ordain and establish this constitution.

1. Refer to Language Arts Guide starting on page 8.
2. Make a list of blizzard survival tips.
3. Interview someone who has lived through a blizzard. Write a story based on the interview.

Character

The motto for North Dakota - *Liberty and union, now and forever, one and inseparable* - is a partial quote from Daniel Webster and was suggested by Dr. Joseph Ward.

The citizens of a nation must be **attentive** to what is happening around them in order to preserve our liberty. It is important to teach our children to be attentive to their surroundings for their safety and prosperity in life.

- **Attentiveness** – Heedfulness; being intent; observance; regarding with care; contemplation; observing with fixed attention.

State Creed

We believe in North Dakota,
in the beauty of her skies,
and in the glory of her prairies

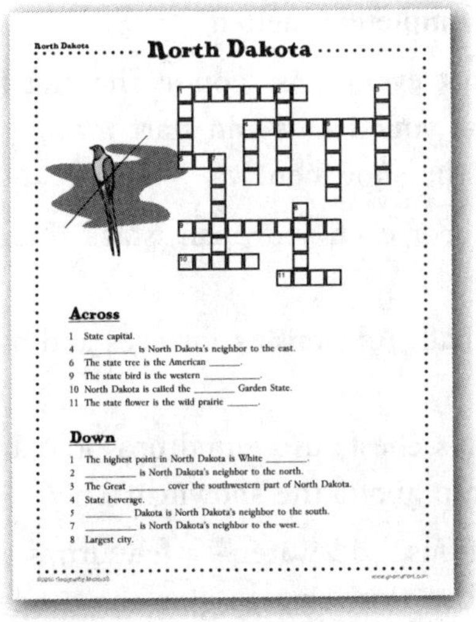

North Dakota

North Dakota

Across

1 State capital.
4 ______ is North Dakota's neighbor to the east.
6 The state tree is the American ______.
9 The state bird is the western ______.
10 North Dakota is called the ______ Garden State.
11 The state flower is the wild prairie ______.

Down

1 The highest point in North Dakota is White ______.
2 ______ is North Dakota's neighbor to the north.
3 The Great ______ cover the southwestern part of North Dakota.
4 State beverage.
5 ______ Dakota is North Dakota's neighbor to the south.
7 ______ is North Dakota's neighbor to the west.
8 Largest city.

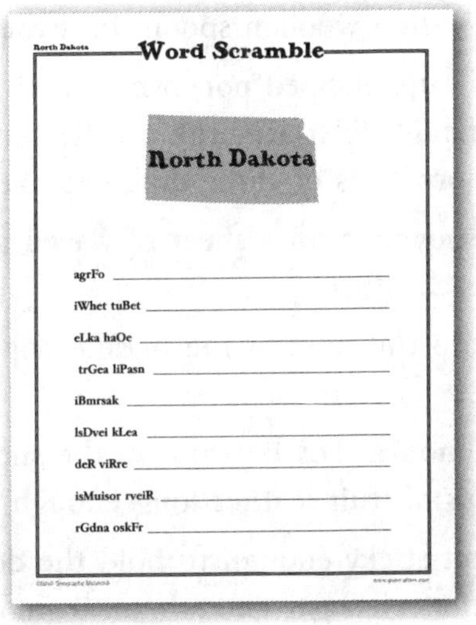

North Dakota

Word Scramble

North Dakota

agrFo ______
iWhet tuBet ______
eLka haOe ______
trGea liPasn ______
iBmrsak ______
lsDvei kLea ______
deR viRre ______
isMuisor rveiR ______
rGdna oskFr ______

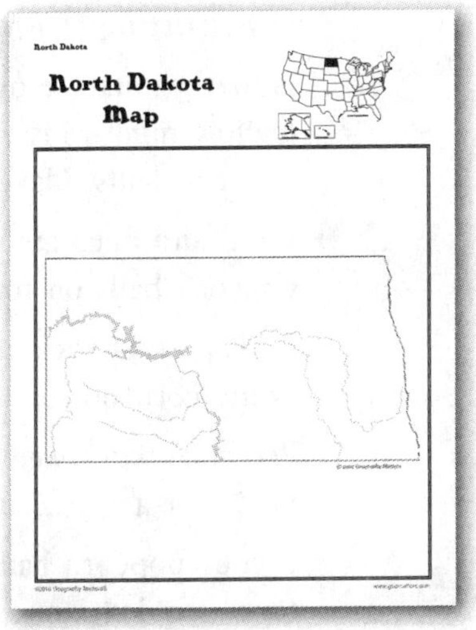

North Dakota

North Dakota Map

Activities

1. Color or label a map of North Dakota.
2. Label Lake Sakakawea on a map of the United States.
3. Locate and label Rugby, North Dakota, as the geographic center of North America.
4. Go to http://www.kidzone.ws/geography/usa/ for printable flag and state symbol coloring pages.
5. Prepare a meal in *Eat Your Way Through the U.S.A.* from the state of North Dakota.
6. Make a snowman.
   - Fill a white sock about a third of the way with beans. Tie sock closed with yarn or rubber bands. Repeat this process, creating a middle section for your snowman. Tie middle section closed. Create head by filling a third section with cotton balls, and make sure that you tie it closed. You should have a little bit of the top of the sock left.
   - Use the bit of sock at the top, yarn, and fabric paint to create a hat.
   - Use buttons, felt, fabric scraps, etc. to decorate your snowman.

7. Make popcorn ball snowmen.
   - Melt one stick of butter in a nonstick saucepan over medium-low heat. Add 20 oz. marshmallows, stirring continually with a wooden spoon until they're completely melted.
   - Pour the mixture over 15 cups popped popcorn and stir to coat evenly. As soon as the marshmallow mixture is cool enough to touch, rub a little butter on your hands and start making popcorn balls. Make popcorn balls of three different sizes for the snowmen.
   - Build and decorate your snowmen on a sheet of waxed paper. For each snowman, stack three popcorn balls on top of each other.
   - Push pretzel stick arms into the sides of the middle popcorn ball. Add raisins for eyes and a candy corn nose.
   - Red hots work well for a mouth. For buttons on the snowman's chest, use gumdrops or red hots. For a scarf, cut strips of fruit leather long enough to wrap about the snowman's neck.
   - If your popcorn balls aren't sticky enough to hold the decorations, add water - a few drops at a time - to 1/4 cup confectioners' sugar and stir until smooth. Use this icing to glue the candy in place.

Ohio

Buckeye State

The first state to be carved out of the Northwest Territory, on March 1, 1803, Ohio became the 17th state to join the Union. The name "*Ohio*" comes from an Iroquois word meaning "something great." Ohio's state capital is Columbus.

Ohio is the only state with a pennant-shaped flag. It was derived from a cavalry guidon. The seventeen stars represent Ohio as the 17th state, and the circle or "O" stands for the state's initial.

Most of Ohio is made up of plains and gently rolling hills and valleys. Western Ohio is part of the Midwestern Corn Belt. Lake Erie forms most of Ohio's northern border. The Ohio River, one of the country's main rivers, flows along Ohio's southern and southeastern borders.

Interesting Facts:

- The first ambulance service was established in Cincinnati in 1865.
- Cleveland boasts America's first traffic light, which began operating on August 5, 1914.
- Akron was the first city to use police cars.
- Cleveland became the world's first city to be lighted electrically in 1879.
- Charles Goodyear of Akron developed the process of vulcanizing rubber in 1839.

General Reference

❑ *Ohio* – Paul Joseph

❑ *Ohio Facts and Symbols* – Emily McAuliffe

Geography

❑ Ohio River

History & Biographies

- ❑ Shawnee
- ❑ Tecumseh
  - *Tecumseh: Shawnee War Chief* – Jane Fleischer
  - *Tecumseh* – Zachary Kent
- ❑ Charles Goodyear
  - *Oh, What an Awful Mess: A Story of Charles Goodyear* – Robert Quackenbush
- ❑ James A. Garfield
  - www.jamesgarfield.org
- ❑ Annie Oakley
  - *Annie Oakley: Little Sure Shot* – Ellen Wilson
  - *Little Sure Shot* – Stephanie Spinner
  - *Bull's-Eye* – Sue Macy

Science

- ❑ owls
  - *The Owl Book* – Laura Storms
  - *Marvels of Creation, Breathtaking Birds* - Buddy and Kay Davis
  - www.enchantedlearning.com/painting/birds.shtml
  - *Zoo Guide*, page 129
  - www.coloring.ws/birds.htm
  - www.daniellesplace.com/html/birdcrafts.html
- ❑ Ohio buckeye (state tree)
- ❑ scarlet carnation (state flower)
- ❑ Ohio flint (state gemstone)
- ❑ fox
  - *Foxes* – Emilie U. Lepthien and Joan Kalbacken
  - http://www.coloring.ws/t/animals/color-fox.htm

Literature

- ❑ *Nothing Here But Trees* – Jean Van Leeuwen
- ❑ *Lentil* – Robert McCloskey
- ❑ *Aurora Means Dawn* – Scott Russell Sanders
- ❑ *Adventures of Reddy Fox* – Thornton W. Burgess
- ❑ *Freedom River* – Doreen Rappaport (RA)
- ❑ *By Wagon & Flatboat* – Enid Meadowcraft
- ❑ *G. A. Henty's Short Stories Vol. 1* – book on tape – Audio by Jim Weiss

Language Arts

Preamble to the State Constitution:
We, the people of the State of Ohio, grateful to Almighty God for our freedom, to secure its blessings and promote our common welfare, do establish this Constitution.

1. Refer to Language Arts Guide starting on page 8.

Character

The original motto for Ohio - *An empire within an empire* - was repealed in 1868. The state was without a motto until the 1950s, when a statewide contest was held to select a new motto. The motto - *With God all things are possible* - was submitted by a 12-year-old from Cincinnati. The motto, inspired by Matthew 19:26, was adopted in 1959. In 1997, the ACLU filed a lawsuit which challenged the constitutionality of the motto. The original panel of judges agreed with the ACLU; however, on March 16, 2001 the entire 6th U.S. Court of Appeals reversed the ruling with a 9–4 decision. The ACLU decided not to appeal the decision to the U.S. Supreme Court for fear that it would set a national precedent that "...takes a skeptical view of church and state separation."

This would be an interesting case to research and debate with older children. This is also a great time to study and discuss **mercy**. You can also discuss the importance of being merciful towards others.

- **Mercy** – Compassion; tenderness; disposition to pity offenders and to forgive their offenses.

State Flag Pledge

I salute the flag of the state of Ohio
and pledge to the Buckeye State respect and loyalty

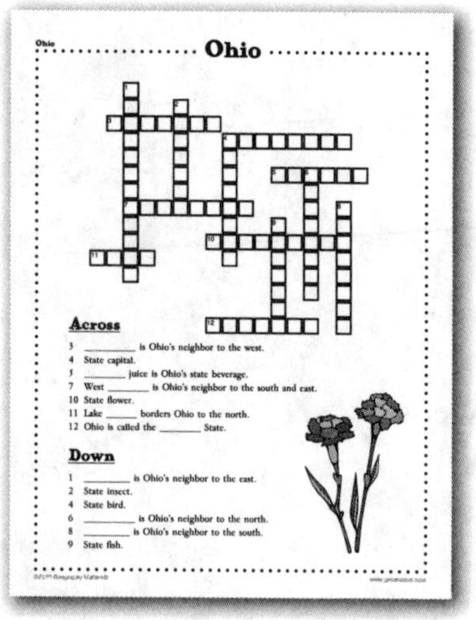

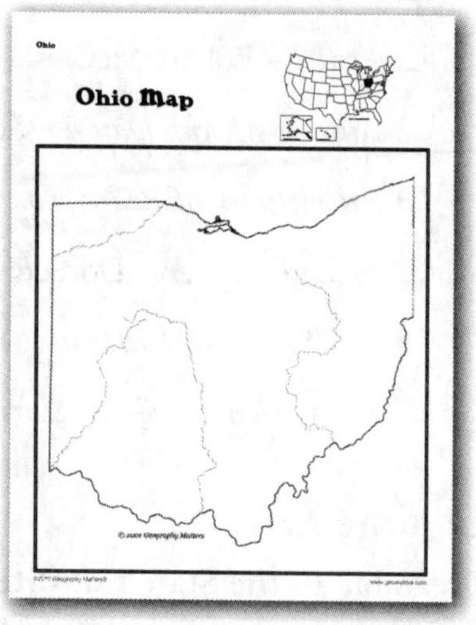

Activities

1. Color or label a map of Ohio.
2. Label the Ohio River on a map of the United States.
3. Go to http://www.kidzone.ws/geography/usa/ for printable flag and state symbol coloring pages.
4. Prepare a meal in *Eat Your Way Through the U.S.A.* from the state of Ohio.

Oklahoma

Sooner State

Oil-rich Oklahoma became the 46th state on November 16, 1907. The name "Oklahoma" comes from two Choctaw words – ***okla***, meaning "people," and ***homma***, which means "red." Oklahoma is called the Sooner State because, when the government first opened the area to white settlement, some settlers were there "sooner" than they were supposed to be. Oklahoma City is the state capital.

The flag of Oklahoma emerged from a design competition and was adopted in 1925. The flag was revised to add the name Oklahoma in 1941. The flag shows two symbols of peace – the olive branch and the peace pipe. The shield behind these symbols stands for defensive warfare.

Most of Oklahoma is prairie broken by mountain ranges. The Ouachita Mountains rise in the southeastern part of the state on the border shared with Arkansas. The Arbuckle Mountains are wedged into an area of south-central Oklahoma. Black Mesa, the highest point in Oklahoma, is in the panhandle, a strip of land 34 miles wide that makes up the northwestern part of the state.

Interesting Facts:

- There is an operating oil well on state capitol grounds called Capitol Site No. 1.
- Boise City, Oklahoma, was the only city in the United States to be bombed during World War II. On Monday night, July 5, 1943, at approximately 12:30 a.m., a B-17 Bomber based at Dalhart Army Air Base (50 miles to the south of Boise City) dropped six practice bombs on the sleeping town.
- The town of Beaver claims to be the Cow Chip Throwing Capital of the World. It is here that the World Championship Cow Chip Throw is held each April.
- Oklahoma is one of only two states whose capital cities name includes the state name. The other is Indianapolis, Indiana.

General Reference

- ❑ *Oklahoma* - Paul Joseph
- ❑ *Oklahoma Facts and Symbols* – Karen Bush Gibson
- ❑ www.statesymbolsusa.org/Oklahoma/StateSymbolsOklahoma.html
- ❑ http://www.state.ok.us/osfdocs/stinfo2.html
- ❑ http://www.ok.gov/kids/

Geography

- ❑ plateau
  - *Geography From A to Z,* page 35
- ❑ Ouachita Mountains

History & Biographies

- ❑ Pawnee
  - *The Pawnee* – Dennis B. Fradin
- ❑ Will Rogers
  - *Will Rogers: Young Cowboy* – Guernsey Van Riper, Jr.
- ❑ Karl Jansky
- ❑ Dust Bowl

Science

- ❑ scissor-tailed flycatcher (state bird)
  - http://www.coloring.ws/birds.htm
- ❑ eastern redbud (state tree)
- ❑ mistletoe (state floral emblem)
- ❑ rose rock/barite rose (state rock)
- ❑ raccoon (state fur-bearing animal)
  - *Marvels of Creation, Magnificent Mammals* - Buddy and Kay Davis
  - *Clever Raccoons* – Kristin L. Nelson
  - *Raccoons* – K. M. Kostyal
  - www.coloring.ws/animals.html
- ❑ buffalo (state animal)
  - *Buffalo* – Emilie U. Lepthien
  - *Marvels of Creation, Magnificent Mammals* - Buddy and Kay Davis
  - http://colortheanimals.com/set1.html
- ❑ radio astronomy
  - http://www.nrao.edu/whatisra/index.shtml

Literature

- ❑ *Dust for Dinner* - Ann Turner
- ❑ *I Have Heard of a Land* - Joyce Carol Thomas
- ❑ "Howdy Folks" - poem by Will Rogers (can be found online)
- ❑ *Wait Till the Moon is Full* - Margaret Wise Brown

Language Arts

Preamble to the State Constitution:

Invoking the guidance of Almighty God, in order to secure and perpetuate the blessing of liberty; to secure just and rightful government; to promote our mutual welfare and happiness, we, the people of the State of Oklahoma, do ordain and establish this Constitution

1. Refer to Language Arts Guide starting on page 8.

Character

The motto for Oklahoma - *Labor conquers all things* - focuses on work as the answer. We do want to instill a strong work ethic in our children. Traits that encourage and focus on the importance of work and labor are **punctuality** and **skillfulness**.

Being punctual demonstrates respect for the persons and events involved. Punctuality involves learning time management and organizational skills. Some children have tendencies towards these skills, and other children are the complete opposite. It is important to realize this when trying to teach your children to be punctual. Skillfulness is also inherent; however, every individual has unique talents and abilities.

- **Punctuality** - Exactness, observance; punctiliousness, particularly in observing time, appointments, or promises.
- **Skillfulness** - Knowledge; being well versed in any art; ability in management; ability to perform nicely any manual operations.

State Flag Pledge

I salute the flag of the State of Oklahoma.
Its symbols of peace unite all people.

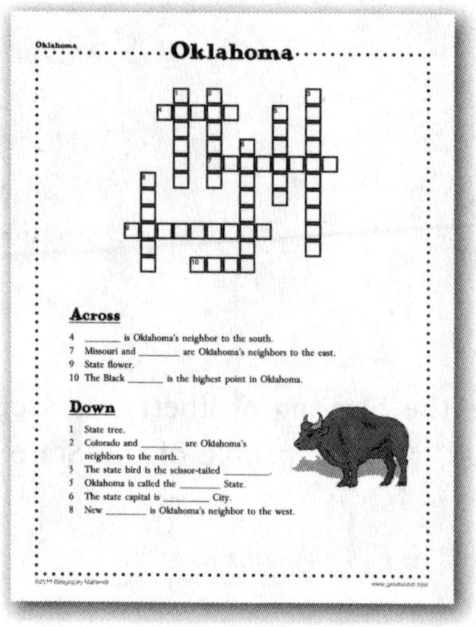

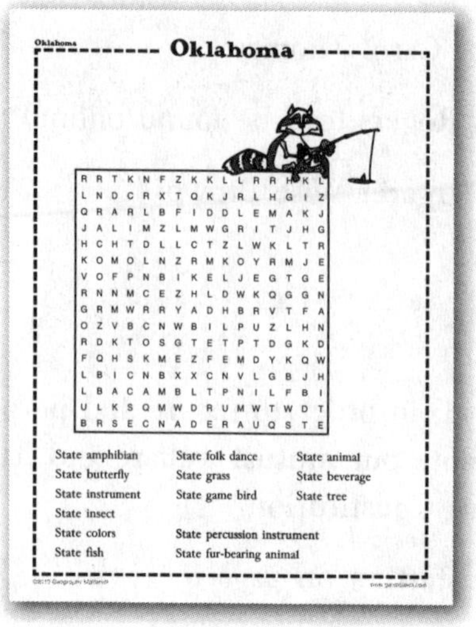

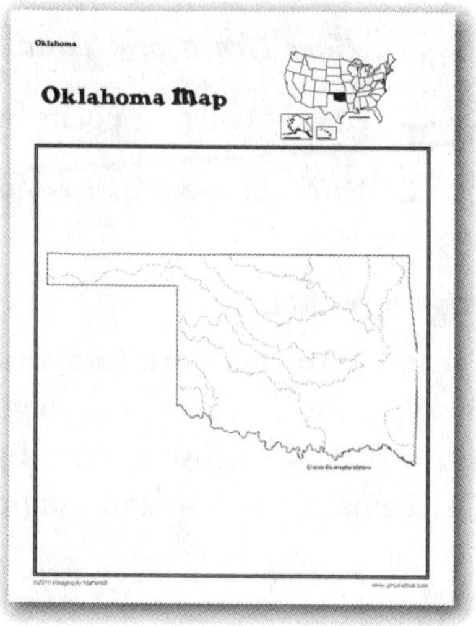

Activities

1. Color or label a map of Oklahoma.
2. Label the Ouachita Mountains and the Ozark Plateau on a map of the United States.
3. Go to www.kidzone.ws/geography/usa/ for printable flag and state symbol coloring pages.
4. Prepare a meal in *Eat Your Way Through the U.S.A.* from the state of Oklahoma.
5. Make a raccoon puppet. Go to www.enchantedlearning.com/crafts/puppets/paperbag/ for instructions.
6. Listen to the state song, "Oklahoma."

Oregon

Beaver State

Often called the "Pacific Wonderland," Oregon joined the Union on February 14, 1859, making it the 33rd state. The name "Oregon" is from the French word *ouragan,* which means "hurricane." The capital of Oregon is Salem.

The flag of Oregon is the only state flag with a different design on each side. On one side is the state seal within 33 stars, the state's name, and date of admission to the Union. The stars represent Oregon as the 33rd state. The departing British man-of-war and the arriving American merchant ship symbolize the end of British influence and the rise of American power. The sheaf of grain, the plow, and the pickax represent Oregon's mining and agricultural resources. The reverse side of the flag shows a beaver. The flag was adopted in 1925.

Oregon's natural wonders include Crater Lake in the Cascade Mountains, the Columbia River Gorge, and Hells Canyon on the Snake River. Mount Hood and other snow-capped peaks rise majestically in the Cascade Mountains. Steep cliffs rise above much of Oregon's coast, where the Pacific Ocean brings moisture and mild temperatures. East of the Cascade Mountains, the land is much drier and the temperature varies more.

Interesting Facts:

- Crater Lake, the deepest lake in the United States, is nearly 2,000 feet deep.
- At 8,000 feet deep, Hells Canyon is the deepest river gorge in North America.
- Haystack Rock off Cannon Beach is 235 feet high and is the 3rd largest coastal monolith in the world.
- The Columbia River gorge is considered by many to be the best place in the world for windsurfing.
- Ninety-nine percent of the entire commercial hazelnut crop of the United States is grown in Oregon.

General Reference

- ❑ *Oregon* – Paul Joseph
- ❑ *Oregon Facts and Symbols* – Emily McAuliffe
- ❑ http://www.oregon.gov/kids_korner.shtml

Geography

- ❑ Cascade Mountains

History & Biographies

- ❑ Jesse Applegate
    - *Profiles from History* - Volume 1, pages 163-170
- ❑ John Jacob Astor
    - *John Jacob Astor: Boy Trader* – Dorothy S. Anderson
- ❑ Dr. John McLoughlin
- ❑ Eliza Hart Spalding

Science

- ❑ ducks
    - *A Duckling Is Born* – Hans-Heinrich Isenbart
    - *Ducks Don't Get Wet* – Augusta Goldin
    - *Marvels of Creation, Breathtaking Birds* - Buddy and Kay Davis
    - *A Duck in a Tree* – Jennifer Loomis
    - www.enchantedlearning.com/painting/birds.shtml
    - http://www.coloring.ws/birds.htm
- ❑ Douglas fir (state tree)
- ❑ Oregon grape (state flower)
- ❑ sunstone (state gemstone)
- ❑ beaver (state animal)
    - *Marvels of Creation, Magnificent Mammals* - Buddy and Kay Davis
    - *Beavers* – Deborah Hodge
    - *The Beaver* – Margaret Lane
    - *Beaver* – Glen Rounds
    - *Beaver Business* – Glen Rounds
    - *Zoo Guide,* page 23
    - www.coloring.ws/animals.html
    - www.dltk-kids.com/animals/mcircle_beaver.htm
- ❑ cougar (also called puma, panther, mountain lion)
    - *Cougars* – Jalma Barrett
    - *Zoo Guide,* page 165

Literature

- ❑ *Purple Delicious Blackberry Jam* – Lisa Westberg Peters
- ❑ *Five Little Ducks* – PamelaPaparone
- ❑ *Wow! It's Great Being a Duck* – Joan Rankin
- ❑ *Trouble for Lucy* – Carla Stevens
- ❑ *To Be a Logger* – Lois Lenski (RA)
- ❑ *Emily's Runaway Imagination* – Beverly Cleary - (RA)
- ❑ *Mississippi Mud* – Ann Turner
- ❑ *Beaver at Long Pond* – William T. George
- ❑ *Blaze and the Mountain Lion* – C. W. Anderson

Language Arts

Preamble to the State Constitution:

We the people of the State of Oregon to the end that justice be established, order maintained, and liberty perpetuated, do ordain this Constitution.

1. Refer to Language Arts Guide starting on page 8.

Character

The current motto for Oregon - *She flies with her own wings* - was the original motto for the Oregon Territory and was adopted in 1854. The motto was chosen in 1843 when the settlers were divided over whether their future lay beneath the wing of Britain or the wing of the United States. The settlers had gathered and voted to form a provisional government which was dependent on neither nation. It was a testament to the independent character of the Oregon people. In 1957 the motto was changed to *the Union,* which was intended to reflect the conflict over the issue of slavery. In 1987, the State Senate voted to re-adopt the original motto, which reflected the independence and **innovation** of the people of Oregon.

- **Innovation** – Changing or altering by introducing something new.

Activities

1. Color or label a map of Oregon.
2. Label the Pacific Ocean and the Cascade Mountains on a map of the United States.
3. Go to http://www.kidzone.ws/geography/usa/ for printable flag and state symbol coloring pages.
4. Prepare a meal in *Eat Your Way Through the U.S.A.* from the state of Oregon.

5. Make ice cream ducks.
    - For the body, place a large scoop of ice cream on a small plate.
    - Use a small scoop of ice cream for the head.
    - Place chocolate chips or raisins for eyes.
    - For a beak, use a candy orange slice or an orange gumdrop and cut it into two pieces.
    - For the webbed feet, use candy orange slices, orange gumdrops, or pieces of fruit leather.

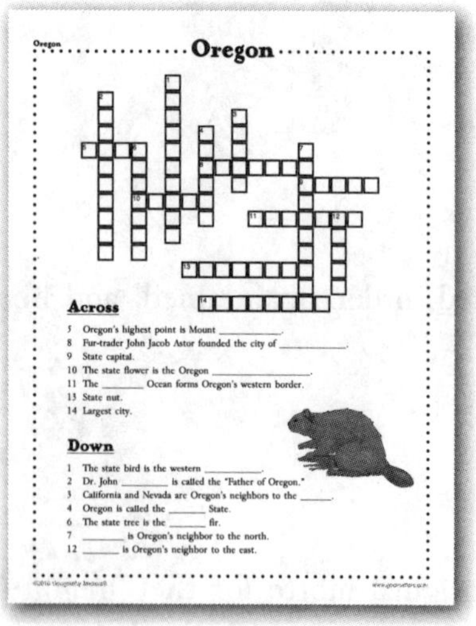

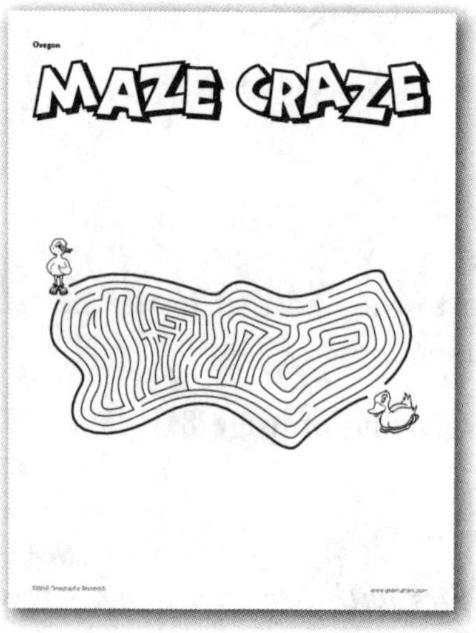

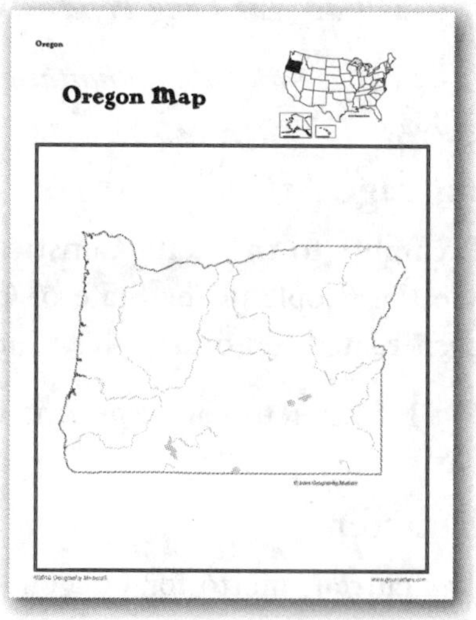

Pennsylvania

Keystone State

Founded as a haven for the religiously persecuted, Pennsylvania became the 2nd state on December 12, 1787. The name "Pennsylvania" means "Penn's woods" and was chosen in honor of the colony's founder, William Penn's father. Pennsylvania is nicknamed the Keystone State because it was the center, or keystone, of the "arch" created by the original thirteen states. Harrisburg is the state capital.

The state flag, adopted in 1907, shows the state's coat of arms supported by two horses on a blue field. The eagle represents speed, strength, bravery, and wisdom. The ship, plow, and bundles of wheat stand for commerce and agriculture. The cornstalk and olive branch symbolize prosperity and peace.

Pennsylvania is made up primarily of hills, plateaus, ridges, and valleys, although the southeastern and northwestern corners of the state are low and flat. Much of the state has rich farmland; the southeastern portion has some of the richest soil in the country. Forests cover about half of Pennsylvania, and the Allegheny Mountains have extensive deposits of anthracite, or hard coal.

Interesting Facts:

- The first daily newspaper was published in Philadelphia on September 21, 1784.
- Pennsylvania is the only original colony not bordered by the Atlantic Ocean.
- Pennsylvania is the first state of the 50 United States to list its web site URL on a license plate.
- Hershey is considered the chocolate capital of the United States.
- KDKA radio in Pittsburgh produced the first commercial radio broadcast.
- Punxsutawney citizens are proud to be overshadowed by their town's most famous resident, the world-renowned weather forecasting groundhog, Punxsutawney Phil. Punxsutawney is billed as the weather capital of the world.

General Reference

- ❑ *Pennsylvania* – Anne Welsbacher
- ❑ *Pennsylvania Facts and Symbols* – Emily McAuliffe
- ❑ http://www.statesymbolsusa.org/Pennsylvania/State_Symbols.html
- ❑ http://sites.state.pa.us/kids/

Geography

- ❑ Lake Erie
- ❑ Liberty Bell
  - *The Liberty Bell* – Gail Sakurai
  - *The Great Big Wagon that Rang: How the Liberty Bell Was Saved* – Joseph Slate
  - http://members.enchantedlearning.com/history/us/monuments/libertybell/index.shtml

History & Biographies

- ❑ William Penn
  - *William Penn: Founder of Pennsylvania* – Steven Kroll
- ❑ Benjamin Franklin
  - *Profiles from History* - Volume 1, pages 97-104
  - *Young Ben Franklin* – Laurence Santrey
  - *Meet Benjamin Franklin* – Maggi Scarf
- ❑ Benjamin West
  - *Benjamin West: Gifted Young Painter* – Dorothea J. Snow
  - *The Boy Who Loved to Draw* - by Barbara Brenner
- ❑ William H. McGuffey
  - *William H. McGuffey: Boy Reading Genius* – Barbara Williams
- ❑ Mary Cassatt
  - *Mary Cassatt* – Ernestine Giesecke
- ❑ Milton Hershey
  - *Chocolate by Hershey* – Betty Burford
- ❑ Stan & Jan Berenstain
  - *Stan & Jan Berenstain* – Mae Woods

Science

- ❑ ruffed grouse (state bird)
  - http://www.coloring.ws/birds.htm
- ❑ eastern hemlock (state tree)
- ❑ buttercup
- ❑ chabazite
- ❑ ground hog
  - *Woodchucks* – Emilie U. Lepthien
  - www.coloring.ws/animals.html

Literature

- ❑ *Ben and Me* – Robert Lawson (RA)
- ❑ *Benjamin West and his Cat Grimalkin* - Marguerite Henry
- ❑ *The Cabin Faced West* – Jean Fritz (RA)
- ❑ *Berenstain Bears* series – Stan & Jan Berenstain
- ❑ *Chocolate Fever* – Robert Kimmel Smith (RA)
- ❑ *The Day It Rained Forever: A Story of the Johnstown Flood* – Virginia Gross (RA)
- ❑ *Thee, Hannah* – Marguerite de Angeli
- ❑ *Silver at Night* – Susan Bartoletti
- ❑ *Bread and Butter Indian* – Anne Colver
- ❑ *Bread and Butter Journey* – Anne Colver

Language Arts

Preamble to the State Constitution:
WE, the people of the Commonwealth of Pennsylvania, grateful to Almighty God for the blessings of civil and religious liberty, and humbly invoking His guidance, do ordain and establish this Constitution.

1. Refer to Language Arts Guide starting on page 8.
2. Write a story about owning your own chocolate factory.

Character

The origin of the motto - *Virtue, Liberty and Independence* - is unclear. The traits in this motto have already been studied, so this would be a good time to review these traits and discuss them again for reinforcement.

The new traits to study are **thoughtfulness** and **creativity**. Children are naturally creative, and it is important to let them express their creativity in a nonjudgmental environment. Being a thoughtful person is a learned behavior, and we should reinforce and encourage thoughtful acts in our children. When children exhibit thoughtfulness, make a point to notice and reward it.

- **Thoughtfulness** – Being full of thought, considerate, attentive, careful; showing care or attention to others.
- **Creativity** – Making or inventing something; putting together; having imagination and ability.

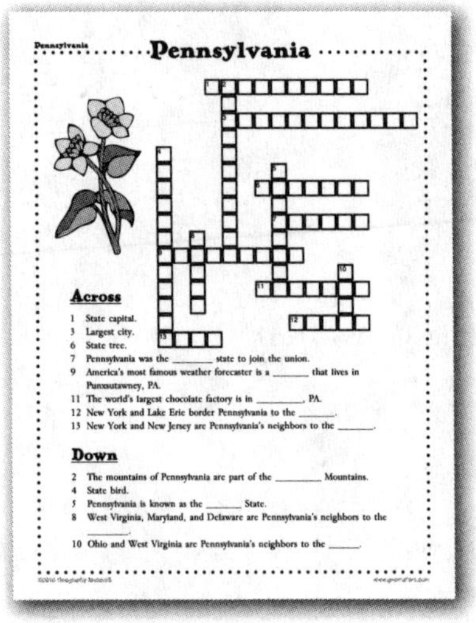

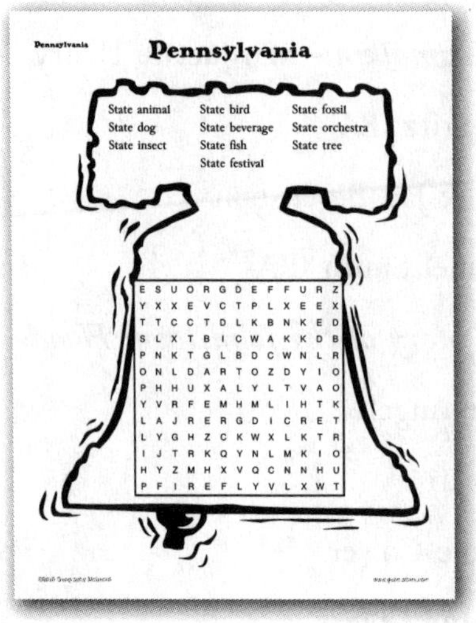

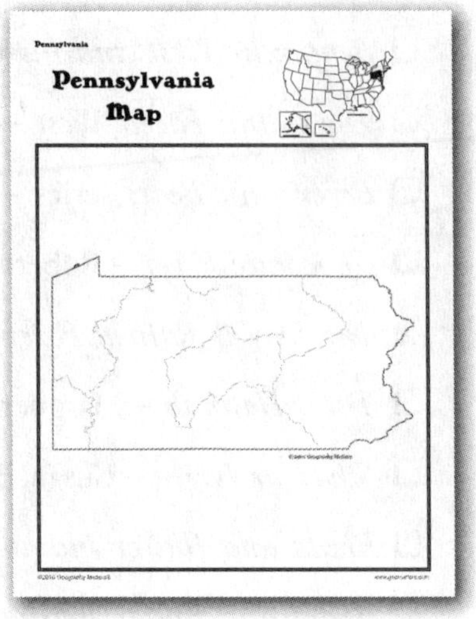

Activities

1. Color or label a map of Pennsylvania.
2. Label Lake Erie on a map of the United States.
3. Go to http://www.kidzone.ws/geography/usa/ for printable flag and state symbol coloring pages.
4. Prepare a meal in *Eat Your Way Through the U.S.A.* from the state of Pennsylvania.
5. If studying Benjamin West, paint a portrait or historical scene.
6. If studying Milton Hershey, eat Hershey candy.
7. If studying Milton Hershey, go to www.hersheys.com and take a virtual tour of the Hershey Chocolate factory.
8. If studying Mary Cassatt, paint a picture in the Impressionist style.
9. Go to http://www.dltk-kids.com/animals/mgroundhog.html for a groundhog craft idea.

Rhode Island

Ocean State

The smallest state, Rhode Island was the last of the thirteen colonies to ratify the Constitution and join the Union, on May 29, 1790. Rhode Island's official name, "State of Rhode Island and Providence Plantations," gives the smallest state the longest official name. Rhode Island was originally the name of the largest islands in Narragansett Bay. Dutch explorers called it *roodt eylandt*, which means "red island." The capital of Rhode Island is Providence.

Based on a Revolutionary War flag, the flag of Rhode Island shows an anchor, a symbol of hope, encircled by thirteen stars on a white field. The stars stand for the thirteen original colonies, and the white field represents the white uniforms worn by Rhode Island soldiers during the Revolutionary War. The flag was adopted in 1877 and modified in 1897.

Extending 28 miles inland, Narragansett Bay almost cuts Rhode Island in two. The state has 36 islands, most of which are in the bay. Sandy beaches and rocky cliffs line the shores. Inland, the land east of Narragansett Bay is low and has few trees. West of the bay, the land rises to forested slopes.

Interesting Facts:

- Rhode Island founder Roger Williams established the first Baptist church in America in 1638. The existing structure was built in 1775.
- Rhode Island has no county government. It is divided into 39 municipalities, each having its own form of local government.
- The first circus in the United States was in Newport in 1774.
- George M. Cohan was born in Providence in 1878. He wrote "I'm a Yankee Doodle Dandy" and "You're a Grand Old Flag."

General Reference

- ❑ *Rhode Island* – Paul Joseph
- ❑ *Rhode Island Facts and Symbols* – Kathy Feeney
- ❑ www.ri.gov/kids/

Geography

- ❑ Narragansett Basin
- ❑ Narragansett Bay

History & Biographies

- ❑ Roger Williams
  - *Finding Providence* – Avi
  - *Roger Williams* – Mark Ammerman
- ❑ George Cohan
- ❑ Gilbert Stuart
- ❑ Oliver H. Perry
  - *Oliver Hazard Perry: Boy of the Sea* – Laura Long

Science

- ❑ Rhode Island Red chicken (state bird)
  - *Chickens* – Sara Swan Miller
  - www.enchantedlearning.com/painting/birds.shtml
  - http://www.coloring.ws/birds.htm
  - www.daniellesplace.com/html/birdcrafts.html
- ❑ red maple (state tree)
- ❑ early blue violet (state flower)
- ❑ cumberlandite (state rock)
- ❑ quahaug (state shell)

Literature

- ❑ *Sailor Song* – Nancy Jewell

Language Arts

Preamble to the State Constitution:

We, the people of the State of Rhode Island and Providence Plantations, grateful to Almighty God for the civil and religious liberty which He hath so long permitted us to enjoy, and looking to Him for a blessing upon our endeavors to secure and to transmit the same, unimpaired, to succeeding generations, do ordain and establish this Constitution of government.

1. Refer to Language Arts Guide starting on page 8.
2. If studying Roger Williams, write a story about starting a colony.
3. If studying Oliver Perry, write an adventure story about a sea captain.

Character

The origin of the Rhode Island motto – *Hope* - is unverifiable.

Hope is a trait that we should encourage in our children. The other trait that complements hope is **optimism**.

- **Hope** – A desire of some good, accompanied with at least a slight expectation of obtaining it; or a belief that it is obtainable; confidence in a future event.
- **Optimism** – The opinion or doctrine that everything in nature is ordered for the best.

Activities

1. Color or label a map of Rhode Island.
2. Label Narragansett Bay on a map of the United States.
3. Go to http://www.kidzone.ws/geography/usa/ for printable flag and state symbol coloring pages.
4. Prepare a meal in *Eat Your Way Through the U.S.A.* from the state of Rhode Island.
5. Roger Williams, founder of Rhode Island, established the first practical working model of democracy after he was banished from Plymouth, Massachusetts, because of his "extreme views" concerning freedom of speech and religion. Thomas Jefferson and John Adams publicly acknowledged Roger Williams as the originator of the concepts and principles reflected in the First Amendment. Among those principles were freedom of religion, freedom of speech, and freedom of public assembly. Discuss the importance of these freedoms.
6. Listen to "I'm a Yankee Doodle Dandy" and "You're a Grand Old Flag."
7. If studying Gilbert Stuart, draw or paint a portrait.
8. Make a maple leaf candle.
   - Place dried or silk maple leaves between two pieces of brown paper bag and press with a dry iron on low temperature. Iron on a hard surface with a towel on it.
   - Melt paraffin wax in a disposable container (glass or metal is best). Cool for 5 minutes.
   - Paint wax onto leaves with a paint brush. Press onto a 3-inch or 4-inch candle. Seal with wax.

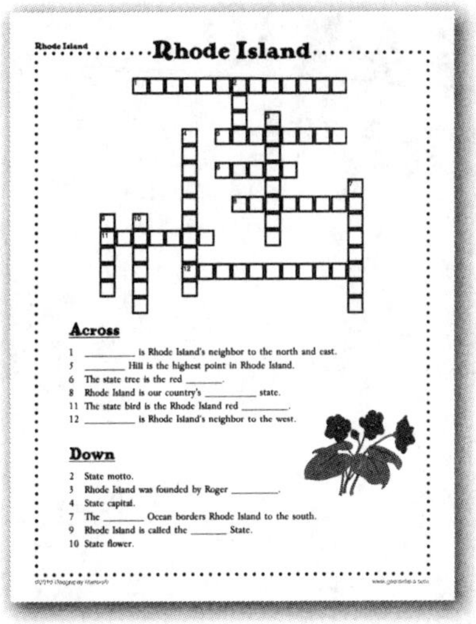

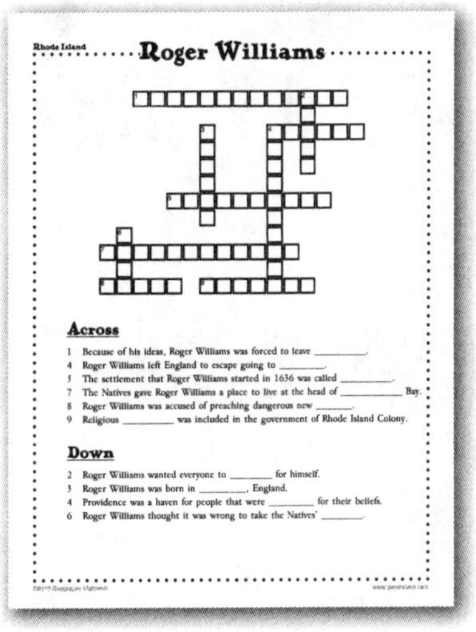

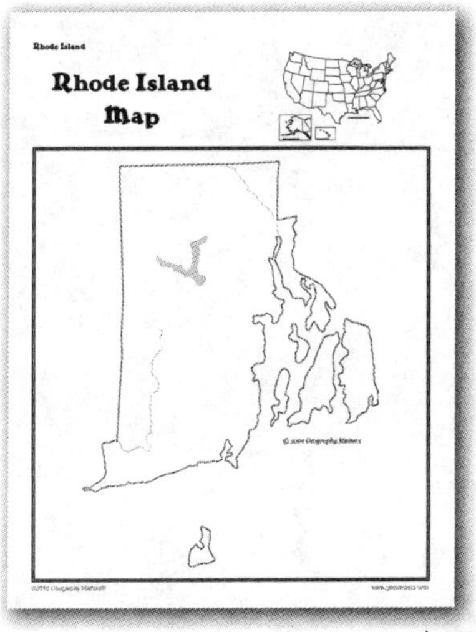

South Carolina

Palmetto State

A picture of Southern pride and tradition, South Carolina joined the Union, on May 23, 1788 making it the 8th state. In 1629, South Carolina was named for King Charles I of England. "Charles" translates to "Carolina" in Latin. "South" was added in 1730, when North and South Carolina became separate colonies. Legend has it that the state earned its nickname, the Palmetto State, during the Revolutionary War. It is said that in 1776, colonists on Sullivan Island in a small fort built from palmetto trees defeated a British fleet that tried to capture Charleston Harbor. Columbia is the capital of South Carolina.

The flag of South Carolina was adopted in 1861 at the start of the Civil War but contains emblems from the Revolutionary War. The blue field signifies the uniforms worn by South Carolina soldiers during the Revolution, and the crescent is from the silver emblem on their caps. The palmetto is the state tree and also represents the victory on Sullivan Island.

Eastern South Carolina is a lowland that borders the Atlantic Ocean. Swamps cover much of the land near the coast and extend inland along the rivers. Moving northwest across the state, the land slowly rises to rolling hills then to the Blue Ridge Mountains. With few peaks in South Carolina rising more than 3,000 feet, the Blue Ridge Mountains of South Carolina are less rugged and more easily crossed than those of North Carolina.

Interesting Facts:

- Senator Strom Thurmond was the longest serving and oldest Senator. He had served 48 years when he retired from the Senate in January 2003 at age 100.
- At the Riverbanks Zoological Park in Columbia, more than 2,000 animals thrive in recreated natural habitats with no bars or cages.

General Reference

- ❑ *South Carolina* – Paul Joseph
- ❑ *South Carolina Facts and Symbols* – Bill McAuliffe
- ❑ *South Carolina* – Charles Fredeen

Geography

- ❑ coastal plain

History & Biographies

- ❑ Fort Sumter
  - *Fort Sumter* – Brendan January
- ❑ Mary McLeod Bethune
  - *Mary McLeod Bethune* – Eloise Greenfield
  - *Mary McLeod Bethune: A Great Teacher* – Patricia and Frederick McKissack
- ❑ Bernard Baruch
  - *Bernard Baruch: Boy from South Carolina* – Joanne Landers Henry
- ❑ James Strom Thurmond

Science

- ❑ Carolina wren (state bird)
  - http://www.coloring.ws/birds.htm
- ❑ palmetto (state tree)
- ❑ yellow jessamine (state flower)
- ❑ blue granite (state stone)
- ❑ thunderstorms
  - *Lightning* – Seymour Simon
  - *Storms* – Seymour Simon
  - *Flash, Crash, Rumble, and Roll* – Franklyn M. Branley
  - *Earth Science for Every Kid,* Experiment #83
- ❑ coyotes
  - *Zoo Guide,* page 33

Literature

- ❑ *Defeat of the Ghost Riders* – Dave & Neta Jackson - Story of Mary McLeod Bethune (RA)

Language Arts

Preamble to the State Constitution:
We, the people of the State of South Carolina, in Convention assembled, grateful to God for our liberties, do ordain and establish this Constitution for the preservation and perpetuation of the same.

1. Refer to Language Arts Guide starting on page 8.
2. Make a list of words that describe rain.
   - Cut raindrops from blue construction paper.
   - Write one word from the list on each raindrop.
   - Glue or tape clothes pins or paperclips to the back side of the raindrops.
   - Attach to an umbrella.

Character

South Carolina has two mottoes: *Prepared in mind and resources* and *While I breathe I hope.* The state seal also has two more mottoes engraved upon it: *Who shall separate us* and *Having fallen, it has set up a better one.* The official state motto varies according to the resource utilized. The important traits to gain from these mottoes are **resourcefulness** and **unity**.

- **Resourcefulness** – Being full of resources; ability to deal promptly and effectively with problems, difficulties.
- **Unity** – Oneness of sentiment, affection or behavior.

State Flag Pledge

I salute the flag of South Carolina
and pledge to the Palmetto State love, loyalty and faith.

Activities

1. Color or label a map of South Carolina.
2. Label the coastal plain on a map of the United States.
3. Go to http://www.kidzone.ws/geography/usa/ for printable flag and state symbol coloring pages.
4. Prepare a meal in *Eat Your Way Through the U.S.A.* from the state of South Carolina.
5. South Carolina was the first state to grow tea. Enjoy a glass of iced tea. Southerners drink sweet iced tea all year long. To make a gallon of sweet tea:
    - Put 6 regular sized tea bags (tags removed) and 8 cups of water in a pot on the stove. Turn on high heat and bring almost to a boil. Turn off heat and allow to steep for 1-2 hours.
    - Put 1 1/3 cups sugar in gallon sized pitcher along with tea. Stir until sugar is dissolved. Add 8 cups water and stir. Chill.

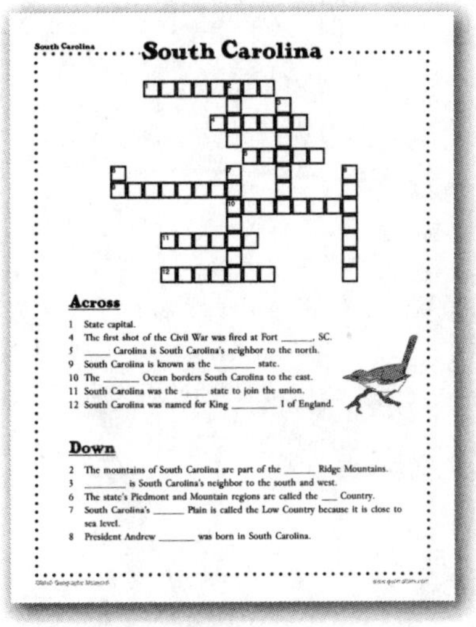

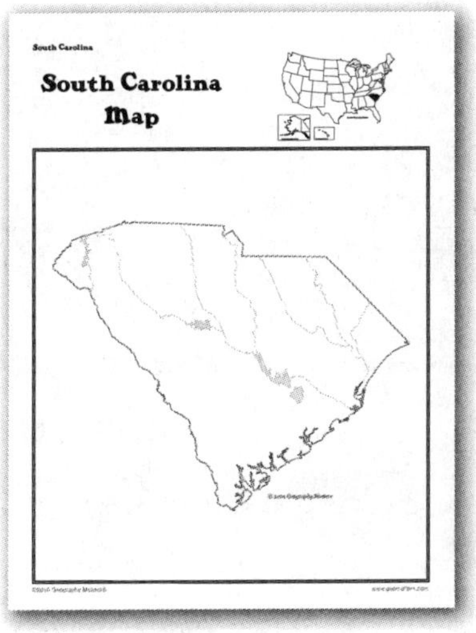

South Dakota

Mount Rushmore State

Low in population, but high in natural and man-made wonders, South Dakota became the 40th state on November 2, 1889. As with its neighbor to the north, South Dakota was named for the Sioux that once roamed the region. Pierre is the state capital.

The flag of South Dakota, adopted in 1963, was modified in 1992 to change the state nickname around the seal from The Sunshine State to The Mount Rushmore State. On the seal, the smelter chimney represents mining, the plowman stands for farming, and the riverboat represents transportation. The gold circle around the seal depicts the blazing rays of the sun. The blue field symbolizes South Dakota's clear skies.

South Dakota is a midwestern state of startling contrasts. The wide Missouri River flows southward through the middle of the state. Low hills, lakes, and vast stretches of prairie lie east of the river. West of the river are deep canyons and rolling plains. Tucked in the state's southwest corner, the Black Hills rise abruptly. Southeast of the Black Hills are the strangely beautiful Badlands. Just west of Castle Rock is the geographic center of all 50 states.

Interesting Facts:

- The faces of George Washington, Thomas Jefferson, Theodore Roosevelt, and Abraham Lincoln are sculpted into Mount Rushmore, the world's greatest mountain carving. Sculptor Gutzon Borglum began drilling into the 6,200-foot Mount Rushmore in 1927. The project took fourteen years and cost $1 million, though it's now deemed priceless.
- Badlands National Park consists of nearly 244,000 acres of sharply eroded buttes, pinnacles, and spires blended with the largest protected mixed-grass prairie in the United States.
- The name "Black Hills" comes from the Lakota words *Paha Sapa,* which mean "hills that are black." Seen from a distance, these pine-covered hills, rising several thousand feet above the surrounding prairie, appear black.
- Harney Peak, at 7,242 above sea level, is the highest point in the United States east of the Rockies.

General Reference

- ❑ *South Dakota* – Anne Welsbacher
- ❑ *South Dakota Facts and Symbols* – Kathy Feeney
- ❑ http://www.state.sd.us/governor/main/kids/k1.htm

Geography

- ❑ badland
  - *Geography From A to Z,* page 9
- ❑ Badlands National Park
- ❑ Black Hills
- ❑ Mount Rushmore
  - *Mount Rushmore* – Lola Schaefer
  - *Mount Rushmore* – Andrew Santella
  - *Rushmore* – Lynn Curlee
  - http://members.enchantedlearning.com/history/us/monuments/mtrushmore/

History & Biographies

- ❑ Sioux
  - *Sioux* – Richard M. Gaines
  - *The Sioux* – Alice Osinski
- ❑ Sitting Bull
  - *Sitting Bull: Courageous Sioux Chief* – Diane Shaughnessy
  - *Sitting Bull: Dakota Boy* – Augusta Stevenson
- ❑ George Custer
  - *George Custer: Boy of Action* – Augusta Stevenson
  - Battle of Little Big Horn
- ❑ Gutzon Borglum

Science

- ❑ ring-necked pheasant (state bird)
  - http://www.coloring.ws/birds.htm
- ❑ Black Hills spruce (state tree)
- ❑ American pasqueflower (state flower)
- ❑ rose quartz (state mineral)
- ❑ coyotes (state animal)
  - *Coyotes* – Cherie Winner
  - *Coyotes* – Emilie U. Lepthien
- ❑ wolves
  - *Zoo Guide,* page 49

Literature

- ❑ *Prairie School* – Lois Lenski (RA)
- ❑ *By the Shores of Silver Lake* – Laura Ingalls Wilder (RA)
- ❑ *The Long Winter* – Laura Ingalls Wilder (RA)
- ❑ *Little Town on the Prairie* – Laura Ingalls Wilder (RA)
- ❑ *These Happy Golden Years* – Laura Ingalls Wilder (RA)

Language Arts

Preamble to the State Constitution:
We, the people of South Dakota, grateful to Almighty God for our civil and religious liberties, in order to form a more perfect and independent government, establish justice, insure tranquility, provide for the common defense, promote the general welfare and preserve to ourselves and to our posterity the blessings of liberty, do ordain and establish this Constitution for the state of South Dakota.

1. Refer to Language Arts Guide starting on page 8.

Character

The state motto - *Under God the people rule* - was adopted as part of the state seal in 1885. The origin of the statement is unverifiable. The motto portrays a deep understanding of the success of a democracy. People must be **cooperative** and **forgiving** in order to exist in a civilized, free society. Our children learn cooperation and forgiveness in the family first, and then those qualities expand into their friendships. We should cultivate an atmosphere in our homes that models cooperation and forgiveness.

- **Cooperation** – Operating jointly to the same end; working together; laboring towards a unified goal.
- **Forgiveness** – Inclination to overlook offenses; mildness; mercy; compassion.

State Flag Pledge

I pledge loyalty and support to the flag and state of South Dakota,
land of sunshine, land of infinite variety.

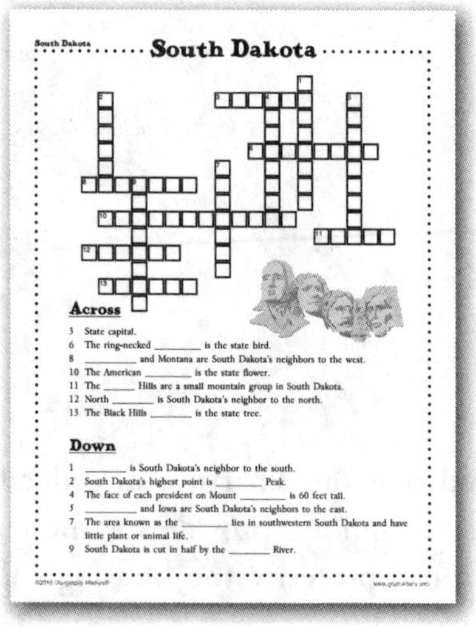

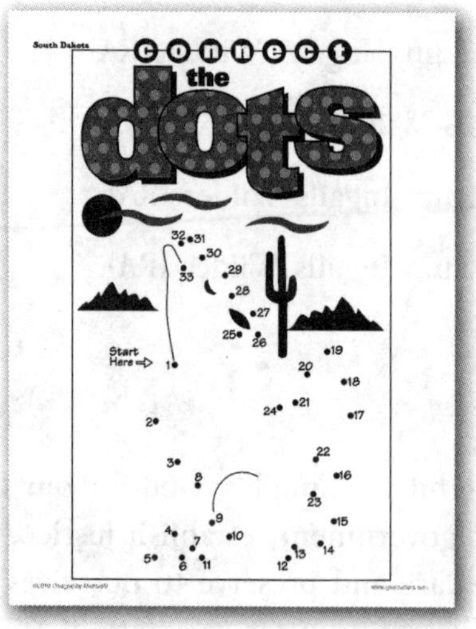

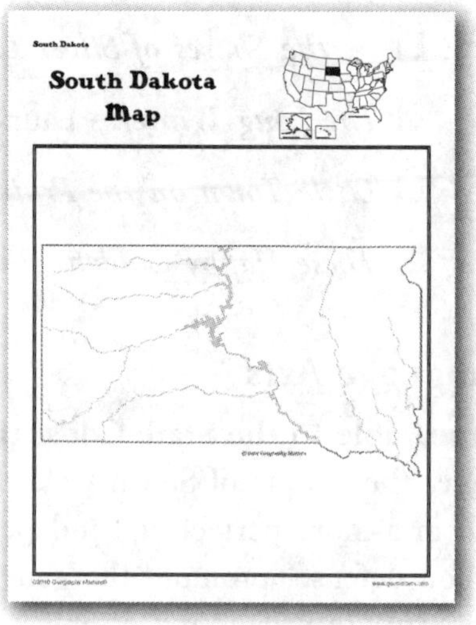

Activities

1. Color or label a map of South Dakota.
2. Label the Badlands and Black Hills on a map of the United States.
3. Locate Castle Rock on a map of South Dakota. Label on a map of the United States.
4. Go to http://www.kidzone.ws/geography/usa/ for printable flag and state symbol coloring pages.
5. Prepare a meal in *Eat Your Way Through the U.S.A.* from the state of South Dakota.
6. Make a paper model of Mount Rushmore. Go to http://papertoys.com/rushmore.htm for a template.
7. Enjoy the state bread of South Dakota, fry bread.
   http://www.statesymbolsusa.org/South_Dakota/bread_frybread.html
   http://www.globalgourmet.com/food/special/2001/prairie/fry.html

Tennessee

Volunteer State

Known as the Volunteer State because of its outstanding military traditions, Tennessee became the 16th state on June 1, 1796. The name Tennessee comes from *Tanasie*, a Cherokee village in the region. The state capital is Nashville.

The state flag of Tennessee was adopted in 1905. The three stars represent east, middle, and west Tennessee. The circle stands for unity.

A long, narrow state, Tennessee starts high in the mountains and gradually becomes lower until it reaches the banks of the Mississippi River. Named for the haze that often hangs over them making them appear smoky, the Great Smoky Mountains dominate the eastern portion of the state. Middle Tennessee is rolling hills. The Tennessee and Mississippi Rivers make western Tennessee the most fertile land in the state.

Interesting Facts:

- Davy Crockett was not born on a mountaintop in Tennessee, as the song says. He was born on the banks of Nolichucky River in Greene County, where a replica of his birthplace stands today.
- Oak Ridge National Laboratory is the largest energy research laboratory in the country.
- The Copper Basin is so different from the surrounding area that it has been seen and is recognizable by American astronauts. The stark landscape was caused by 19th-century mining practices.
- There were more National Guard soldiers deployed from Tennessee for the Gulf War than any other state.
- The Ocoee River in southeastern Tennessee is rated among the top white-water recreational rivers in the nation and was the site for the Olympic white-water canoe/kayak competition in the 1996 summer Olympics.

General Reference

- ❑ *Tennessee* – Paul Joseph
- ❑ *Tennessee Facts and Symbols* – Kathy Feeney
- ❑ www.statesymbolsusa.org/Tennessee/Tennesseestatesymbols.html
- ❑ www.tnhistoryforkids.org/home

Geography

- ❑ Smoky Mountains
  - *Great Smoky Mountains National Park* – David Petersen

History & Biographies

- ❑ Davy Crockett
  - *Davy Crockett: Young Pioneer* – Laurence Santrey
  - *Davy Crockett: Hero of the Wild Frontier* – Elizabeth R. Moseley
  - http://members.enchantedlearning.com/history/us/people/c/crockett/cloze.shtml
- ❑ Alvin C. York
  - *Alvin C. York: Young Marksman* – Ethel H. Weddle
  - *Sergeant York: Reluctant Hero* – Peter Andrews
- ❑ the Scopes Trial

Science

- ❑ black walnut
- ❑ iris (state flower)
- ❑ tufted titmouse
- ❑ limestone (state rock)
- ❑ wolves
  - *Wolves* – Seymour Simon
  - *The Gray Wolf* – Carol Greene
  - www.coloring.ws/animals.html

Literature

- ❑ *When Uncle Took the Fiddle* – Libba Moore Gray
- ❑ *Daniel's Duck* – Clyde Robert Bulla
- ❑ *Flossie & the Fox* – Patricia C. McKissack
- ❑ *The Three Little Wolves and the Big Bad Pig* – Eugene Trivizas
- ❑ *The Buffalo Knife* – William O. Steele (RA)

Language Arts

Preamble to the State Constitution (partial excerpt):

We, the Delegates and Representatives of the people of the State of Tennessee, duly elected, and in Convention assembled, in pursuance of said Act of Assembly, have ordained and established the following Constitution and form of government for this State, which we recommend to the people of Tennessee for their ratification.

1. Refer to Language Arts Guide starting on page 8.
2. If participating in the activity on volunteering, write a story or report about your experience.

Character

For Tennessee, we will focus on the state nickname rather than the motto. While not the original intent of the nickname, the term Volunteer State can also imply a people ready and willing to offer their services in any cause. Take this time to discuss volunteering with your children. The older children can research some of the many agencies run by volunteers. Volunteers are unselfish and caring. Our children should be taught to be **unselfish** and **caring**. A good way to do this is to reach out to others in need.

- **Unselfishness** – Without selfishness or self-seeking; without undue attachment to one's own interests and desires.
- **Care** – Concern; regard.

State Flag Pledge

Flag of Tennessee, I salute thee.
To thee I pledge my allegiance
with my affection, my service, and my life.

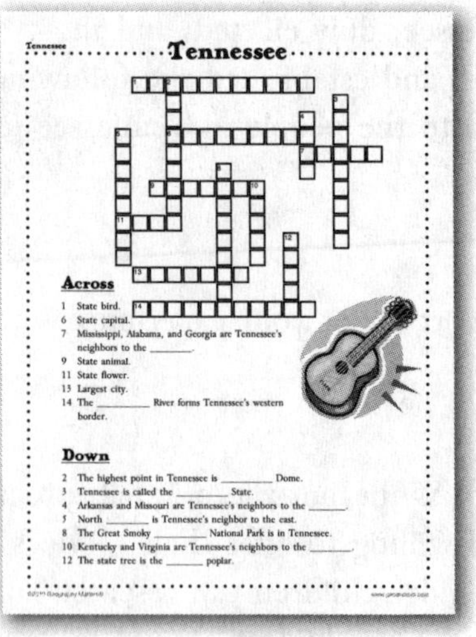

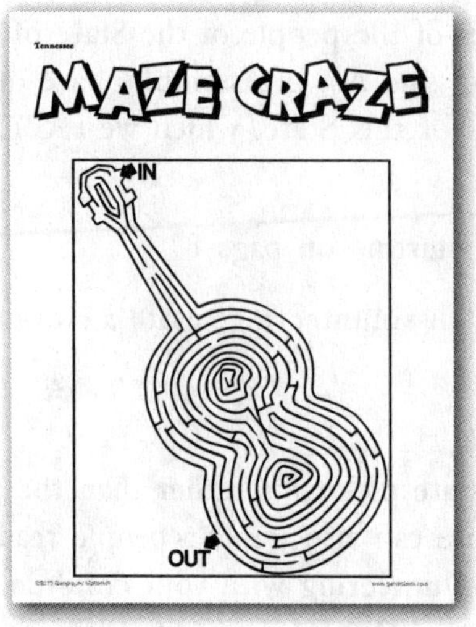

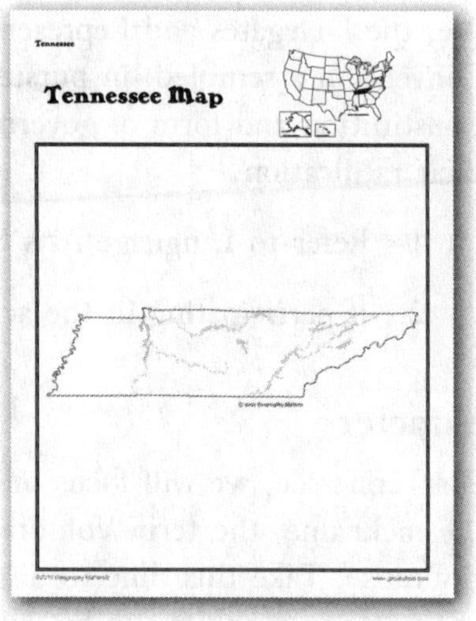

Activities

1. Color or label a map of Tennessee.
2. Go to http://www.kidzone.ws/geography/usa/ for printable flag and state symbol coloring pages.
3. Prepare a meal in *Eat Your Way Through the U.S.A.* from the state of Tennessee.
4. If you study the Scopes Trial and you feel your children are mature enough, hold a mock trial and debate evolution. Go to http://www.answersingenesis.org/ for great resources for this sort of debate.
5. Listen to the song "Rocky Top."
6. Tennessee is the Volunteer State. Volunteer at a local soup kitchen, food bank, etc.

Texas

Lone Star State

Known for cattle ranching and oil wells, Texas became the 28th state on December 29, 1845. Texas is the 2nd largest state. It is larger than Illinois, Indiana, Iowa, Michigan, and Wisconsin combined, and it is 220 times larger than Rhode Island. Texas received its name from the Spanish pronunciation of the Caddo word *tejas*, which means "friends" or "allies." Texas is called the Lone Star State because of the single star on its flag and seal. The capital of Texas is Austin.

The Texas state flag takes its colors from the national flag. Blue stands for loyalty, white represents strength, and red is for courage. The large white star was first used on flags carried by Texas during the Texas Revolution against Mexico in the 1830s. Adopted on January 25, 1839 as the national flag of the Republic of Texas, the flag was later adopted as the state flag when Texas became the 28th state in 1845.

Texas is bordered by Mexico to the southwest and the Gulf of Mexico to the southeast. Its vast area encompasses forests, mountains, deserts and dry plains, and subtropical coastal lowland. The rich soil of the plains provides fertile farmland. Texas has more farms than any other state, and huge cattle and sheep ranches are scattered over the prairie.

Interesting Facts:

- According to the terms of an 1845 treaty with the United States, Texas has the right to divide into five states.
- The Alamo, located in San Antonio, is where Texas defenders fell to Mexican General Santa Anna and the phrase "Remember the Alamo" originated. The Alamo is considered the cradle of Texas liberty and is the state's most popular historic site.
- The King Ranch in Texas is bigger than the state of Rhode Island.
- Dr Pepper was invented in Waco in 1885.
- El Paso is closer to Needles, California, than it is to Dallas.
- Johnson Space Center, near Houston, is the center of operations for all manned space U.S. space flights.

General Reference

- ❑ *Texas* – Anne Welsbacher
- ❑ *Texas Facts and Symbols* – Emily McAuliffe
- ❑ www.statesymbolsusa.org/Texas/state_symbols.html
- ❑ www.senate.state.tx.us/kids/
- ❑ www.tpwd.state.tx.us/kids/

Geography

- ❑ Rio Grande

History & Biographies

- ❑ Sam Houston
  - *Sam Houston: Boy Chieftain* – Augusta Stevenson
  - *I Am Houston* – Mary Dodson Wade
- ❑ Stephen Austin
- ❑ Jim Bowie
  - *Jim Bowie: Boy with a Hunting Knife* – Gertrude Hecker Winders
- ❑ the Alamo
  - *The Battle of the Alamo* – Andrew Santella
  - http://members.enchantedlearning.com/history/us/monuments/alamo/
- ❑ rodeos
  - *Rodeos* – James W. Fain
- ❑ Lyndon B. Johnson
  - www.whitehouse.gov/history/presidents/
  - www.presidentialavenue.com/lbj.cfm
  - www.homeofheroes.com/e-books/presidents/36_johnson.html
- ❑ George W. Bush
  - www.whitehouse.gov/history/presidents/
  - www.presidentialavenue.com/gwb.cfm
  - www.homeofheroes.com/e-books/presidents/43_bush.html

Science

- ❑ longhorn (state large mammal)
- ❑ pecan tree (state tree)
- ❑ bluebonnet (state flower)
- ❑ prairie chicken
  - www.enchantedlearning.com/painting/birds.shtml
- ❑ blue topaz (state gem)
- ❑ prairie dog
  - *The Friendly Prairie Dog* – Denise Casey
  - *Zoo Guide*, page 75
- ❑ armadillo (state small animal)
  - *Zoo Guide*, page 77
- ❑ tornadoes
  - *Tornadoes* – Arlene Erlbach
  - *Tornado Alert* – Franklyn M. Branley
  - *Tornado* – Stephen Kramer
  - *Do Tornadoes Really Twist?* - Melvin and Gilda Berger, pages 4-23

Literature

- ❑ *Texas Tomboy* – Lois Lenski (RA)
- ❑ *Old Yeller* – Fred Gipson (RA)
- ❑ *The Day the Circus Came to Lone Tree* – Glen Rounds
- ❑ *Cowpokes* – Caroline Stutson
- ❑ *Saving Sweetness* – Diane Stanley
- ❑ *Raising Sweetness* – Diane Stanley

Language Arts

Preamble to the State Constitution:

Humbly invoking the blessings of Almighty God, the people of the State of Texas, do ordain and establish this Constitution.

1. Refer to Language Arts Guide starting on page 8.
2. Write a story about the Alamo.
3. Write a story about a tornado.

Character

Adopted in 1930, the motto - *Friendship* - was derived from *Tejas,* the Spanish pronunciation of a Caddo Indian word meaning "friends" or "allies." True friendship encompasses many character traits. True friends are willing to give of themselves and expect nothing in return. Being **friendly** and **hospitable** is the starting place of a relationship.

- **Friendliness** – The temper and disposition of a friend; kindness; favorableness; disposition to promote the good of another.
- **Hospitality** – Receiving and entertaining others with kindness and without reward; kindness to strangers and guests.

State Flag Pledge

Honor the Texas flag; I pledge allegiance to thee,
Texas, one and indivisible.

Activities

1. Color or label a map of Texas.
2. Label the Rio Grande on a map of the United States.
3. Go to http://www.kidzone.ws/geography/usa/ for printable flag and state symbol coloring pages.
4. Prepare a meal in *Eat Your Way Through the U.S.A.* from the state of Texas.
5. Listen to the song "The Yellow Rose of Texas."
6. Have a tornado drill.
7. Drink Dr. Pepper.

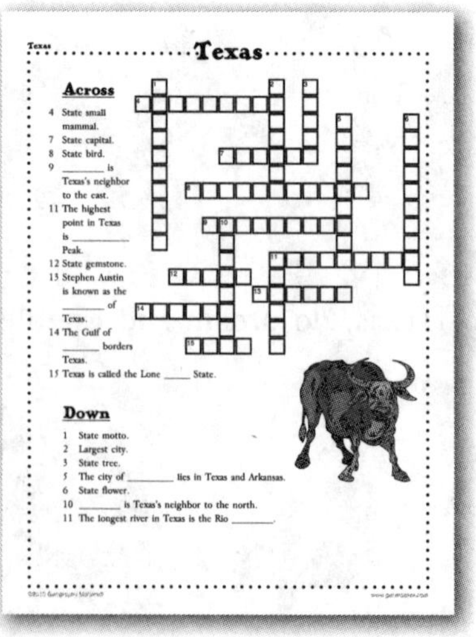

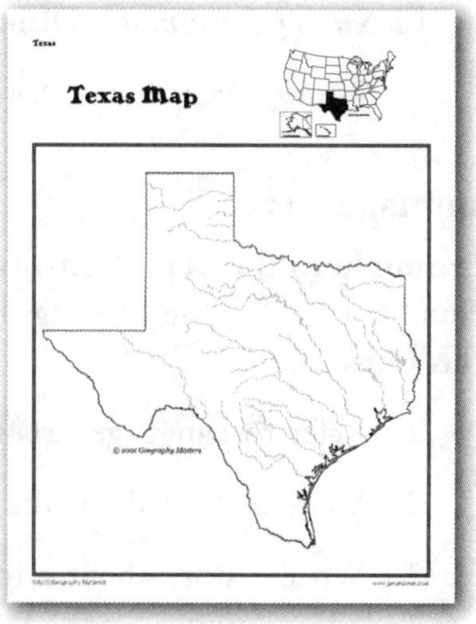

Utah

Beehive State

Although Utah became part of the United States in 1848 by the Treaty of Guadalupe Hidalgo, which ended the Mexican War, it was not granted statehood until January 4, 1896, when it became the 45th state. Congress named the territory "Utah" in 1850 after the Ute tribe that lived in the region. Utah is known as the Beehive State after the Mormon word *deseret,* which means "honeybee" and stands for hard work and industry. Salt Lake City is the capital of Utah.

The flag of Utah was adopted in 1913. The beehive on the shield represents industry. The sego lilies symbolize the time that Mormon settlers ate lily bulbs to avoid starvation. *Industry* is the state motto, and 1847 is the year that Mormons first came to Utah.

Utah has colorful canyons and snow-covered mountains. Wind and rain have eroded rock into arches and natural bridges. Deserts cover much of the state, and western Utah is one of the driest areas in the country. The Rocky Mountains rise in the northeastern portion of the state. Great Salt Lake is the largest natural lake west of the Mississippi. The salt concentration is four to seven times greater than the ocean, so high that swimmers float like corks.

Interesting Facts:

- Completion of the world's first transcontinental railroad was celebrated at Promontory, where the Central Pacific and Union Pacific Railroads met on May 10, 1869. It is now known as Golden Spike National Historic Site.
- Levan is "navel" spelled backwards. It is so named because it is in the middle of Utah.
- Annual precipitation varies from less than five inches in Utah's arid Great Salt Lake Desert to more than 60 inches in the northern mountain ranges.

General Reference

- ❑ *Utah* – Paul Joseph
- ❑ *Utah Facts and Symbols* – Kathy Feeney
- ❑ *Utah* – Karen Sirvaitis (contains evolution)

Geography

- ❑ Zion National Park
  - *Zion National Park* – David L. Petersen
- ❑ Bryce Canyon
- ❑ Great Salt Lake
- ❑ Arches National Park

History & Biographies

- ❑ Promontory Point
- ❑ John Moses Browning
- ❑ Philo Farnsworth

Science

- ❑ Utah juniper
- ❑ sea gull (state bird)
  - *Gulls...Gulls...Gulls* – Gail Gibbons
  - www.enchantedlearning.com/painting/birds.shtml
  - http://www.coloring.ws/birds.htm
- ❑ sego lily (state flower)
- ❑ copper (state mineral)
- ❑ bobcats
  - *Bobcat* – Jalma Barrett
  - *Zoo Guide*, page 161

Literature

- ❑ *Grandfather's Gold Watch* – Louise Garff Hubbard
- ❑ *Blaze and the Lost Quarry* – C. W. Anderson

Language Arts

Preamble to the State Constitution:
Grateful to Almighty God for life and liberty, we, the people of Utah, in order to secure and perpetuate the principles of free government, do ordain and establish this CONSTITUTION.

1. Refer to Language Arts Guide starting on page 8.

Character

Adopted in 1959, the motto – *Industry* - is associated with the symbol of the beehive. The motto is a tribute to the early settlers who had to rely on their own industry in order to survive.

The new trait is **curiosity**. Curiosity sometimes has a negative connotation; however, it can be a very beneficial quality. Many inventions and discoveries were made by curious people. It is important to distinguish the difference between being curious and being nosy. Curiosity relates to how things work or why things are done a certain way. Nosiness is wanting to be involved in others' business and know everything about them.

- **Curiosity** – A strong desire to see something novel, or to discover something unknown, either by research or inquiry; a desire to gratify the senses with a sight of what is new or unusual, or to gratify the mind with new discoveries.

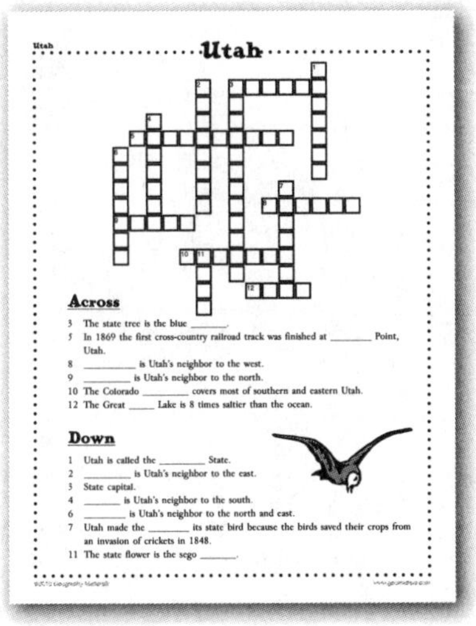

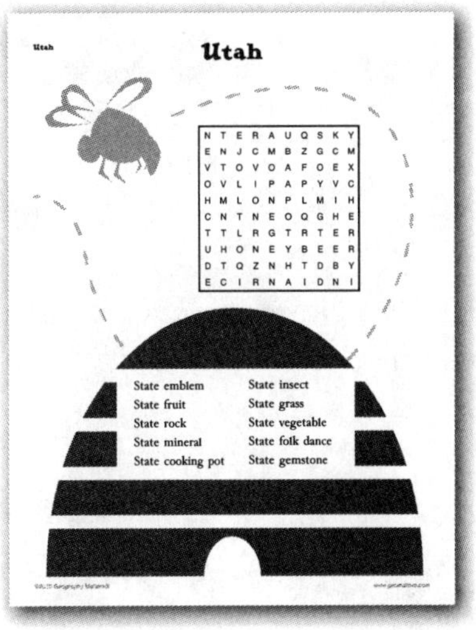

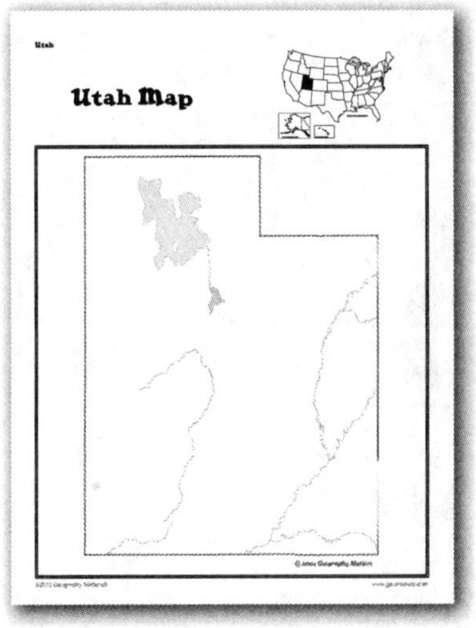

Activities

1. Color or label a state map of Utah.
2. Label the Great Salt Lake on a map of the United States.
3. Go to http://www.kidzone.ws/geography/usa/ for printable flag and state symbol coloring pages.
4. Prepare a meal in *Eat Your Way Through the U.S.A.* from the state of Utah.
5. Visit a bee keeper.

Vermont

Green Mountain State

Famous for spectacular colors of autumn foliage, Vermont became the 14th state on March 4, 1791. The name "Vermont" comes from two French words – *vert*, meaning "green," and *mont*, which means "mountain." Montpelier is the state capital.

The state flag, adopted in 1923, bears the Vermont coat of arms and shows a view of the Green Mountains. The cow and sheaves of wheat represent dairy and agriculture.

The Green Mountains run the entire length of central Vermont and divide the state into eastern and western sections. In addition to the Green Mountains, Vermont has many other mountains and hills, including the Taconic Mountains and Granite Hills. Vermont is the only New England state that does not have a border formed by the Atlantic Ocean. However, water does border half the state. The Connecticut River forms Vermont's entire eastern border, and Lake Champlain makes up half of the western border.

Interesting Facts:

- Ben & Jerry's Ice Cream factory is in Waterbury.
- Ben & Jerry's Ice Cream gives their ice cream waste to local farmers, who use it to feed their hogs. The hogs seem to like all of the flavors except Mint Oreo.
- Montpelier, Vermont, is the smallest state capital in the U.S.
- Until 1996, Vermont was the only state without a Wal-Mart.
- President Calvin Coolidge was the only U.S. president born on the Fourth of July.

General Reference

- ❑ *Vermont* – Paul Joseph
- ❑ *Vermont Facts and Symbols* – Kathy Feeney
- ❑ www.sec.state.vt.us/kids/index.html

Geography

- ❑ Green Mountains

History & Biographies

- ❑ Chester A. Arthur
  - www.whitehouse.gov/history/presidents/
- ❑ Calvin Coolidge
  - www.whitehouse.gov/history/presidents/
  - www.calvin-coolidge.org
- ❑ Wilson Bentley
  - *Snowflake Bentley* – Jacqueline Briggs Martin
- ❑ Norman Rockwell

Science

- ❑ hermit thrush (state bird)
  - http://www.coloring.ws/birds.htm
- ❑ sugar maple (state tree)
  - *Maple Trees* – Marcia S. Freeman
  - *Maple Tree* – Millicent E. Selsam
- ❑ maple syrup
  - *Sugaring Time* – Kathryn Lasky
  - *Maple Harvest* – Elizabeth Gemming
- ❑ red clover (state flower)
- ❑ talc (state mineral)
- ❑ timber
  - *Timber!* – William Jaspersohn

Literature

- ❑ *Sugaring* – Jessie Haas
- ❑ *Understood Betsy* – Dorothy Canfield (RA)
- ❑ *Faraway Summer* – Johanna Hurwitz
- ❑ *Least of All* – Carol Purdy
- ❑ *Jip: His Story* – Katherine Paterson

Language Arts

Preamble to the State Constitution:

1. Refer to Language Arts Guide starting on page 8.
2. Write a story about gathering sap and making maple syrup.

Character

The motto - *Freedom and unity* - was adopted with the state seal in 1779.The motto may have been adopted due to a desire by Vermonters to be free and united, or more likely, due to the desire that individual states should be free, but united. It has been suggested that this motto may have been the verbal source for the "Liberty and Union" speech of Daniel Webster. We have already discussed the meanings of freedom and unity. In order to have a free nation, the citizens must have **integrity** and **reverence** for authority.

- **Integrity** – The entire unimpaired state of anything, particularly of the mind; moral soundness or purity; incorruptness; uprightness; honesty. Integrity comprehends the whole moral character, but has a special reference to uprightness in mutual dealings, transfers of property, and agencies for others.
- **Reverence** – Fear mingled with respect, esteem, and affection.

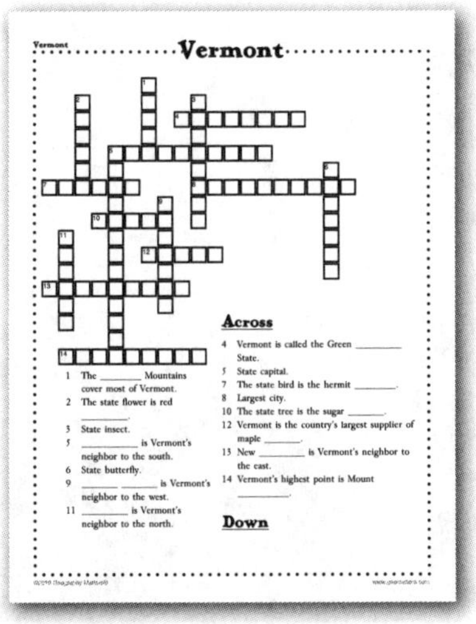

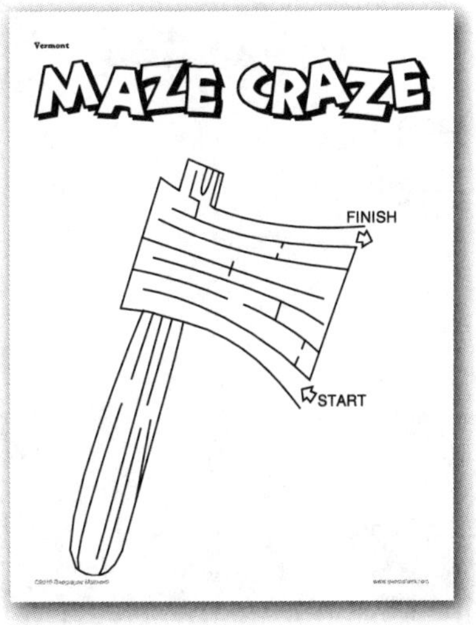

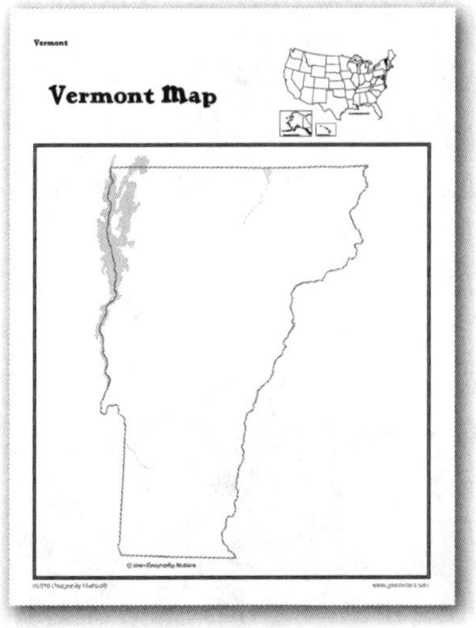

Activities

1. Color or label a map of Vermont.
2. Label the Green Mountains on a map of the United States.
3. Go to http://www.kidzone.ws/geography/usa/ for printable flag and state symbol coloring pages.
4. Prepare a meal in *Eat Your Way Through the U.S.A.* from the state of Vermont.
5. Eat Ben & Jerry's Ice Cream.
6. Paint in the style of Norman Rockwell.

Virginia

Old Dominion

Also known as the "Mother of Presidents" and the "Mother of States, "Virginia was the 10th state to join the Union, on June 25, 1788. Virginia was named for Queen Elizabeth I of England, who was known as the "Virgin Queen." Historians believe the name was suggested by Sir Walter Raleigh in 1584. Virginia was given the nickname Old Dominion by King Charles II because it remained loyal to the crown during the English Civil War of the mid-1600s. Virginia's capital is Richmond.

The flag of Virginia was designed and first used in 1861 but was not officially adopted until 1930. The figures represent Virtue triumphant over Tyranny. The Latin motto translates as "Thus always to tyrants."

Along Virginia's western border a series of parallel mountain ridges extend northeast and southwest. The Great Valley, a series of separate river valleys, lies in this region. The largest of these is the beautiful Shenandoah Valley. Central Virginia is covered with gently rolling plains, rivers, and streams. Eastern Virginia is bordered by the Atlantic Ocean and Chesapeake Bay. This lowland region has many salt marshes and swamps.

Interesting Facts:

- Virginia is the birthplace of eight U.S. presidents: George Washington, Thomas Jefferson, James Madison, James Monroe, William Henry Harrison, John Tyler, Zachary Taylor, and Woodrow Wilson.
- Six Presidents' wives were born in Virginia: Martha Washington, Martha Jefferson, Rachel Jackson, Letitia Tyler, Ellen Arthur, and Edith Wilson.
- Seven Presidents are buried in Virginia: George Washington, Thomas Jefferson, James Madison, James Monroe, John Tyler, William H. Taft, and John F. Kennedy.
- All or part of eight states were formed from land once claimed by Virginia. These states are Illinois, Indiana, Kentucky, Michigan, Minnesota, Ohio, West Virginia, and Wisconsin.
- Bristol is legally two cities, but they share the same main street - one in Virginia and one in Tennessee, each with its own government and city services.

General Reference

- ❑ *Virginia* – Paul Joseph
- ❑ *Virginia Facts and Symbols* – Bill McAuliffe
- ❑ *Virginia* – Karen Sirvaitis (contains evolution)

Geography

- ❑ Blue Ridge Mountains
- ❑ Shenandoah Valley

History & Biographies

- ❑ George Washington
    - *George Washington* – Lola M. Schaefer
    - *George Washington* – Garnet Jackson
    - *Young George Washington* – Andrew Woods
    - http://members.enchantedlearning.com/history/us/pres/washington/cloze/
    - www.whitehouse.gov/history/presidents/
    - www.mountvernon.org
- ❑ Thomas Jefferson
    - *Profiles from History* - Volume 1, pages 123-130
    - *Young Thomas Jefferson* – Francene Sabin
    - *Meet Thomas Jefferson* – Marvin Barrett
    - www.whitehouse.gov/history/presidents/
    - www.monticello.org
- ❑ John Smith
    - *Profiles from History* - Volume 1, pages 53-60
- ❑ Pocahontas
    - *Profiles from History* - Volume 1, pages 69-77
- ❑ James Monroe
    - *James Monroe: Good Neighbor Boy* – Mabel Cleland Widdemer
    - www.whitehouse.gov/history/presidents/
- ❑ William Harrison
    - *William Henry Harrison: Young Tippecanoe* – Howard Peckham
    - www.whitehouse.gov/history/presidents/
    - www.presidentialavenue.com/wh.cfm
- ❑ Zachary Taylor
    - *Zack Taylor: Young Rough and Ready* – Katharine E. Wilkie
    - www.whitehouse.gov/history/presidents/
    - www.presidentialavenue.com/zt.cfm
- ❑ Woodrow Wilson
    - *Woodrow Wilson: Boy President* – Helen Albee Monsell
    - www.whitehouse.gov/history/presidents/

- www.presidentialavenue.com/ww.cfm
- www.woodrowwilson.org

❑ Cyrus McCormick

- *Cyrus McCormick: Farmer Boy* – Lavinia Dobler

❑ Robert E. Lee

- *Robert E. Lee: Brave Leader* – Rae Bains
- *Robert E. Lee: Boy of Old Virginia* – Helen Albee Monsell

Science

❑ dogwood (state tree & flower)

❑ purple martin

❑ apophyllite

❑ hay

- *The Story of Hay* – Geoffrey Patterson

Literature

❑ *George Washington's Mother* – Jean Fritz

❑ *Shenandoah Noah* – Jim Aylesworth

❑ *The Blue Hill Meadows* – Cynthia Rylant (RA)

❑ *Misty of Chincoteague* – Marguerite Henry (RA)

Language Arts

Preamble to the State Constitution:
A declaration of rights made by the good people of Virginia in the exercise of their sovereign powers, which rights do pertain to them and their posterity, as the basis and foundation of government.

1. Refer to Language Arts Guide starting on page 8.

Character

The state motto - *Thus always to tyrants* - was adopted in 1776 as part of the state seal. The motto was recommended by George Mason to symbolize victory over tyranny.

As citizens of America we should **grateful** for the liberty and freedoms our forefathers fought and died to obtain. We also must be **discerning** of the times and remain ever watchful to guard our liberty and freedom. Our children should learn to be grateful for all the many blessings bestowed upon them.

- **Gratefulness** – Having a due sense of benefits; being kindly disposed towards one from whom a favor has been received.
- **Discernment** - Seeing or understanding the difference; making distinction; as, discern between good and evil, truth and falsehood.

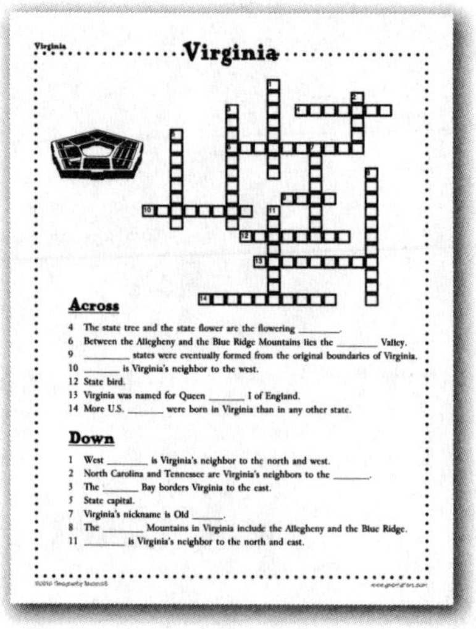
Virginia

Virginia

Across

4 The state tree and the state flower are the flowering _______.
6 Between the Allegheny and the Blue Ridge Mountains lies the _______ Valley.
9 _______ states were eventually formed from the original boundaries of Virginia.
10 _______ is Virginia's neighbor to the west.
12 State bird.
13 Virginia was named for Queen _______ I of England.
14 More U.S. _______ were born in Virginia than in any other state.

Down

1 West _______ is Virginia's neighbor to the north and west.
2 North Carolina and Tennessee are Virginia's neighbors to the _______.
3 The _______ Bay borders Virginia to the east.
5 State capital.
7 Virginia's nickname is Old _______.
8 The _______ Mountains in Virginia include the Allegheny and the Blue Ridge.
11 _______ is Virginia's neighbor to the north and east.

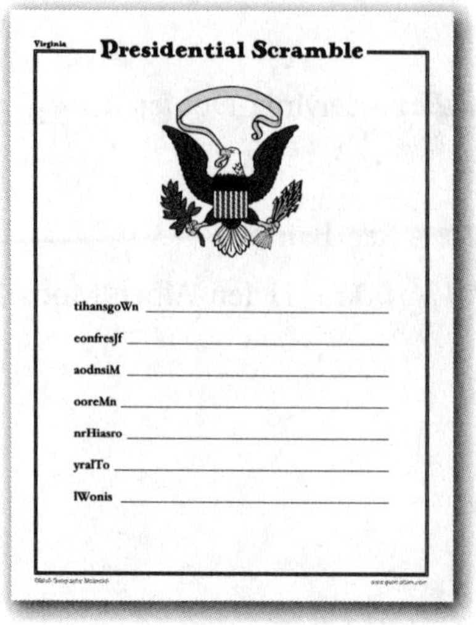
Virginia

Presidential Scramble

tihansgoWn
confresJf
aodnsiM
ooreMn
nrHiasro
yralTo
lWonis

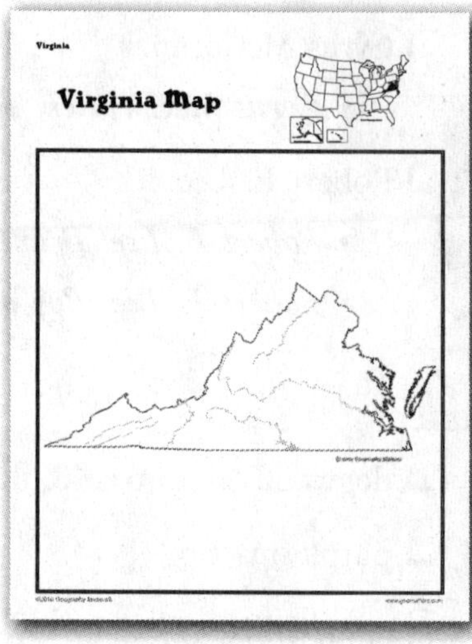
Virginia

Virginia Map

State Flag Pledge

I salute the flag of Virginia, with reverence and patriotic devotion
to the "Mother of States and Statesmen" which it represents –
the "Old Dominion," where liberty and independence were born.

Activities

1. Color or label a map of Virginia.
2. Label the Blue Ridge Mountains and the Shenandoah Valley on a map of the United States.
3. Go to http://www.kidzone.ws/geography/usa/ for printable flag and state symbol coloring pages.
4. Prepare a meal in *Eat Your Way Through the U.S.A.* from the state of Virginia.
5. Listen to the state song, "Carry Me Back to Old Virginia."

Washington

Evergreen State

Washington became the 42nd state on November 11, 1889. The only state to be named for a president, Washington was named in honor of George Washington. The capital of Washington is Olympia.

Washington is known as the Evergreen State, and this is reflected in its flag. It is the only state with a green flag. The state seal bearing a portrait of George Washington is in the center. The flag was adopted in 1925.

The Cascade Mountains divide Washington into two geographical regions. The western part of the state is lush and green. High mountains rise above evergreen forests and sparkling coastal waterways. The forests of the Olympic Peninsula are among the wettest places in the world. East of the Cascades, however, the region is semi-desert. The flat land stretches for long distances without a single tree.

Interesting Facts:

- Acting on the idea of Sonora Louise Smart Dodd of Spokane, Washington was the first state to celebrate Father's Day, on June 18, 1910.
- The Olympic Peninsula is home to one of America's few temperate rain forests.
- The northwestern most point in the contiguous United States is Cape Flattery on the Olympic Peninsula.
- The highest point in Washington is Mount Rainier.
- The world's first soft-serve ice cream machine was in an Olympia Dairy Queen.

General Reference

- ❑ *Washington* – Paul Joseph
- ❑ *Washington Facts and Symbols* – Emily McAuliffe

Geography

- ❑ Mount St. Helens
  - *Volcano: The Eruption and Healing of Mount St. Helens* – Patricia Lauber
- ❑ Mount Rainier
- ❑ Puget Sound

History & Biographies

- ❑ Marcus & Narcissa Whitman
  - *Narcissa Whitman: Pioneer Girl* – Ann Spence Warner
- ❑ Chester Carlson
  - *Book of Inventors* - Usborne, page 23
- ❑ Bill Gates
  - *Bill Gates: Billionaire Computer Whiz* – David Marshall

Science

- ❑ ravens
  - *Marvels of Creation, Breathtaking Birds* - Buddy and Kay Davis
  - www.daniellesplace.com/html/birdcrafts.html
- ❑ western hemlock (state tree)
- ❑ red maids
- ❑ petrified wood (state rock)
- ❑ apples (state fruit)
  - *Apple Tree* – Barrie Watts
  - *The Life and Times of the Apple* – Charles Micucci
  - *Apple Trees* – Dorothy Hinshaw Patent
  - *Picking Apples* – Gail Saunders-Smith
  - *Apple* - Angela Royston
  - *How Do Apples Grow* – Betsy Maestro
  - http://members.enchantedlearning.com/subjects/plants/cloze/apple/
- ❑ otters
  - *Otters* – Emilie U. Lepthien
  - *Zoo Guide*, page 85
  - www.coloring.ws/animals.html

Literature

- ❑ *The Apple Pie Tree* – Zoe Hall
- ❑ "Father, We Thank You" – Ralph Waldo Emerson

Language Arts

Preamble to the State Constitution:
We, the people of the State of Washington, grateful to the Supreme Ruler of the Universe for our liberties, do ordain this constitution.

1. Refer to Language Arts Guide starting on page 8.
2. Write a newspaper article about the eruption of Mount St. Helens.
3. Write a poem about an apple.

Character

The motto – *Alki* - a Chinook word for "by and by," first appeared on the territorial seal. The word *Alki* was first used by settlers when they named the settlement Alki Point New York. The new settlement didn't grow as quickly as its East Coast counterpart, however, so the name was changed to New York-Alki, which means "New York, by and by."

Settlers in the region dreamed of expansion and growth. Our children should dream big and work hard to achieve those dreams. To achieve success our children must remain **dedicated** to their ambitions, even in the midst of trials and setbacks.

- **Dedication** – Appropriating to any person or purpose; devoting wholly or chiefly to.

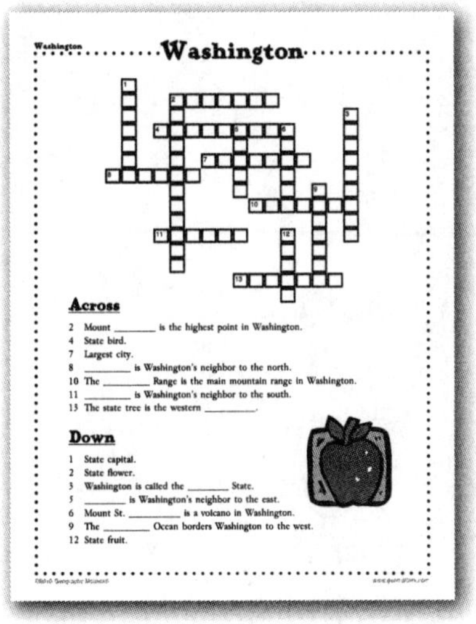

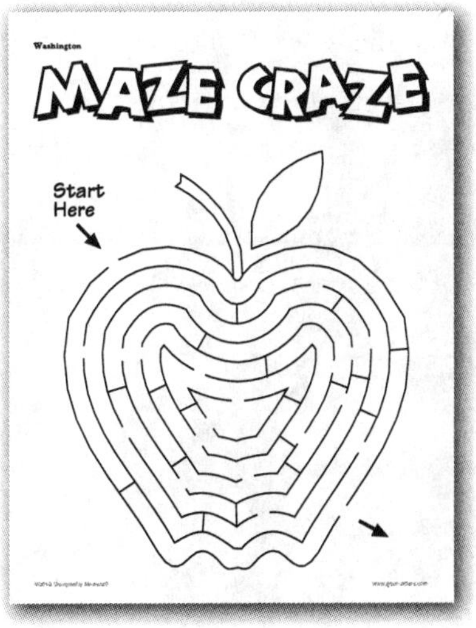

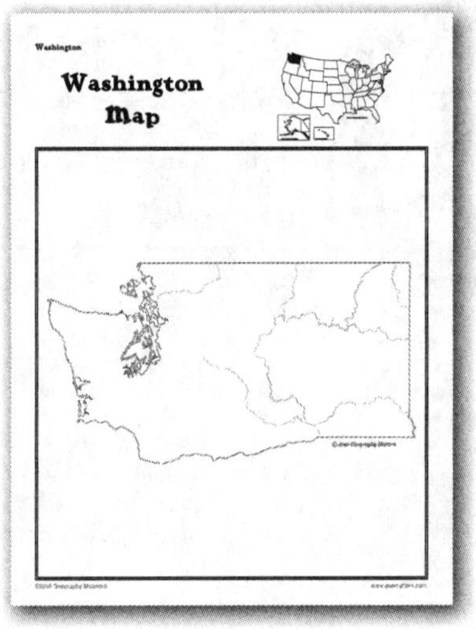

Activities

1. Color or label a map of Washington.
2. Label Mount Rainier, Puget Sound, and the Columbia River on a map of the United States.
3. Go to http://www.kidzone.ws/geography/usa/ for printable flag and state symbol coloring pages.
4. Prepare a meal in *Eat Your Way Through the U.S.A.* from the state of Washington.
5. Make a mosaic apple.
   - Tear red paper into small pieces and glue them all over a paper plate in mosaic fashion until the entire plate is covered.
   - Make a stem from brown paper or a brown pipe cleaner and a leaf from green paper. Glue to the top of the plate.
6. Go to http://familycrafts.about.com/od/applecrafts/ for other apple craft ideas.

West Virginia

Mountain State

West Virginia was part of Virginia until the Civil War. Virginia sided with the Confederacy, but the western counties remained loyal to the Union. They broke away from Virginia and formed their own government. West Virginia became the 35th state on June 20, 1863. Charleston is the capital of West Virginia.

The flag of West Virginia – the state coat of arms in a wreath of rhododendron, the state flower – was adopted in 1929. The rock and ivy symbolize stability and continuity. The rock bears the inscription "June 20, 1863," the date that West Virginia joined the Union. The farmer and miner represent the state's industries.

West Virginia, a region of forest-covered mountains, deep gorges, and mineral springs, has some of the steepest and most rugged land in the United States. In fact, there are no large areas of level ground. West Virginia is the highest state east of the Rocky Mountains.

Interesting Facts:

- Bluefield, with an elevation of 2,558 feet, is the highest town east of Denver.
- West Virginia is considered the southernmost northern state and the northernmost southern state.
- Mother's Day was first observed at Andrews Church in Grafton on May 10, 1908.
- West Virginia was the first state to have a sales tax. It became effective July 1, 1921.

General Reference

- ❑ *West Virginia* – Paul Joseph
- ❑ *West Virginia Facts and Symbols* – Kathy Feeney

Geography

- ❑ Appalachian Mountains

History & Biographies

- ❑ Appalachian culture
  - *Mist Over the Mountains: Appalachia and Its People* – Raymond Bial
- ❑ Hatfield & McCoy feud
- ❑ Chuck Yeager

Science

- ❑ blackgum
- ❑ turkey
  - *Marvels of Creation, Breathtaking Birds* - Buddy and Kay Davis
  - *Turkeys That Fly and Turkeys That Don't* – Allan Fowler
  - *All About Turkeys* – Jim Arnosky
  - *Zoo Guide*, page 159
  - www.enchantedlearning.com/painting/birds.shtml
  - http://members.enchantedlearning.com/subjects/birds/printouts/Turkeyprintout.shtml
  - http://members.enchantedlearning.com/subjects/birds/label/turkey/index.shtml
  - http://members.enchantedlearning.com/subjects/birds/colorbynumber/turkey.shtml
  - http://members.enchantedlearning.com/connectdots/turkey/
  - http://www.coloring.ws/birds.htm
- ❑ rhododendron (state flower)
- ❑ coal
  - *Coal* – Bill Gunston
- ❑ black bears (state animal)
  - *Black Bear* – Tom and Pat Leeson
  - *Zoo Guide*, page 25
  - www.coloring.ws/animals.html

Literature

- ❑ *The Rag Coat* – Lauren Mills
- ❑ *Appalachia: The Voices of Sleeping Birds* – Cynthia Rylant
- ❑ *Little Fur Family* – Margaret Wise Brown

Language Arts

West Virginia's constitution has no preamble.

1. Refer to Language Arts Guide starting on page 8.

Character

West Virginia's state motto - *Mountaineers are always free* - was proposed by Joseph H. DisDebar, who also designed the state seal.

When we think of mountaineers, we think of **strong**, **adventurous** people. Children in modern society have a very easy life compared to other times in our history. Our children need to learn inner strength so that when hard times come, they don't give up and quit. Teaching our children to be adventurous and explore new areas in their lives helps them gain confidence.

- **Strength** – Power of mind; intellectual force; soundness.
- **Adventurousness** – Inclination or willingness to encounter danger; boldness; daring; courage.

State Flag Pledge

I pledge allegiance to the flag of West Virginia,
which serves as a constant reminder that
"Mountaineers Are Always Free,"
which stands as a symbol of her majestic mountains,
fertile forests, rich veins of coal, and the pride of her people.

Activities

1. Color or label a map of West Virginia.
2. Label the Appalachian Mountains on a map of the United States.
3. Go to http://www.kidzone.ws/geography/usa/ for printable flag and state symbol coloring pages.
4. Prepare a meal in *Eat Your Way Through the U.S.A.* from the state of West Virginia.
5. Make a model Appalachian log cabin. For instructions go to www.craftsforkids.com/projects/cinnamon_log_cabin.htm.

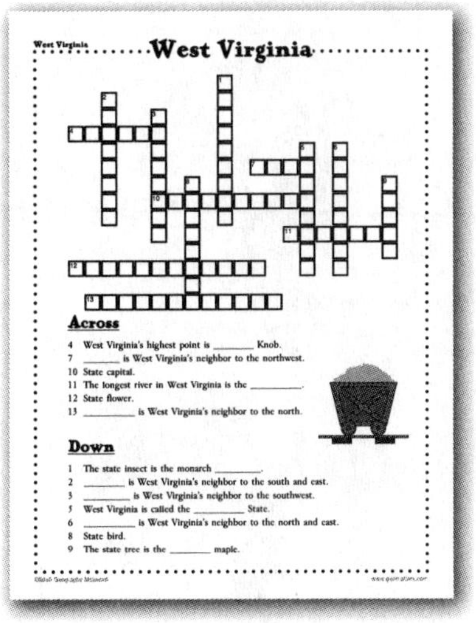

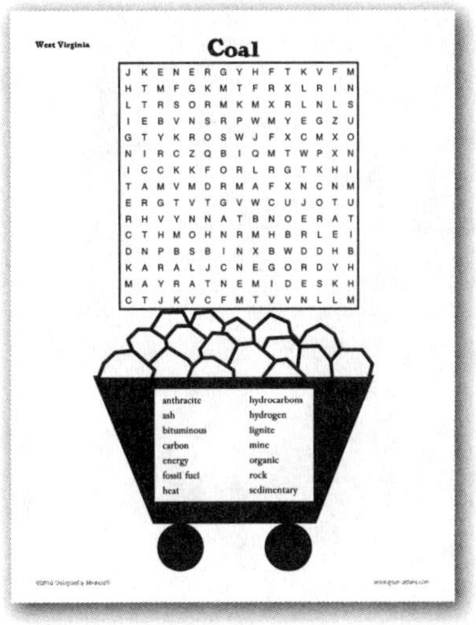

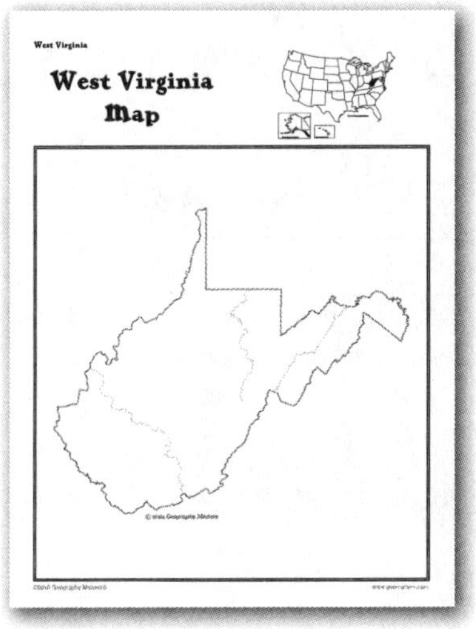

Wisconsin

Badger State

Often referred to as "America's Dairyland," Wisconsin was granted statehood on May 25, 1848, making it the 30th state. The name "Wisconsin" has two possible sources, both from the Ojibwa language. The first, ***ouisconsin***, means "the gathering of waters." The second, ***wishkonsing***, means "place of the beavers." Madison is the capital of Wisconsin.

The state flag of Wisconsin was adopted in 1913 and modified in 1981 to add the state name and the year 1848, the year of statehood. The sailor and miner represent Wisconsin's agriculture, mining, manufacturing, and navigation. The horn of plenty symbolizes prosperity. The pyramid of pig lead stands for the state's mineral wealth. The badger represents Wisconsin's nickname.

With Lake Michigan to the east, Lake Superior to the north, and the Mississippi and St. Croix Rivers forming its western border, Wisconsin is nearly surrounded by water. A land of rolling hills, ridges, and fertile plains and valleys, Wisconsin was once covered with forests. Farms now cover much of the countryside. Wisconsin generally has warm summers and long, severe winters.

Interesting Facts:

- In 1882, the world's first hydroelectric plant began in Appleton.
- Wisconsin has 7,446 streams and rivers. End-to-end they would stretch 26,767 miles - that is more than enough to circle the globe at the equator.
- The Republican Party was founded in Ripon in 1854.

General Reference

- ❑ *Wisconsin* – Paul Joseph
- ❑ *Wisconsin Facts and Symbols* – Emily McAuliffe
- ❑ www.statesymbolsusa.org/Wisconsin/WisconsinSymbols.html
- ❑ www.wisconsin.gov/state/core/kids_page.html

Geography

- ❑ Lake Michigan

History & Biographies

- ❑ Laura Ingalls Wilder
  - *Meet Laura Ingalls Wilder* – S. Ward
  - *Laura Ingalls Wilder* – Mae Woods
  - *Laura Ingalls Wilder* – Alexandra Wallner
  - *Laura Ingalls Wilder* – Carol Greene

Science

- ❑ American basswood
- ❑ wood violet (state flower)
- ❑ American tree sparrow
  - www.enchantedlearning.com/painting/birds.shtml
- ❑ galena (state mineral)
- ❑ cows
  - *Baby Calf* – P. Mignon Hinds
  - *The Milk Makers* – Gail Gibbons
  - *Cows* – Sara Swan Miller (beginning on page 16)
  - *Milking Machines* – Hal Rogers
  - *Life on a Cattle Farm* – Judy Wolfman
  - *Milk: From Cow to Carton* – Aliki
  - http://www.kiddyhouse.com/Farm/Cows/
  - www.coloring.ws/animals.html
- ❑ badgers (state animal)
  - *Discovering Badgers* – Martin Banks
  - *Zoo Guide,* page 19
  - www.coloring.ws/animals.html
- ❑ forest
  - *Geography From A to Z,* page 18
  - *Wonders of the Forest* – Francene Sabin
  - *Our Living Forests* – Allan Fowler
  - *I Can Be a Forest Ranger* – Carol Greene
  - *How the Forest Grew* – William Jaspersohn

Literature

- ❑ *Minnie and Moo Go to the Moon* – Denys Cazet
- ❑ *Badger's Bad Mood* – Hiawyn Oram
- ❑ *First Farm in the Valley* – Anne Pellowski (RA)
- ❑ *Thimble Summer* – Elizabeth Enright (RA)
- ❑ *Rascal* – Sterling North (RA)
- ❑ *Caddie Woodlawn* – Carol Brink (RA)
- ❑ *Little House in the Big Woods* – Laura Ingalls Wilder (RA)
- ❑ *Summertime in the Big Woods* – adapted from the Little House Books by Laura Ingalls Wilder
- ❑ *Dance at Grandpa's* – adapted from the Little House Books by Laura Ingalls Wilder
- ❑ *The Deer in the Wood* – adapted from the Little House Books by Laura Ingalls Wilder
- ❑ *Going to Town* – adapted from the Little House Books by Laura Ingalls Wilder
- ❑ *Winter Days in the Big Woods* – adapted from the Little House Books by Laura Ingalls Wilder
- ❑ *Going West* – adapted from the Little House Books by Laura Ingalls Wilder
- ❑ *Blaze and the Forest Fire* – C. W. Anderson

Language Arts

Preamble to the State Constitution:
We, the people of Wisconsin, grateful to Almighty God for our freedom, in order to secure its blessings, form a more perfect government, insure domestic tranquility and promote the general welfare, do establish this Constitution.

1. Refer to Language Arts Guide starting on page 8.
2. Laura Ingalls Wilder wrote stories from her life. Have your child write a story from his own life.

Character

The motto – *Excelsior* – was selected when John Lathrop designed the new state seal in 1851. When Governor Dewey went to New York to have the seal engraved, he changed the motto to Forward. To make forward progress in any endeavor, one must not be lazy but remain **busy**.

- **Busyness** – Active employment with constant attention; being occupied without cessation.

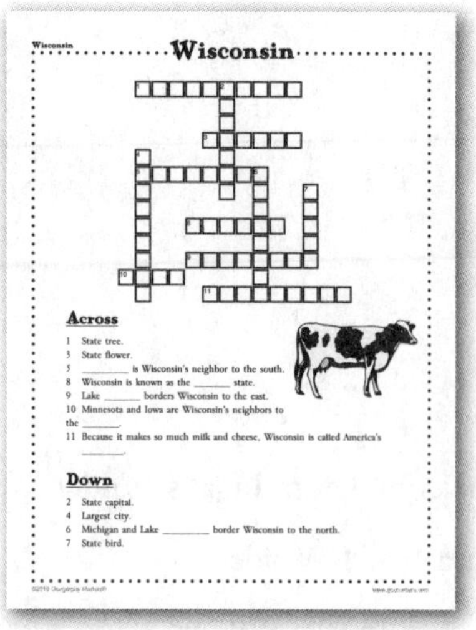

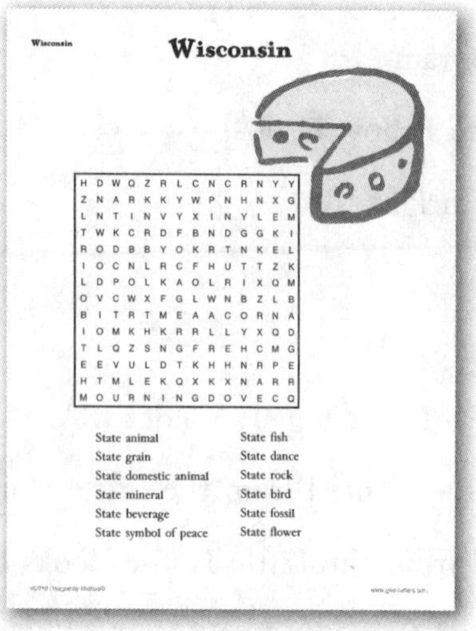

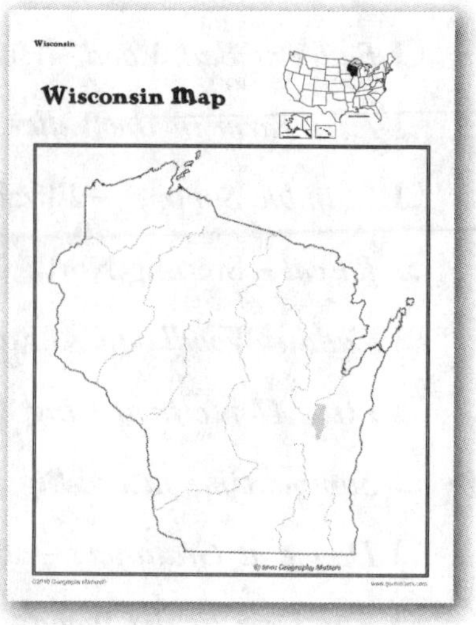

Activities

1. Color or label a map of Wisconsin.
2. Label Lake Michigan on a map of the United States.
3. Go to http://www.kidzone.ws/geography/usa/ for printable flag and state symbol coloring pages.
4. Prepare a meal in *Eat Your Way Through the U.S.A.* from the state of Wisconsin.
5. Learn the polka, the state dance.
6. Make butter.
   - Pour 1 cup heavy cream into a clean pint-sized jar; screw lid on tightly.
   - Shake, shake, shake until a ball of butter forms.
   - Remove butter from jar and allow to drain on a tea towel, cheesecloth, or very small-holed colander.
   - Salt butter and refrigerate.
   - Remaining liquid is buttermilk and may be used for cooking.
7. Sample different varieties of cheese.
8. Wisconsin is the leading producer of carrots. See http://coloringbookfun.com/vegy/index.htm.
9. For instructions on a chemistry experiment with milk, go to http://pbskids.org/zoom/activities/sci/plasticmilk.html.

Wyoming

Equality State

With more than 80% of its land devoted to ranching, Wyoming became the 44th state on July 10, 1890. The name "Wyoming" comes from a Delaware word meaning "upon the great plain." Wyoming women were the first in the nation to vote, hold public office, and serve on juries, earning the state the nickname the Equality State. The state capital is Cheyenne.

The flag of Wyoming emerged from a design competition and was adopted in 1917. The flag shows the state seal on a buffalo to represent the branding of livestock. On the seal, the woman and the motto symbolize the equal rights women have had in the state. The two men represent Wyoming's livestock and mining industries. The dates are those on which Wyoming became a territory and a state. The flag's red border symbolizes Native Americans and the blood of pioneers.

Wyoming is famous for the beauty of its mountains. The peaks of the Rocky Mountains tower over the landscape and provide the setting for the nation's oldest national park – Yellowstone. Not all of Wyoming is mountainous, though. Between the mountains lie broad, flat, treeless basins, some of which are dotted with buttes.

Interesting Facts:

- Devils Tower is a natural column of rock that stands 865 feet high.
- In 1870, Esther Morris became the country's first female justice of the peace.
- In 1924, Wyoming elected the nation's first woman governor, Nellie Taylor Ross.
- The Red Desert in south central Wyoming drains neither to the east nor to the west. The Continental Divide splits and goes around the desert on all sides, leaving the basin without normal drainage.

General Reference

- ❑ *Wyoming* – Paul Joseph
- ❑ *Wyoming Facts and Symbols* – Muriel L. Dubois
- ❑ *Wyoming* – Carlienne Frisch (contains evolution)
- ❑ www.wyoming.gov/kids.aspx

Geography

- ❑ Yellowstone
  - *Yellowstone National Park* – David Petersen
  - *Yellowstone's Cycle of Fire* – Frank Staub
  - http://www.nps.gov/yell/forkids/index.htm
- ❑ Red Desert
- ❑ Alpine tundra
  - *One Day in the Alpine Tundra* – Jean Craighead George

History & Biographies

- ❑ cowboys
  - *Life on the Ranch* – Bobbie Kalman
  - *Yippee–Yay! A Book About Cowboys and Cowgirls* – Gail Gibbons
  - *Cowboys* – Teri Martini
  - *Cowboy* – David H. Murdoch
  - *Cowboy Cooking* – Mary Gunderson
  - *A Cowboy in the Wild West* – Adam Woog
- ❑ Buffalo Bill Cody
  - *Buffalo Bill* – Dan Zadra
  - *Buffalo Bill and the Pony Express* – Eleanor Coerr
  - *Buffalo Bill* – Ingri & Edgar Parin d'Aulaire
  - *Buffalo Bill: Frontier Daredevil* – Augusta Stevenson
- ❑ Jim Bridger
  - *Jim Bridger* – Willard and Celia Luce
  - *Jim Bridger: Mountain Boy* – Gertrude Hecker Winders
- ❑ Red Cloud
- ❑ Washakie
- ❑ Richard "Dick" Cheney
  - *Dick Cheney* – Elaine Andrews

Science

- ❑ falcons
  - *The Peregrine Falcon* - Carol Greene (Preview page 13. It may be too graphic for some children.)
  - *Falcons Nest on Skyscrapers* – Priscilla Belz Jenkins
  - *Zoo Guide,* page 145
  - www.enchantedlearning.com/painting/birds.shtml
- ❑ plains cottonwood (state tree)
- ❑ Indian paintbrush (state flower)
- ❑ jade (state stone)
- ❑ lynx
  - *Lynx* – Jalma Barrett
  - *Hunter in the Snow: The Lynx* – Susan Bonners
  - www.coloring.ws/animals.html
- ❑ geyser
  - *Geography From A to Z,* page 19
  - *Letting Off Steam* – Linda Jacobs Altman
  - *Earth Science for Every Kid,* Experiment #24
  - http://www.nps.gov/yell/photosmultimedia/yellowstonelive.htm

Literature

- ❑ *Cowboys* – Glen Rounds
- ❑ *Four Dollars and Fifty Cents* – Eric A. Kimmel
- ❑ *Whitey and the Wild Horse* – Glen Rounds
- ❑ *True Heart* – Marissa Moss
- ❑ *A Fourth of July on the Plains* – Jean Van Leeuwen
- ❑ *Blaze and Thunderbolt* – C. W. Anderson

Language Arts

Preamble to the State Constitution:

We, the people of the State of Wyoming, grateful to God for our civil, political and religious liberties, and desiring to secure them to ourselves and perpetuate them to our posterity, do ordain and establish this Constitution.

1. Refer to Language Arts Guide starting on page 8.
2. Keep a journal of a cowboy on a cattle drive.
3. Write a story about a pioneer coming across Old Faithful.

Character

The motto - *Equal Rights* - was adopted in 1955. This refers to Wyoming being the first state to give women the right to vote. We have already studied being fair and just in relation to others. **Meekness** is a quality that is often overlooked or viewed as a weakness. In order to treat others equally, we must teach our children to be meek when dealing with the differences among individuals.

- **Meekness** – Softness of temper; mildness; gentleness; humility.

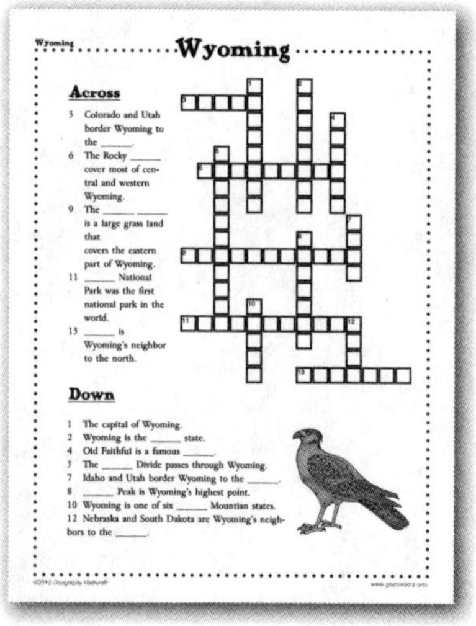
Wyoming

Wyoming

Across

3 Colorado and Utah border Wyoming to the ______.

6 The Rocky ______ cover most of central and western Wyoming.

9 The ______ is a large grass land that covers the eastern part of Wyoming.

11 ______ National Park was the first national park in the world.

13 ______ is Wyoming's neighbor to the north.

Down

1 The capital of Wyoming.

2 Wyoming is the ______ state.

4 Old Faithful is a famous ______.

5 The ______ Divide passes through Wyoming.

7 Idaho and Utah border Wyoming to the ______.

8 ______ Peak is Wyoming's highest point.

10 Wyoming is one of six ______ Mountain states.

12 Nebraska and South Dakota are Wyoming's neighbors to the ______.

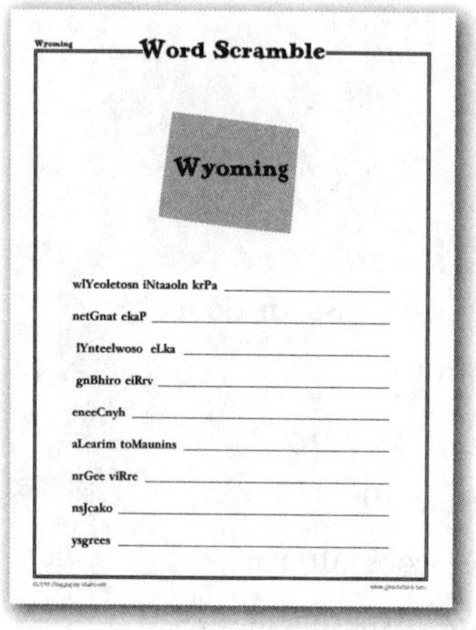
Wyoming

Word Scramble

Wyoming

wlYeoletosn iNtaaoln krPa ______

netGnat ekaP ______

lYnteelwoso eLka ______

gnBhiro eiRrv ______

eneeCnyh ______

aLearim toMaunins ______

nrGee viRre ______

nsJcako ______

ysgrees ______

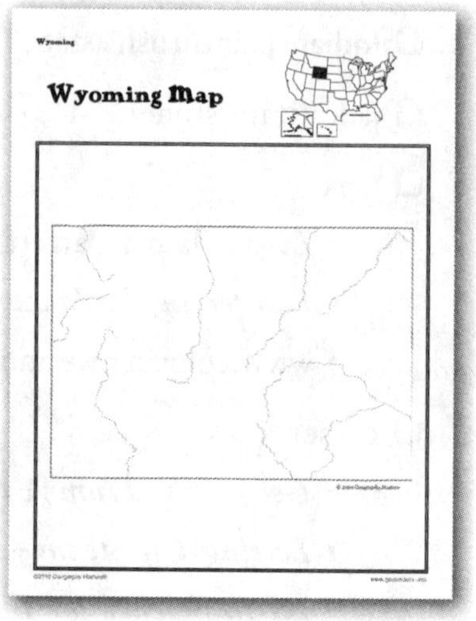
Wyoming

Wyoming Map

Activities

1. Color or label a map of Wyoming.
2. Color map of United States to show the range of the Alpine tundra.
3. Go to http://www.kidzone.ws/geography/usa/ for printable flag and state symbol coloring pages.
4. Prepare a meal in *Eat Your Way Through the U.S.A.* from the state of Wyoming.

Washington D.C.

The capital of our great nation, Washington, D.C., is one of the country's most majestic and historic cities. Also known as the District of Columbia, Washington, D.C. is the seat of our federal government. The President, Congress, Supreme Court, and a myriad of other federal employees work in Washington, D.C.

The red and white flag of the District of Columbia is based on a banner of the arms of the Washington family, which dates back to 1592, England. Congress adopted the flag in 1938.

Washington, D.C., one of the few cities in the world that was designed before it was built, lies in the southeastern United States between Maryland and Virginia. It is the only city in America that is not part of a state.

Interesting Facts:

- George Washington chose the site for the city in 1791.
- Pierre Charles L'Enfant, a French engineer, was hired to design the city.
- Washington, D.C., replaced Philadelphia as the nation's capital in 1800.
- The Capitol building is visible from almost every point in the city.
- The Smithsonian Institution is the world's largest museum complex. It is made up of fourteen museums and the National Zoo.
- The White House has served as the home and office of every U.S. President except George Washington.

General Reference

- ❑ *Washington, D.C.* – Anne Welsbacher
- ❑ *Washington, D.C. Facts and Symbols* – Kathy Feeney
- ❑ *Washington, D.C.* – Nancy Loewen
- ❑ *Washington, D.C.* – Joyce Johnston
- ❑ *Capital* – Lynn Curlee

Geography

- ❑ time zones
  - www.time.gov
  - http://tycho.usno.navy.mil/time.html

Buildings & Monuments

- ❑ Arlington National Cemetery and the Tomb of the Unknown Soldier
  - www.arlingtoncemetery.org
- ❑ Capitol building
  - *The U.S. Capitol* – Lola Schaefer
  - *The Story of the Capitol* – Marilyn Prolman
  - www.aoc.gov
  - www.senate.gov/vtour/
- ❑ Lincoln Memorial
  - *The Lincoln Memorial* – Lola Schaefer
- ❑ National Mall
  - *The National Mall* – Brendan January
  - *On the Mall in Washington D.C.* – Brent Ashabranner
- ❑ Naval Observatory
  - www.usno.navy.mil/
- ❑ Smithsonian Institute
  - www.si.edu
- ❑ Washington Monument
  - *The Washington Monument* – Lola Schaefer
  - http://members.enchantedlearning.com/history/us/monuments/washingtonmonument/
- ❑ White House
  - *The White House* – Lola Schaefer
  - *The White House* – Paula Guzzetti
  - *Woodrow the White House Mouse* – Peter W. Barnes
  - http://members.enchantedlearning.com/history/us/monuments/whitehouse/
  - www.whitehouse.gov (Please be careful when entering the White House web address. Using anything other than .gov can have distasteful results.)

History & Biographies

- ❑ American flag
  - *The American Flag* – Patricia Ryon Quiri
  - *The Flag of the United States* – Dennis B. Fradin
  - *Stars and Stripes: The Story of the American Flag* – Sarah L. Thompson
  - *Red, White, and Blue* – John Herman
  - *Stars & Stripes* – Leonard Everett Fisher
  - http://members.enchantedlearning.com/books/geography/usflag/
- ❑ Pledge of Allegiance
- ❑ Great Seal of the United States of America
  - http://members.enchantedlearning.com/crafts/books/julyfourth/Greatseal.shtml
- ❑ U.S. Postal Service
  - *The Post Office Book* – Gail Gibbons
  - *Postal Workers* – Paulette Bourgeois
  - www.usps.com/postalhistory/welcome.htm
- ❑ U.S. Mint
  - www.usmint.gov

The motto IN GOD WE TRUST was placed on United States coins largely because of the increased religious sentiment existing during the Civil War. Secretary of the Treasury Salmon P. Chase received many appeals from devout persons throughout the country urging that the United States recognize the deity on United States coins. From Treasury Department records, it appears that the first such appeal came in a letter dated November 13, 1861, written to Secretary Chase by the Rev. M. R. Watkinson, Minister of the Gospel from Ridleyville, Pennsylvania. It read:

> *Dear Sir:*
>
> *You are about to submit your annual report to the Congress respecting the affairs of the national finances.*
>
> *One fact touching our currency has hitherto been seriously overlooked. I mean the recognition of the Almighty God in some form on our coins.*
>
> *You are probably a Christian. What if our Republic were not shattered beyond reconstruction? Would not the antiquaries of succeeding centuries rightly reason from our past that we were a heathen nation? What I propose is that instead of the goddess of liberty we shall have next inside the 13 stars a ring inscribed with the words PERPETUAL UNION; within the ring the allseeing eye, crowned with a halo; beneath this eye the American flag, bearing in its field stars equal to the number of the States united; in the folds of the bars the words GOD, LIBERTY, LAW.*
>
> *This would make a beautiful coin, to which no possible citizen could object. This would relieve us from the ignominy of heathenism. This would place us openly under the Divine protection we have personally claimed. From my hearth I have felt our national shame in disowning God as not the least of our present national disasters.*
>
> *To you first I address a subject that must be agitated.*

As a result, Secretary Chase instructed James Pollock, Director of the Mint at Philadelphia, to prepare a motto, in a letter dated November 20, 1861:

Dear Sir:

No nation can be strong except in the strength of God, or safe except in His defense. The trust of our people in God should be declared on our national coins. You will cause a device to be prepared without unnecessary delay with a motto expressing in the fewest and tersest words possible this national recognition.

It was found that the Act of Congress dated January 18, 1837 prescribed that mottoes and devices that should be placed upon the coins of the United States. This meant that the mint could make no changes without the enactment of additional legislation by the Congress. In December 1863, the Director of the Mint submitted designs for a new one-cent coin, two-cent coin, and three-cent coin to Secretary Chase for approval. He proposed that upon the designs either OUR COUNTRY; OUR GOD or GOD, OUR TRUST should appear as a motto on the coins.

In a letter to the Mint Director on December 9, 1863, Secretary Chase stated:

I approve your mottoes, only suggesting that on that with the Washington obverse the motto should begin with the word OUR, so as to read OUR GOD AND OUR COUNTRY. And on that with the shield, it should be changed so as to read: IN GOD WE TRUST.

The Congress passed the Act on April 22, 1864. This legislation changed the composition of the one-cent coin and authorized the minting of the two-cent coin. The Mint Director was directed to develop the designs for these coins for final approval of the Secretary. IN GOD WE TRUST first appeared on the 1864 two-cent coin.

Another Act of Congress passed on March 3, 1865. It allowed the Mint Director, with the Secretary's approval, to place the motto on all gold and silver coins that "shall admit the inscription thereon." Under the Act, the motto was placed on the gold double-eagle coin, the gold eagle coin, and the gold half-eagle coin. It was also placed on the silver dollar coin, the half-dollar coin, and the quarter-dollar coin, and on the nickel three-cent coin beginning in 1866. Later, Congress passed the Coinage Act of February 12, 1873. It also said that the Secretary "may cause the motto IN GOD WE TRUST to be inscribed on such coins as shall admit of such motto."

❑ Francis Scott Key

- *Francis Scott Key* – Melissa Whitcraft
- *Francis Scott Key and the Star Spangled Banner* – Lynea Bowdish
- *Francis Scott Key: Poet and Patriot* – Lillie Patterson

❑ "The Star-Spangled Banner"

- *By the Dawn's Early Light* – Steven Kroll
- *The Star-Spangled Banner* – Deborah Kent

❑ Benjamin Banneker

- *What Are You Figuring Now?* – Jeri Ferris

❑ John Philip Sousa

- *John Philip Sousa* – Mike Venezia
- *John Philip Sousa: Marching Boy* – Ann Weil

Civics

- ☐ Constitution
  - *If You Were There When They Signed the Constitution* – Elizabeth Levy
  - *Shh! We're Writing the Constitution* – Jean Fritz
  - *The Story of the Constitution* – Marilyn Prolman
  - *The Bill of Rights* – Warren Colman
- ☐ government
  - http://bensguide.gpo.gov/
- ☐ bill becoming a law
  - *House Mouse, Senate Mouse* – Peter W. Barnes
- ☐ executive branch
  - *The President's Cabinet and How It Grew* – Nancy Winslow Parker
- ☐ legislative branch
  - *Congress* – Carol Greene
- ☐ judicial branch
  - *Supreme Court Book* – Paul J. Deegan
  - *The Supreme Court* – Carol Greene
  - *Meet My Grandmother: She's a Supreme Court Justice* – Lisa Tucker McElroy with Courtney O'Connor
  - *The Story of the FBI* – Jim Hargrove
- ☐ elections
  - *Voting and Elections* – Dennis B. Fradin
  - *America Votes* – Linda Granfield
  - *Woodrow for President* – Peter W. Barnes

Science

- ☐ bald eagle
  - *Zoo Guide*, page 113
  - *Marvels of Creation, Breathtaking Birds* - Buddy and Kay Davis
  - *Bald Eagles* – Emilie U. Lepthien
  - *Eagles* – Deborah Hodge
  - *Bald Eagle* – Gordon Morrison
  - www.enchantedlearning.com/painting/birds.shtml
  - http://members.enchantedlearning.com/subjects/birds/printouts/Eaglecoloring.shtml
- ☐ cherry tree
- ☐ American Beauty rose

- ❑ vivianite
- ❑ fireworks
  - *From Rock to Fireworks* – Gary W. Davis
  - *Fireworks: The Science, the Art, and the Magic* – Susan Kuklin

Literature

- ❑ *America: A Patriotic Primer* – Lynne Cheney
- ❑ *The Yearling* by Marjorie Rawlings
- ❑ *Duke Ellington: The Piano Prince and His Orchestra* – Andrea Davis Pinkney
- ❑ *When Marian Sang* – Pam Munoz Ryan

Language Arts

Preamble to Constitution of the United States:

We the people of the United States, in order to form a more perfect union, establish justice, insure domestic tranquility, provide for the common defense, promote the general welfare, and secure the blessings of liberty to ourselves and our posterity, do ordain and establish this Constitution for the United States of America.

1. Refer to Language Arts Guide starting on page 8.
2. Write a letter to the president.
3. Write a bill that you would like to become a law in your family.
4. Copy the Pledge of Allegiance.
5. Copy the Presidential Oath of Office.

Character

The motto - *Justice for all* - was adopted in 1871 as the first act passed by the District's first legislative assembly on August 3, 1871.

Review the traits discussed and have the children pick their favorite and give a presentation on the importance of that trait in the founding of our country.

Activities

1. Color or label a map of Washington, D.C.
2. Draw and label time zones on a map of the United States.
3. Label Washington D.C. on a map of the United States.
4. Memorize the Pledge of Allegiance.
5. Learn "The Star Spangled Banner."
6. Listen to the music of John Philip Sousa.

7. Sing "This Land Is Your Land" by Woody Guthrie.
8. Go on a field trip to your local post office. Mail the letter from Language Arts activity #2.
9. Make an American flag.
    - Cut a piece of cardboard into a rectangle big enough for six jumbo sticks to fit across.
    - Paint three jumbo sticks red and three white. Let dry.
    - Glue jumbo sticks onto cardboard with hot glue or regular glue. Hot glue works better.
    - Paint seven mini sticks blue and let dry.
    - Glue the sticks vertically in the top left corner of your flag.
    - Glue wooden stars in the blue portion of flag and let dry. Paint glue on stars, then apply silver glitter or use silver glitter glue/paint. Let dry.
    - If desired, glue a pipe cleaner on back for a hanger.
10. Go to http://familycrafts.about.com/od/birdprojects/ for an eagle craft idea.
11. Make a paper model of the U.S. Capitol Building. For a template go to http://papertoys.com/capitol.htm.
12. Hold a campaign and election.
13. Introduce the bill from Language Arts activity #3 into the "family legislature." Take it through the steps to be signed into law or be vetoed by the president (in this case Mom & Dad).

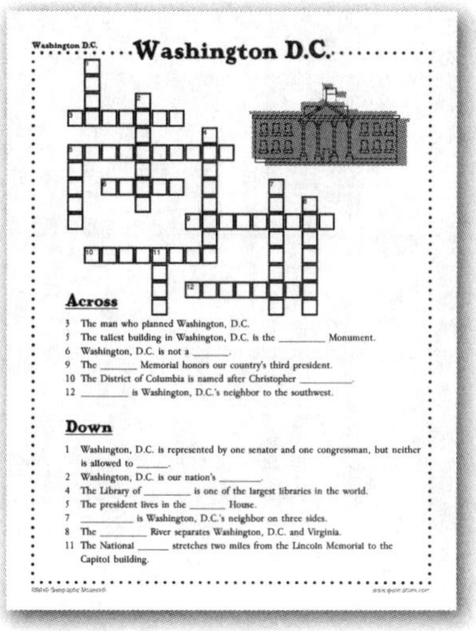

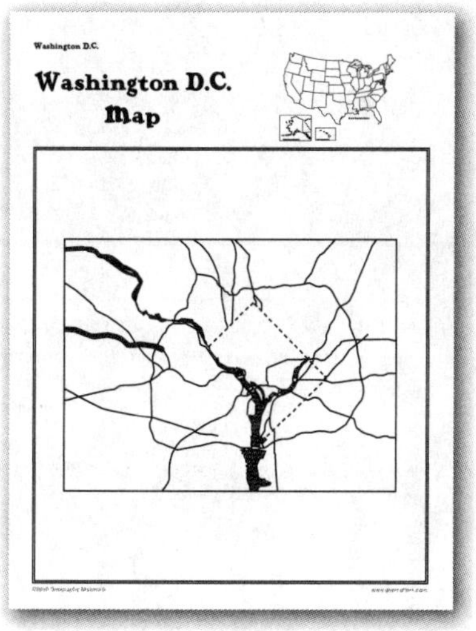

Appendix

Character Trait - A

Character trait:

Definition:

Draw a picture of something you can do to show this trait.

Character Trait -B

Character trait:

Definition:

Story characters that portray this trait:

Something I can do to demonstrate this trait:

State Report

____

Use this space for state map or picture.

State Nickname: ______________________________

Size: ______________________ **Rank:** __________

Population: ______________________ **Rank:** __________

Abbreviation: __________ **Became a state on** __________

Bird: ______________________ **Flower:** ______________________

Tree: ______________________ **Rock:** ______________________

Song: ______________________________

Governor: ______________________ **Capital:** ______________________

Motto: ______________________________

____

____

State Notebook

State Name ________________________

____

Color a map of the state, cut it out, and paste it above.

This state looks like a ________________________

The capital of this state is ________________________

Biography Report

What is my name? ____________________

When was I born? __________ **When did I die?** __________

Where did I live? ____________________

Who were my parents? ____________________

How many brothers and sisters did I have? ____________________

Whom did I marry? ____________________

How many children did we have? ____________________

What kind of work did I do? ____________________

____

Why am I important? ____________________

____

____

Why am I important? ____________________

____

____

What mistakes did I make? ____________________

____

____

What did you learn from me? ____________________

____

____

Animal Report

Name of the animal: ______________________________

Where does the animal live? ______________________________

What is its home like? ______________________________

____

What does it eat? ______________________________

____

This animal is awake during the: __________ **Day Night** __________

What kind of climate does this animal like? ______________________________

____

What special features did God give this animal? ______________________________

____

____

Draw a picture of this animal.

Geography Dictionary

word

Draw a picture of what the word means.

Recipes for Making Maps

Traditional salt dough map

2 parts flour

1 part salt

1 part water

Mix well. Add more water if crumbly.

Cookie Dough

Dough Recipe:

2 c. smooth peanut butter

2 1/2 c. powdered milk

2 1/2 c. powdered sugar

2 c. white corn syrup

Mix all ingredients together and put small portions on waxed paper.

Using the physical map found in your student atlas, place the dough or clay on a piece of cardboard and shape like the state or region you are studying. Tape or trace an outline map of the area on the cardboard for accuracy in forming the general shape of the state or region. Let dry overnight and paint, if desired. Use toothpicks with flags to label the capital, rivers, mountain ranges, etc. and push into map before it dries, or leave unlabeled.

Materials: dough recipe, waxed paper, blue icing, green sprinkles, clear sprinkles, small chocolate chips, red candy strips (licorice strings), M&Ms.

Use these symbols:

blue icing - lakes and oceans

green sprinkles - plains

clear sprinkles - deserts

chocolate chips - mountains

red candy strips - rivers

M&Ms - capitals

**The above information was taken from www.geomatters.com and www.tapestryofgrace.com.

Official State Symbols

State	State Bird	State Tree	State Flower
Alabama	yellowhammer	long leaf pine	camellia
Alaska	willow ptarmigan	sitka spruce	forget-me-not
Arizona	cactus wren	palo verde	saguaro cactus blossom
Arkansas	mockingbird	loblolly pine	apple blossom
California	quail	California redwood	California poppy
Colorado	lark bunting	blue spruce	columbine
Connecticut	robin	white oak	mountain laurel
Delaware	blue hen chicken	American holly	peach blossom
Florida	mockingbird	sabal palm	orange blossom
Georgia	brown thrasher	live oak	Cherokee rose
Hawaii	nene	candlenut	hibiscus
Idaho	mountain bluebird	western white pine	syringa
Illinois	cardinal	white oak	violet
Indiana	cardinal	yellow poplar	peony
Iowa	eastern goldfinch	oak	wild rose
Kansas	western meadowlark	cottonwood	sunflower
Kentucky	cardinal	tulip poplar	goldenrod
Louisiana	brown pelican	bald cypress	magnolia
Maine	chickadee	white pine	white pine cone & tassel
Maryland	Baltimore oriole	white oak	black-eyed Susan
Massachusetts	chickadee	American elm	mayflower
Michigan	robin	white pine	apple blossom
Minnesota	common loon	red pine	lady's slipper
Mississippi	mockingbird	magnolia	magnolia
Missouri	bluebird	flowering dogwood	hawthorn

Official State Symbols

State	State Bird	State Tree	State Flower
Montana	western meadowlark	ponderosa pine	bitterroot
Nebraska	western meadowlark	cottonwood	goldenrod
Nevada	mountain bluebird	single-leaf pinon	sagebrush
New Hampshire	purple finch	paper birch	purple lilac
New Jersey	eastern goldfinch	red oak	purple violet
New Mexico	roadrunner	pinyon pine	yucca flower
New York	bluebird	sugar maple	rose
North Carolina	cardinal	long leaf pine	flowering dogwood
North Dakota	western meadowlark	American elm	wild prairie rose
Ohio	cardinal	buckeye	carnation
Oklahoma	scissor-tailed flycatcher	redbud	Oklahoma rose
Oregon	western meadowlark	Douglas fir	Oregon grape
Pennsylvania	ruffed grouse	hemlock	mountain laurel
Rhode Island	Rhode Island red	red maple	violet
South Carolina	Carolina wren	palmetto	yellow jessamine
South Dakota	ring-necked pheasant	white spruce	American pasqueflower
Tennessee	mockingbird	yellow-poplar	iris
Texas	mockingbird	pecan	bluebonnet
Utah	sea gull	blue spruce	sego lily
Vermont	hermit thrush	sugar maple	red clover
Virginia	cardinal	flowering dogwood	flowering dogwood
Washington	willow goldfinch	western hemlock	pink rhododendron
West Virginia	cardinal	sugar maple	coast rhododendron
Wisconsin	robin	sugar maple	wood violet
Wyoming	meadowlark	cottonwood	Indian paintbrush
Washington DC	wood thrush	scarlet oak	American beauty rose

State Science Chart

science topics studied with each state

State	Tree	Bird	Flower	Rock/ Mineral	Other
Alabama	longleaf pine	yellow-hammer	camellia	marble	boll weevil rockets & spacecraft
Alaska	sitka spruce	willow ptarmigan	forget-me-not	andradite	lemming, sled dogs, polar bears, seals, salmon, oil spills, arctic wolves, narwhals
Arizona	palo verde	cactus wren	saguaro cactus blossom	turquoise	desert ecosystem
Arkansas	pine	mockingbird	apple blossom	diamond	trout
California	redwood	quail	California poppy	gold	goats, computers, earthquakes
Colorado	blue spruce	lark bunting	columbine	aquamarine	pronghorn antelope, marmot
Connecticut	white oak	robin	mountain laurel	garnet	praying mantis, skunk, DNA
Delaware	American holly	blue hen chicken	peach blossom	sillimanite	ladybugs, chemicals
Florida	sabal palm	glossy ibis	orange blossom	agatized coral	space travel, tomatoes, mangroves, manatee
Georgia	live oak	brown thrasher	cherokee rose	staurolite	kudzu, peaches, peanuts, opossum
Hawaii	candlenut	Hawaiian goose	hibiscus	black coral	pineapple, volcanoes
Idaho	western white pine	mountain bluebird	syringa	star garnet	potatoes

State Science Chart

science topics studied with each state

State	Tree	Bird	Flower	Rock/ Mineral	Other
Illinois	weeping willow	cardinal	violet	fluorite	skyscrapers
Indiana	tulip poplar	blue jay	peony	gypsum	squirrel
Iowa	box elder	hawk	wild rose	geode	pigs
Kansas	cottonwood	western meadowlark	sunflower	calcite	salamander, wheat
Kentucky	Kentucky Coffeetree	cardinal	goldenrod	Kentucky agate	horses, bats
Louisiana	bald cypress	pelican	gardenia	agate	frogs, alligators, sugar
Maine	eastern white pine	black-capped chickadee	lupine	tourmaline	lobster, whales, tidal pool, blue-berries
Maryland	white ash	Baltimore oriole	black-eyed susan	sulfur	crabs
Massachusetts	American elm	heron	mayflower	rhodonite	cranberries
Michigan	American beech	woodpecker	daffodil	chlorastrolite	wolverine, combustion engines, automobiles
Minnesota	Norway pine	common loon	lady's slipper	red granite	pond & lake ecosystem
Mississippi	magnolia	snipe	magnolia	bentonite	cotton, hurricanes
Missouri	bitternut	eastern bluebird	hawthorn	mozarkite	mules, rivers
Montana	ponderosa pine	osprey	bitterroot	sapphire	grizzly bears

State Science Chart

science topics studied with each state

State	Tree	Bird	Flower	Rock/ Mineral	Other
Nebraska	hackberry	crow	daisy	prairie agate	corn
Nevada	single-leaf pinyon	vulture	sagebrush	black fire opal	porcupine, dams
New Hampshire	white birch	purple finch	purple lilac	granite	whitetail deer
New Jersey	northern red oak	American gold-finch	morning glory	willemite	bridges, electricity
New Mexico	pinyon	greater roadrunner	yucca	sandstone	hot air balloons
New York	larch	pigeons	rose	shale	photography
North Carolina	Fraser fir	great egret	Queen Anne's lace	emerald	turtles, horseshoe crabs, airplanes & flight
North Dakota	peachleaf willow	barn swallow	wild prairie rose	lignite	blizzards
Ohio	Ohio buckeye	owl	carnation	Ohio flint	fox
Oklahoma	eastern redbud	scissor-tailed flycatcher	mistletoe	barite rose	raccoon, buffalo, radio, astronomy
Oregon	Douglas fir	duck	Oregon grape	sunstone	beaver, cougar
Pennsylvania	eastern hemlock	ruffed grouse	buttercup	chabazite	groundhog
Rhode Island	red maple	Rhode Island red chicken	early blue violet	cumberlandite	quahaug
South Carolina	palmetto	Carolina wren	yellow jessamine	blue granite	thunderstorms

State Science Chart

science topics studied with each state

State	Tree	Bird	Flower	Rock/ Mineral	Other
South Dakota	Black Hills spruce	ring-necked pheasant	American pasqueflower	rose quartz	coyote
Tennessee	black walnut	tufted titmouse	iris	limestone	wolves
Texas	pecan	prairie chicken	bluebonnet	blue topaz	longhorn, armadillo, tornadoes, prairie dogs
Utah	Utah juniper	seagull	sego lily	copper	bobcats
Vermont	sugar maple	mermit thrush	red clover	talc	timber, maple syrup
Virginia	dogwood	purple martin	dogwood	apophyllite	hay
Washington	western hemlock	raven	red maids	petrified wood	apples, otters
Washington, D.C.	cherry	bald eagle	American beauty rose	vivianite	fireworks
West Virginia	blackgum	turkey	coast rhododendron	coal	black bear
Wisconsin	American basswood	American tree sparrow	wood violet	galena	dairy ows, badgers, forest
Wyoming	plains cottonwood	falcon	indian paintbrush	jade	geysers, lynx

Order of Statehood

Order	State	Date of Statehood	Abbreviation	State Capital
1	Delaware	December 7,1787	DE	Dover
2	Pennsylvania	December 12, 1787	PA	Harrisburg
3	New Jersey	December 18, 1787	NJ	Trenton
4	Georgia	January 2, 1788	GA	Atlanta
5	Connecticut	January 9, 1788	CT	Hartford
6	Massachusetts	February 6, 1788	MA	Boston
7	Maryland	April 28, 1788	MD	Annapolis
8	South Carolina	May 23, 1788	SC	Columbia
9	New Hampshire	June 21, 1788	NH	Concord
10	Virginia	June 25, 1788	VA	Richmond
11	New York	July 26, 1788	NY	Albany
12	North Carolina	November 21, 1789	NC	Raleigh
13	Rhode Island	May 29, 1790	RI	Providence
14	Vermont	March 4, 1791	VT	Montpelier
15	Kentucky	June 1, 1792	KY	Frankfort
16	Tennessee	June 1, 1796	TN	Nashville
17	Ohio	March 1, 1803	OH	Columbus
18	Louisiana	April 30, 1812	LA	Baton Rouge
19	Indiana	December 11, 1816	IN	Indianapolis
20	Mississippi	December 10, 1817	MS	Jackson
21	Illinois	December 3, 1818	IL	Springfield
22	Alabama	December 14, 1819	AL	Montgomery
23	Maine	March 15, 1820	ME	Augusta
24	Missouri	August 10, 1821	MO	Jefferson City
25	Arkansas	June 15, 1836	AR	Little Rock
26	Michigan	January 26, 1837	MI	Lansing
27	Florida	March 3, 1845	FL	Tallahassee
28	Texas	December 29, 1845	TX	Austin
29	Iowa	December 28, 1846	IA	Des Moines
30	Wisconsin	May 29, 1848	WI	Madison
31	California	September 9, 1850	CA	Sacramento
32	Minnesota	May 11, 1858	MN	St. Paul
33	Oregon	February 14, 1859	OR	Salem
34	Kansas	January 29, 1861	KS	Topeka
35	West Virginia	June 20, 1863	WV	Charleston
36	Nevada	October 31, 1864	NV	Carson City
37	Nebraska	March 1, 1867	NE	Lincoln
38	Colorado	August 1, 1876	CO	Denver
39	North Dakota	November 2, 1889	ND	Bismarck
40	South Dakota	November 2, 1889	SD	Pierre
41	Montana	November 8, 1889	MT	Helena
42	Washington	November 11, 1889	WA	Olympia
43	Idaho	July 3, 1890	ID	Boise
44	Wyoming	July 10, 1890	WY	Cheyenne
45	Utah	January 4, 1896	UT	Salt Lake City
46	Oklahoma	November 16, 1907	OK	Oklahoma City
47	New Mexico	January 6, 1912	NM	Santa Fe
48	Arizona	February 14, 1912	AZ	Phoenix
49	Alaska	January 3, 1959	AK	Juneau
50	Hawaii	August 21, 1959	HI	Honolulu

Travel & Tourism

Alabama

Alabama Bureau of Tourism & Travel
401 Adams Avenue, Suite 126
P.O. Box 4927
Montgomery, AL 36103-4927

334-242-4169

www.800alabama.com
Alabama state website: www.alabama.gov

Alaska

Alaska Tourism Office
P.O. Box 110801
Juneau, AK 99811-0801

1-800-862-5275

http://www.dced.state.ak.us/tourism/
Alaska state website: www.alaska.gov

Arizona

Arizona Office of Tourism
1110 West Washington, Suite 155
Phoenix, AZ 85007

1-866-275-5816 or 1-602-364-3700

www.arizonaguide.com
Arizona state website:www.az.gov

Arkansas

Arkansas Department of Parks & Tourism
One Capitol Mall
Little Rock, AR 72201

1-800-NATURAL or (501) 682-7777

www.arkansas.com
Arkansas state website: www.arkansas.gov

California

California Tourism
P.O. Box 1499
Sacramento, CA 95812-1499.

(800) 862-2543 or 1-916-444-4429.

www.visitcalifornia.com
California state website: www.ca.gov

Colorado

Colorado Tourism Office
1625 Broadway, Ste 1700
Denver, CO 80202

1-800-COLORADO
303-892-3885

Colorado state website: www.colorado.gov

Connecticut

Connecticut Commission on Culture & Tourism
Tourism Division
505 Hudson Street
Hartford, CT 06106

1-800-CTBOUND
(860)270-8080

www.ctvisit.com/
Connecticut state website: www.ct.gov

Delaware

Delaware Tourism Office
99 Kings Highway
Dover, DE 19901

(302) 739-4271 or 866-284-7483

www.visitdelaware.com
Delaware state website: www.delaware.gov

Florida

Visit Florida
P.O. Box 1100
Tallahassee, FL 32302-1100

888-7FLAUSA

www.visitflorida.com
Florida state website: www.myflorida.com

Georgia

Chamber of Commerce
235 International Blvd.
Atlanta, GA 30303

800-VISITGA

www.exploregeorgia.org
Georgia state website: www.georgia.gov

Travel & Tourism

Hawaii

Hawaii Visitors & Convention Bureau
1001 Bishop Street
Pauahi Tower, Suite 950
Honolulu, HI 96813

(808) 539-3409

www.gohawaii.com
Hawaii state website: www.ehawaii.gov

Idaho

Division of Tourism Development
700 West State Street
P.O. Box 83720
Boise, ID 83720-0093

(208) 334-2470

www.visitidaho.org
Idaho state website: www.Idaho.gov

Illinois

Illinois Department of Commerce &
Community Affairs
620 E. Adams St.
Springfield, IL 62701

800-2-CONNECT

www.enjoyillinois.com
Illinois state website: www.illinois.gov

Indiana

Indiana Office of Tourism Development
One North Capitol, Suite 700
Indianapolis, IN 46204-2288

888-ENJOY-IN

www.in.gov/visitindiana
Indiana state website: www.in.gov

Iowa

Iowa Department of Economic Development
Iowa Tourism Office
200 East Grand Avenue
Des Moines, IA 50309

(515) 242-4705
888-472-6035

www.traveliowa.com
Iowa state website: www.iowa.gov

Kansas

Kansas Department of Commerce
1000 S.W. Jackson Street, Suite 100
Topeka, KS 66612-1354

(785) 296-8478
800-2-kansas

www.travelks.com
Kansas state website: www.kansas.gov

Kentucky

Kentucky Department of Tourism
Capital Plaza Tower, 22nd Floor
500 Mero Street
Frankfort, KY 40601

(502) 564-4930

www.travel.ky.gov
Kentucky state website: www.kentucky.gov

Louisiana

Office of Tourism
P.O. Box 94291
Baton Rouge, LA 70804-9291

(225) 342-8119
800-677-4082

Louisiana state website: www.louisiana.gov

Travel & Tourism

Maine

Maine Office of Tourism
#59 State House Station
Augusta, ME 04333-0059

888-624-6345

www.visitmaine.com
Maine state website: www.maine.gov

Maryland

Maryland Office of Tourism Development
217 East Redwood Street, 9th Floor
Baltimore, MD 21202

800-634-7386

www.visitmaryland.org
Maryland state website: www.maryland.gov

Massachusetts

Massachusetts Office of Travel & Tourism
10 Park Plaza, Suite 4510
Boston, MA 02116 U.S.A.

(617) 973-8500
800-227-MASS

www.mass-vacation.com
Massachusetts state website: www.mass.gov

Michigan

Travel Michigan
300 N. Washington Square
Second Floor
Lansing, MI 48913

888-784-7328

www.travelmichigan.org
Michigan state website: www.michigan.gov

Minnesota

Explore Minnesota Tourism
100 Metro Square, 121 7th Place E.
St. Paul, MN 55101

800-657-3700
888-TOURISM

www.exploreminnesota.com
Minnesota state website: www.state.mn.us

Mississippi

Division of Tourism Development
P.O. Box 849
Jackson, MS 39205

(866) SEE-MISS (733-6477)

www.visitmississippi.org
Mississippi state website: www.mississippi.gov

Missouri

Missouri Division of Tourism
P.O. Box 1055
Jefferson City, MO 65102

800-519-2100

www.missouritourism.org
Missouri state website: www.state.mo.us

Montana

Travel Montana
301 South Park
P.O. Box 200533
Helena, MT 59620-0133

800-VISIT-MT (800-847-4868)
(406) 841-2870

www.visitmt.com
Montana state website: www.mt.gov

Nebraska

Nebraska Division of Travel & Tourism
P.O. Box 98907
Lincoln, NE 68509-8907

877-NEBRASKA

www.visitnebraska.org
Nebraska state website: www.nebraska.gov

Nevada

Nevada Commission on Tourism
401 North Carson Street
Carson City, NV 89701

800-NEVADA-8

www.travelnevada.com
Nevada state website: www.nv.gov

Travel & Tourism

New Hampshire

State of New Hampshire Division of Travel & Tourism Development
172 Pembroke Road, P.O. Box 1856
Concord, NH 03302-1856

800-FUN-IN-NH (386-4664)
(603) 271-2665

www.visitnh.gov
New Hampshire state website: www.nh.gov

New Jersey

New Jersey Commerce & Economic Growth Commission
P.O. Box 820
Trenton, NJ 08625-0820

800-VISITNJ
(609) 777- 0885

www.state.nj.us/travel/
New Jersey state website: www.state.nj.us

New Mexico

New Mexico Tourism Department
491 Old Santa Fe Trail
The Lamy Building
Santa Fe, NM 87503

800-733-6396 ext 0643

www.newmexico.org
New Mexico state website: www.newmexico.gov

New York

NYS Division of Tourism
30 S. Pearl Street
Main Concourse, Rm 110
Albany, NY 12245

(518) 474-4116
800-CAL-LNYS

www.iloveny.com
New York state website: www.state.ny.us

North Carolina

North Carolina Department of Commerce
Division of Tourism
301 North Wilmington Street
Raleigh, NC 27601

800-VISITNC

www.visitnc.com
North Carolina state website: www.ncgov.com

North Dakota

Tourism Division
Century Center
1600 E. Century Ave., Suite 2
P.O. Box 2057
Bismarck, ND 58503-2057

800-435-5663
(701) 328-2525

www.ndtourism.com
North Dakota state website:
www.discovernd.com

Ohio

Ohio Department of Development
Travel & Tourism Division
P.O. Box 1001
Columbus, OH 43216-1001

(614) 466-8844
1-800-BUCKEYE

www.discoverohio.com
Ohio state website: www.ohio.gov

Oklahoma

Oklahoma Tourism and Recreation Department
15 N. Robinson, Suite 100
Oklahoma City, OK 73102

800-652-6552

www.tourism.state.ok.us
Oklahoma state website: www.state.ok.us

Travel & Tourism

Oregon

State of Oregon, Economic & Community Development Department.
775 Summer St., NE, Suite 200,
Salem, OR 97301-1280

503-986-0123 or 800-735-2900

www.traveloregon.com
Oregon state website: www.oregon.gov

Pennsylvania

Pennsylvania Tourism Office
Department of Community & Economic Development
4th Floor, Commonwealth Keystone Building
400 North Street
Harrisburg, PA 17120-0225

800-237-4363

www.visitpa.com
Pennsylvania state website: www.pa.gov

Rhode Island

Rhode Island Tourism Division
One West Exchange Street
Providence, RI 02903

800-556-2484

www.visitrhodeisland.com
Rhode Island state website: www.ri.gov

South Carolina

SC Department of Parks, Recreation & Tourism
1205 Pendleton St., Room 505
Columbia, SC 29201

(803) 734-1700

www.discoversouthcarolina.com
South Carolina website: www.sc.gov

South Dakota

Department of Tourism & State Development
711 E. Wells Ave.
Pierre, SD 57501-3369

(605) 773-3301

www.travelsd.com
South Dakota state website: www.sd.gov

Tennessee

State of Tennessee Department of Tourist Development
Tennessee Tower
312 8th Avenue North, 25th Floor
Nashville, TN 37243

(615) 741-2159

www.tnvacation.com
Tennessee state website: www.state.tn.us

Texas

Chamber of Commerce
900 Congress
Suite 501
Austin, TX, 78701

1-800-8888-TEX

www.traveltx.com
Texas state website:
www.texasonline.com/portal/tol

Utah

Utah Travel Council
P.O. Box 147420
Salt Lake City, UT 84114-7420

800-200-1160
801-538-1030

www.utah.com
Utah state website: www.utah.gov

Travel & Tourism

Vermont

Vermont Dept. of Tourism & Marketing
6 Baldwin St., Drawer 33
Montpelier, VT 05633-1301

(802) 828-3676
1-800-VERMONT

www.travel-vermont.com
Vermont state website: www.vermont.gov

Virginia

Virginia Tourism Corporation
901 E. Byrd St.
Richmond, VA 23219

800-VISIT VA (800-847-4882)

www.virginia.org
Virginia state website: www.virginia.gov

Washington

Department of Community, Trade & Economic Development
P.O. Box 42525
Olympia, WA 98504-2525

800-544-1800

www.experiencewa.com
Washington state website: www.access.wa.gov

West Virginia

West Virginia Division of Tourism
90 MacCorkle Ave. SW
South Charleston, WV 25303

304-558-2200
800-CALL WVA (800-225-5982)

www.wvtourism.com
West Virginia state website: www.wv.gov

Wisconsin

Wisconsin Department of Tourism
201 West Washington Avenue
P.O. Box 8690
Madison, WI 53708-8690

800-432-8747
(608) 266-2161

www.travelwisconsin.com
Wisconsin state website: www.wisconsin.gov

Wyoming

Wyoming Travel & Tourism
I-25 at College Drive
Cheyenne, WY 82002

(307) 777-7777
800-225-5996

www.wyomingtourism.org
Wyoming state website: www.wyoming.gov

Washington, D.C.

Washington, D.C. Convention & Tourism Corporation
901 7th Street NW, 4th Floor
Washington, DC 20001-3719

(202) 789-7000
800-422-8644

www.washington.org

- Trail Guide to Geography Series -

by Cindy Wiggers

The *Trail Guide to Geography* series is a multi-level geography curriculum guide for 2nd grade through High School. Three books in the *Trail Guide to ...Geography* series include U.S., World, and Bible geography. Each book provides clear directions and assignment choices to encourage self-directed learning as students create their own personal geography notebooks. Daily atlas drills, mapping activities, and various weekly assignment choices address learning styles in a way that has kids asking for more!

***Trail Guide* features:**

- Weekly lesson plans – for 36 weeks
- 5-minute daily atlas drills (2 questions/day, four days/week)
- 3 levels of difficulty – all ages participate together
- Weekly mapping assignments
- A variety of weekly research and hands-on activity choices

Student Notebooks are available on CD-ROM

Trail Guide Levels

The *Trail Guide* Levels are just a guide. Select a level according to student ability, and match level with the appropriate atlas or student notebook.

- Primary: grades 2–4
- Intermediate: grades 5–7
- Secondary: grades 8–12

All 3 levels in each book!

Note: Primary is ideal for independent 4th graders. Second and third graders will need plenty of guidance. If your oldest is 2nd–3rd grade range, please consider *Galloping the Globe* or *Cantering the Country* first.

Trail Guide to U.S. Geography

Grades 2 - 12

"The *Trail Guide to U.S. Geography* provides lots of guidance while allowing for (and encouraging) flexibility and this is just the balance most homeschool moms need! The manual is easy to navigate and I am very impressed with how thoroughly material is covered. This resource is destined to be a favorite with homeschool families for years to come!"
–Cindy Prechtel, homeschoolingfromtheheart.com

Paperback, 144 pages, $18.95

Trail Guide to World Geography

Grades 2 - 12

"We have the *Trail Guide to World Geography* and **love** it!! We are using it again this year just for the questions... I will never sell this guide!! I am looking forward to doing the U.S. one next year."
–Shannon, OK

Paperback, 128 pages, $18.95

Trail Guide to Bible Geography

Grades 2 - 12

"Here is another winner from Geography Matters! *Trail Guide to Bible Geography* is multi-faceted, user-friendly, and suited to a wide range of ages and abilities."
–Jean Hall, Eclectic Homeschool Association

Paperback, 128 pages, $18.95

Galloping the Globe

Grades K - 4

by Loreé Pettit and Dari Mullins

"If you've got kindergarten through fourth grade students, and are looking for unit study material for geography, hold on to your hat and get ready for *Galloping the Globe!* Loreé Pettit and Dari Mullins have written this great resource to introduce children to the continents and some of their countries. This book is designed to be completed in one to three years, depending on how much time you spend on each topic. And for each continent, there are suggestions and topics galore." –Leslie Wyatt, www.homeschoolenrichment.com

Organized by continent, incorporates student notebooking, and covers these topics:

• Basic Geography	• History and Biographies	• Literature	• Science
• Bible	• Activities	• Internet Sources	• Language Arts

This new 2010 edition of *Galloping the Globe* includes an Activity CD-ROM jam-packed with all the reproducible activity sheets found in the book plus added bonus pages. Paperback with CD-ROM, 272 pages, $29.95

Cantering the Country

Grades 1-5

by Loreé Pettit and Dari Mullins

Saddle up your horses and strap on your thinking caps. Learning geography is an adventure. From the authors who brought you *Galloping the Globe,* you'll love its U.S. counterpart, *Cantering the Country.* This unit study teaches a wide range of academic and spiritual disciplines using the geography of the U.S. as a starting point. With this course, you won't have to put aside one subject to make time for another. They're all connected! This comprehensive unit study takes up to three years to complete and includes all subjects except math and spelling. Incorporates student notebooking and covers these topics:

• U.S. Geography	• Character	• Science	• Language Arts
• Activities	• Literature	• Civics	• History and Biographies
• Internet Sources	• Bible		

In addition to the 250+ page book, you will receive a CD-ROM packed full of reproducible outline maps and activities. Dust off your atlas and get ready to explore America! Paperback with CD-ROM, 254 pages, $29.95

Adventures of Munford Series

by Jamie Aramini

Although he's just two parts hydrogen and one part oxygen, Munford is all adventure. He can be rain, snow, sleet, or steam. He has traveled the world in search of excitement. Throughout history, he has been present at some of the most important and world-changing events.

Fun and educational, Munford will inspire your children to learn more about many of history's greatest events. These readers make a great addition to your learning experience in areas such as history, geography, and science. This book series was written on an elementary reading level, but provides plenty of read-aloud entertainment for the entire family! Paperback, $8.95

The Klondike Gold Rush

In this adventure, Munford travels to colonial America and experiences first hand the events leading to the American Revolution. He meets famed American Founding Fathers, such as Samuel Adams, Thomas Jefferson, and George Washington. He joins the Sons of Liberty under cover of night to dump tea into Boston Harbor. He tags along for Paul Revere's most famous ride, and even becomes a part of the Declaration of Independence in a way that you might not expect!

The American Revolution

In this adventure, Munford finds himself slap into the middle of the Klondike Gold Rush. He catches gold fever on this dangerous, yet thrilling, adventure. Meet some of the Gold Rush's most famous characters, like gold baron Alex McDonald or the tricky villain named Soapy Smith. Take a ride on the Whitehorse Rapids, and help Munford as he pans for gold. This is an adventure you won't soon forget!

Munford Meets Lewis & Clark

Join Munford on an epic adventure with Meriwether Lewis and William Clark, as they make their perilous journey in search of the Northwest Passage to the Pacific Ocean.

. . . More to Come!

Look for more adventures in this exciting series as Munford's journey through time and territory continues around the world.

Eat Your Way Through the USA

by Loreé Pettit

Taste your way around the U.S.A. without leaving your own dining room table! Each state has its unique geographical features, culinary specialities, and agricultural products. These influence both the ingredients that go into a recipe and the way food is prepared. Compliment your geography lesson and tantalize your tastebuds at the same time with this outstanding cookbook.

This cookbook includes a full meal of easy to follow recipes from each state. Recipes are easy to follow. Though they aren't written at a child's level, it's easy to include your students in the preparation of these dishes. Cooking together provides life skills and is a source of bonding and pride. More than just a cookbook, it is a taste buds-on approach to geography. Spiral bound, 118 pages, $14.95

Eat Your Way Around the World

by Jamie Aramini

Get out the sombrero for your Mexican fiesta! Chinese egg rolls… corn pancakes from Venezuela… fried plantains from Nigeria. All this, and more, is yours when you take your family on a whirlwind tour of over thirty countries in this unique international cookbook. Includes a full meal of recipes from each country. Recipes are easy to follow, and ingredients are readily available. Jam-packed with delicious dinners, divine drinks, and delectable desserts, this book is sure to please.

The entire family will be fascinated with tidbits of culture provided for each country including: Etiquette Hints, Food Profiles, and Culture a la Carté. For more zest, add an activity and violà, create a memorable learning experience that will last for years to come. Some activities include: Food Journal, Passport, and World Travel Night. Spiral bound, 120 pages, $14.95

The Ultimate Geography and Timeline Guide

by Maggie Hogan and Cindy Wiggers

Grades K - 12

Learn how to construct timelines, establish student notebooks, teach geography through literature, and integrate science with activities on volcanoes, archaeology, and other subjects. Use the complete multi-level geography course for middle and high school students. Now includes CD-ROM of all reproducible activity and planning pages. Use for all students kindergarden through high school. Paperback with CD-ROM, 353 pages, $39.95

- 18 Reproducible Outline Maps
- Teaching Tips
- Planning Charts
- Over 150 Reproducible Pages
- Over 300 Timeline Figures
- Lesson Plans
- Scope and Sequence
- Flash Cards
- Games

Mark-It Timeline of History

There's hardly no better way to keep history in perspective than creating a timeline in tandem with your history studies. This poster is just the tool to do so. Write or draw images of events as they are studied, or attach timeline figures to aid student understanding and comprehension of the topic at hand. 23" x 34". Laminated, $10.95, Paper (folded), $5.95

Lewis & Clark - Hands On
Art and English Activities
by Sharon Jeffus

Follow the experiences of Meriwether Lewis and William Clark with hands-on art and writing projects associated with journal entries made during the Corps of Discovery Expedition. Ideal for adding interest to any Lewis and Clark study or to teach drawing and journaling. Includes profiles of American artists, step by step drawing instructions, actual journal entries, and background information about this famous adventure.
Paperback, 80 pages, $12.95

Profiles from History
by Ashley (Strayer) Wiggers

When studying history, a human connection is the most important connection that we can make. In *Profiles from History*, your student will not only learn about twenty famous people – but also why each one is worthy of remembrance. Everyone knows that Benjamin Franklin was a great inventor, but how many realize he was also a great man? He valued helping people more than making money or becoming famous. He refused to patent his popular Franklin stove, so more families could keep their homes warm during the cold, winter months. *Profiles from History* tells stories like this one, stories of greatness and inspiration. Each profile includes fun activities such as crosswords, word search, & timeline usage. Paperback, $16.95

Coming soon *Profiles from History - Volume 2.*

Geography Through Art
by Sharon Jeffus and Jamie Aramini

Geography Through Art is the ultimate book of international art projects. Join your children on an artistic journey to more than twenty-five countries spanning six continents (includes over a dozen United States projects). Previously published by Visual Manna as *Teaching Geography Through Art*, Geography Matters has added a number of enhancements and practical changes to this fascinating art book. Use this book as an exciting way to supplement any study of geography, history, or social studies. You'll find yourself reaching for this indispensable guide again and again to delight and engage students in learning about geography through the culture and art of peoples around the world.
Paperback, 190 pages, $19.95

Timeline Figures on CD-ROM

Kids love the look of their timelines when they add color and variety. Students can draw on their timeline, write events and dates, and add timeline figures. We've created two different sets of color timeline figures that are ready to print from any computer. There are over 350 figures in each set plus templates to create your own. Our figures are appealing in style, simple to use, and include color-coding and icons to aid memory. Available with biblical events and general world events. CD-ROM (Mac & Windows Compatible), $24.95

- Reproducible Outline Maps -

Reproducible outline maps have a myriad of uses in the home, school, and office. Uncle Josh's quality digital maps provide opportunities for creative learning at all ages. His maps feature rivers and grid lines where possible, and countries are shown in context with their surroundings. (No map of Germany "floating" in the center of the page, here!) When students use outline maps and see the places they are studying in context they gain a deeper understanding of the subject at hand.

Uncle Josh's Outline Map Book

Take advantage of those spontaneous teaching moments when you have this set of outline maps handy. They are:

- Over 100 reproducible maps
- 15 world regions
- Continents with and without borders
- 25 countries
- Each of the 50 United States
- 8 U.S. regions

Useful for all grades and topics, this is by far one of the best book of reproducible outline maps you'll find. Paperback, 128 pages, $19.95

Uncle Josh's Outline Map Collection CD-ROM

In addition to all maps in *Uncle Josh's Outline Map Book* the CD-Rom includes color, shaded-relief, and labeled maps. Over 260 printable maps plus bonus activities. CD-ROM (Mac & Windows), $26.95

- Large-scale Maps -

Large-scale maps are great for detail labeling and for family or classroom use. Laminated Mark-It maps can be reused for a variety of lessons. Quality digital map art is used for each of the map titles published and laminated by Geography Matters. Choose from large scale continents, regions, United States, and world maps. US and World available in both outline version and with state, country, and capitals labeled. Ask about our ever expanding library of full, color shaded-relief maps. Paper and laminated, each title available separately or in discounted sets.

About the Authors

Loreé Pettit is a wife and homeschooling mother to three children. Her background as school teacher and administrator helped her see the value in adapting traditional teaching methods for schooling at home. She developed a love for geography as a child traveling throughout the United States and Europe with her family. In 2001 she translated that interest into a geography-based unit study for her own children. That unit study went into publication the following year as *Galloping the Globe. Eat your Way through the USA* and *Cantering the Country* soon followed.

When she is not writing, or involved with the many details of teaching her own children, Loreé presents workshops at home school conferences across the country. There, she helps parents realize that home schooling is more than bringing traditional teaching methods into the home. Her heart is to help parents discover the joys of learning together as a family.

Dari Mullins, author and motivational speaker, has been homeschooling her three teenagers for over ten years. She fell in love with history and geography when she began researching home education in 1995. Dari and her husband, Allen, have taught their children at home since the oldest started kindergarten in 1997.

Realizing early that traditional textbooks were not the route she wanted in educating her children, Dari utilized notebooking and the unit study approach. This passion for non-traditional methods led her to write curriculum for her own family and eventually teaming up with Loree Pettit to write *Galloping the Globe* and *Cantering the Country.*

Dari and her family currently live in Asheville, NC where she teaches several classes and stays active with the local homeschool community. She remains dedicated to helping homeschool families prosper and delight in learning together.